MILITARY FAMILIES

MILITARY FAMILIES

Adaptation to Change

——————➤ ☆ ◄——————

edited by

Edna J. Hunter
D. Stephen Nice

PRAEGER PUBLISHERS
Praeger Special Studies

New York   •   London   •   Sydney   •   Toronto

Library of Congress Cataloging in Publication Data

Main entry under title:

Military families.

   Includes bibliographical references and index.
   1. Soldiers--United States--Family relationships--
Addresses, essays, lectures. 2. United States--
Armed Forces--Military life--Addresses, essays,
lectures. I. Hunter, Edna J. II. Nice, D. Stephen.
U21.5.M46   301.5'93   78-13067
ISBN 0-03-043106-9

PRAEGER PUBLISHERS
383 Madison Avenue, New York, N.Y. 10017, U.S.A.

Published in the United States of America in 1978
by Praeger Publishers,
A Division of Holt, Rinehart and Winston, CBS, Inc.

9   038   98765432

Printed in the United States of America

Dedicated to all military

families; they also serve.

FOREWORD

Military families present many characteristics which set them apart from society. The profession of arms is dangerous, whether in wartime or peacetime. The military member of the family is subject to instant change of duty, whether permanent or temporary. Military families are likely to spend many years living in communities composed entirely, or largely, of other military families, and in an area where they are likely to be supported entirely, or largely, by military facilities.

But while military families have many things in common, they also present great diversity. The problems of family separation and parental role changing which confront, say, the submarine community with patrol cycles of 60 days at sea, 60 days at home, are different from those of families which may rarely be separated. The dynamics of a one-year separation on isolated duty are different from those of a three-month training course. But in which ways are they different? What are the effects on the families and what can be done to modify them? We need answers to a whole range of questions, and we are just beginning to learn what questions we should have been asking and what answers we should have been resolving.

We already know that families are important: We know that 77 percent of the enlisted career navy and 70 percent of the officer corps is married; that families need support facilities; that families must be considered in career planning; and that family attitudes have a great impact on the attitudes of navy personnel. In years past, we have devised programs to provide advice and assistance to families. We have encouraged the activities of wives' clubs, we have sponsored day care centers for the young and teen centers for the restless, and we have been concerned not only with the physical environment, but with the moral and spiritual environment as well. We want our people—and their families—to be pround of their affiliation with the navy, to view the navy not as a job, but as an attractive and meaning-ful way of life.

But, when budget time rolls around each year, the planners, analysts, and civilian and military leaders are for the most part— quite properly—focusing on hardware-oriented military capabilities and the readiness of the services to carry out their combat missions. Budget items not directly coupled to readiness are often vulnerable.

To be honest, we have not been very sophisticated about measur-ing the value or impact of our family support efforts. The lack of solid data has not only made it difficult to define our requirements, but has also made it difficult to defend resulting programs—in competition with programs more obviously related to readiness. For example, in the total research and development budget for the Department of Defense, for every dollar allocated to hardware programs only one half of one cent goes to personnel research.

Furthermore, even though the military family as a class is unique, and even though millions of U.S. families are military families, very little formal research in this area has been conducted in the past, and much of what has been conducted has not reached the people who could put that research into practical application. In the past 25 years, the number of published studies on the military family has averaged about four per year, and very few of those have ever been reviewed by people in my line of work—people who can influence policies which directly affect military families in hundreds of ways. But that situation is changing. In our past efforts, we have perhaps too often tried to deal in isolation with something which cannot truly be isolated. For example, the disciplinary problems of a teen-age son could well have been caused by—or at least aggravated by—a well-intended command effort directed at increased readiness which kept the father hard at work at a critical time for the family. In this example, the son's activities could well have such a strong negative impact on the father's morale and upon his ability to do his job that, on balance, reduced command readiness was the net result.

Treating the disciplinary problem, through traditional means alone—the chaplain, the psychiatrist, the social worker, the family counselor, or the probation officer, important though such help is—may not change the root cause of the problem. Attempting to deal with the father's poor performance through traditional means—such as extra duty, restriction, fines, and reduction in rate—certainly won't raise his morale and will probably have a cumulative negative effect on the son. All the while, readiness suffers further while the commanding officer, the executive officer, the division officer, and the leading chief petty officer have to divert their attention to dealing with personal problems rather than training and maintenance—and with possible negative impact on the health and welfare of their own families. This is a classic "vicious circle," a problem very much in need of solution. I believe that valid research can help us to find, if not a full solution, at least an approach toward resolution.

The military itself is changing. For example, 20,000 enlisted women serve in the navy today, four times as many as we had five years ago. We expect to add another 10,000 in the next few years. This impacts on navy family life in several fairly obvious ways. First, there is the concern of navy wives over the prospect of women serving at sea and the possibilities of family disruption which could ensue. This is an important and sensitive area, and one that we need to study very carefully in the future. Another obvious impact on the navy is that many of our women are, themselves, navy wives or army wives; more than 3,000 navy women are married to servicemen. Many of these couples are career-oriented, as couples, which brings special problems of career progression and assignment.

Then there are the areas of change where the impact on both men and women may not be so obvious (for example, women serving in traditional male jobs and more and more senior women serving in positions of authority). We need to follow these changes very closely.

Another change in the military family is in the growing number of single-parent families—more than 17,000 in the navy, two-thirds of which, incidentally, are led by men. The single-parent family has the same concerns as any family, but some of those concerns—such as child care—can more quickly become critical, if the parent must leave home for temporary duty, or training, or the deployment of a unit. Also, for the parent who is assigned to rotating shift work, such as watches in a communications or operations center, child care is not "day care" but must be available on a 24-hour basis. This is obviously a problem for some of those 17,000 navy men and women, but we do not have sufficient information to support changing any assignment policies or developing new facilities.

The research we need all too often seems to end up in a dusty filing cabinet, to be remembered only as a footnote citation in some future effort. One reason perhaps has been that too often the studies have been framed to serve academic pursuits when our needs are pragmatic. While theory is certainly important in the development of a study, hard data must support the application of the results. While opinions are necessary in forming conclusions, the budget analysts and the Congress want to see measurable payoff. The choice of hardware systems clearly affects combat capability of a ship. The trade-offs, one system against the next, dollar for dollar, are usually specific, and the decision factors are easily reviewed. However, such areas as family support, personnel selection and assignment procedures, special pay and benefits—these are more difficult to quantify and assess. But good, solid, well-constructed and properly coordinated research in these areas will give us the data we need to defend our programs against the most detailed and objective scrutiny.

Vice Admiral James D. Watkins, USN
Chief, Bureau of Naval Personnel
September 1, 1977

ix

PREFACE

A Conference on Current Trends and Directions in Military Family Research was held in San Diego, California, from September 1-3, 1977. The conference was jointly hosted by the Family Studies Branch of the Naval Health Research Center, San Diego, and the Naval Postgraduate School, Monterey, California. Funding was provided by the Office of Naval Research. The meetings afforded an opportunity for researchers and operational decision makers to examine the entire spectrum of military family research: what had been done in the past, what is presently being done, and the directions military family research should pursue in the future. Representatives from all branches of the military services attended the meetings as did representatives from the academic community. Participants and those in attendance included operational, research, and service delivery personnel. The conference gave evidence of the growing interest of top planners and decision makers within the military services in the military family and their recognition that the military organization not only has an impact on family members but that the family also has an impact upon the accomplishment of the military mission.

Keynote speakers representing the three service branches included Vice Admiral James D. Watkins, Chief of the Bureau of Naval Personnel; Brigadier General John H. Johns, Chief of the Human Resources Directorate, United States Army; and Brigadier General Richard Carr, Deputy Chief of Chaplains, United States Air Force. The Opening Plenary Session of the conference was introduced by Rear Admiral D. Earl Brown, Commanding Officer of the Naval Regional Medical Center at San Diego and closed by Rear Admiral John J. O'Connor, Chief of Navy Chaplains. Principal speakers on the opening day of the conference included representatives from both the academic and military communities: Professor Henry B. Biller of the University of Rhode Island and retired Admiral Elmo R. Zumwalt, Jr., Former Chief of Naval Operations. Dr. Edna J. Hunter, Head of the Family Studies Branch of the Naval Health Research Center was General Chairman of the meetings; Dr. D. Stephen Nice, also of the Naval Health Research Center, served as Program Chairman; and Professor C. Brooklyn Derr of the Naval Postgraduate School was Administrative Chairman.

During the three-day conference, issues which require research efforts concerning military families were discussed. Presentations showed that the factors which in prior years made the military community unique, such as prolonged family absence and frequent geographic mobility, are also becoming more apparent in the civilian sector. During the meetings, it became apparent to conference attendees that studies of military families are widely applicable to the civilian community and vice versa.

Presentations also pointed up the fact that it is much more difficult for the military organization to compete with the family than it was in the past. Thus, there is increased need for further research to delineate how the family can be made to function more effectively in support of the military organization, as well as the other way around. That is, the military also must contribute to the family "mission." A balance must be achieved between health-care delivery services and other family support programs and research on the military family. Many questions about changing times and the changing military were raised. For example, do the new marriage relationships (committed, whether legalized or not) which emphasize family loyalty and expectations of interpersonal closeness sustain rather than threaten military functioning? Research can perhaps give us the answer.

For many of the conference participants it appeared that military family research has become a valid area of study and one with operational payoffs. Admiral Zumwalt cautioned that research must also be repeated and ongoing in order to measure the impact of changing times and environments on the navy family. Otherwise, we cannot know whether the solutions of the 1970s will be applicable in the 1980s with regard to specific programs or policies. At present, attitudes toward the family as an institution are ambivalent in both civilian and military settings, with decisions yet to be made as to whether the family is a liability for any organization, civilian or military, or an invaluable morale agency which is well worth the expenditures and emotional supports required.

ACKNOWLEDGMENTS

The editors extend their sincere gratitude to Dr. John A. Nagay of the Office of Naval Research whose support made the publication of this volume possible. We also express our appreciation for the untiring efforts of Lucile Cheng, Fran Jackson, and Barbara Morse whose capable editorial assistance put all the pieces together. The opinions and assertions are those of the authors and are not to be construed as official or as reflecting the views of the Departments of the Army, Navy, or Air Force.

CONTENTS

LIST OF TABLES

LIST OF FIGURES

PART I

CHANGING ATTITUDES

". . . wives' attitudes are indeed a factor in influencing retention of military personnel. . . . A strategy designed to increase satisfaction of undecided [military] wives might also tend to make them more favorable to their husbands' reenlistment."

Gloria Lauer Grace
and Mary B. Steiner

1 Military Family Attitudes Toward Housing, Benefits, and the Quality of Military Life

Susan S. Stumpf

The Office of the Secretary of Defense (OSD) assigned the navy the task of developing this study to obtain data from occupants of both government and civilian family housing in all four branches of service. The primary focus of the study reported in this chapter was upon housing preferences, but OSD was also interested in attitudes toward other military benefits and facilities. The researchers thus expanded the scope of the study to examine the relationship of housing both to perceived quality of life and career motivation among military families. This study was conducted concurrently with the 1975 Study of Department of Defense Housing Programs, which was performed by a task force representing both the Defense Department and the Office of Management and Budget. The findings provided input to this task force and were also utilized in the Quadrennial Review of Military Compensation.

BACKGROUND

The development of quality-of-life measures, or social indicators, is currently a subject of much interest to social scientists. Housing is frequently considered an important component in "objective" quality-of-life indicators. Statistics on housing quantity, quality, and costs are collected and analyzed as a partial measure of the quality of life in various cities and regions and in the United States as a whole (see Oborn 1972, for a literature review on social indicators).

Other researchers have concentrated on subjective measures of quality of life in an effort to determine the factors contributing

The author wishes to express appreciation to William F. Kieckhaefer for his extensive contributions to the study.

to a person's overall perception of well-being. Andrews and Withey (1974) analyzed responses of several national samples to over 100 items concerning satisfaction with various aspects of life (domains). Their preliminary results pointed to housing as one of the 12 domains showing the greatest relationship to overall satisfaction with life.

Career retention is a significant concern to the military services. Previous studies of military personnel have shown that career-motivated individuals are more likely to prefer military housing than the noncareer motivated (Dupuy 1965; U.S. Department of the Army 1966). The noncareer motivated often cite a desire to avoid the military atmosphere as an important reason for preferring civilian housing.

The findings are not as consistent concerning the relationship between housing satisfaction and career motivation. Dupuy (1965) found that junior officers and junior enlisted personnel cited family housing as an important factor in their career decision. However, it was unclear whether they viewed housing as a positive or negative feature of military service. Two army surveys showed that housing was frequently viewed as a major source of dissatisfaction and rarely as a major source of satisfaction for military families (U.S. Department of the Army 1969). However, in a navy survey which asked respondents to choose the most important change that would make a navy career attractive to them, "improve barracks and government family housing" was less important than changes in pay, allowances, leadership, and personnel policies (Knitter, Stumpf and Dow 1969).

MODEL AND STATEMENT OF HYPOTHESES

The findings of previous housing studies were integrated with concepts of psychological theory to develop the model shown in Figure 1.1. This model was used for both the military and spouse data analysis. Since career retention and improvement in the quality of military life are both important Defense Department goals, both variables were investigated in relation to housing and demographic variables. As shown in Figure 1.1 the housing and demographic variables were divided into three categories: personal/situational factors, housing choice behavior, and housing attitudes.

The principal hypothesis of the model was that personal/ situational factors, housing choice behavior, and housing attitudes would all contribute to the explanation of individual differences in career intention (or, for spouses, favorability toward a military career for their partner), and perceived quality of life for both military personnel and spouses. No prior expectations were held as to the strength of these relationships or the particular variables

FIGURE 1.1

Model of Relationships between Housing
Variables, Demographic Variables,
Quality of Life, and Career Intention

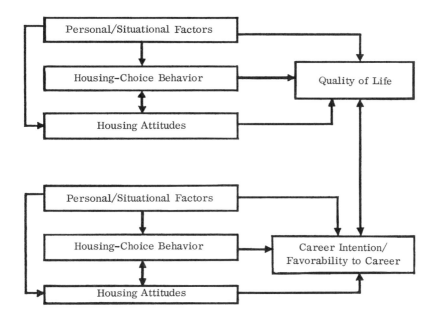

Note: Arrows indicate hypothesized nature and direction of
relationships.

Source: Compiled by the author.

that would be the most useful in predicting either career intention
or quality of life.

It was further hypothesized that:

1. Both housing choice behavior and personal/situational factors
    would be correlated with housing attitudes. Housing type,
    paygrade, and urbanization level were particularly expected
    to be associated with housing attitudes;

2. Career intention and perceived quality of life would be
    correlated; and

3. The various housing attitude variables would be intercorre-
    lated.

QUESTIONNAIRES AND SCALES USED

Development of the questionnaires involved a review of relevant literature, unstructured interviews with military personnel and navy spouses, and discussions with family housing officials from the Department of Defense and the four services. After the questionnaires were developed, further conferences were held with family housing and survey research officials to ensure accuracy and lack of bias in the items.

Early in 1975 the package of materials was mailed to each military family in the sample, addressed to the military member at his/her duty station. A cover letter from the Deputy Assistant Secretary of Defense (Installations and Housing) introduced the questionnaires, explained the purpose of the survey, and requested the cooperation of the military selectees and their spouses. Two different questionnaire forms, one for the military member and one for the spouse, were included with the letter. Selectees and their spouses were each requested to complete the appropriate questionnaire independently. They were assured that all responses would be confidential and would be used for research purposes only.

The two questionnaires were both multiple-choice forms, a 107-item form for military personnel and an 87-item form for their spouses. The primary difference between the two was that, to avoid duplication, certain background items on the military form were not repeated on the spouse form. The attitudinal items were, with few exceptions, identical in both forms.

Most of the attitudinal scales were of four basic types:

1. A 7-point satisfaction scale used for rating various types of housing, various housing characteristics, and quality of life (based upon the work of Andrews and Withey 1974);
2. A 7-point importance scale used for rating various military benefits and facilities and various housing characteristics;
3. A 7-point favorability scale used for rating housing policy proposals which had been suggested in previous housing studies; and
4. Five alternatives that were scaled for use in indicating preference for civilian housing over government quarters.

An important phase in the study involved the recoding of single items to reflect some underlying dimension and the construction of multi-item scales to provide greater measurement reliability. Most of the variables were constructed on an a priori basis. A few of the multi-item scales were contingent upon satisfactory item intercorrelations or response distributions. Where these statistics were required, they were obtained for the military and spouse data separately. In some cases, the data suggested different variable scalings for military and spouse data.

The variables used to investigate the model and hypotheses for both military respondents and spouses are listed in Table 1.1. Although housing-choice behavior variables and many of the personal/situational variables were obtained only from military respondents, they were used in both the military and spouse data analyses. Military respondents were also queried concerning their career intentions, while spouses were asked instead whether they favored a military career for their partners. Housing attitudes and quality-of-life data were obtained from both military and spouse respondents.

TABLE 1.1

Variables Used in Investigation of
Model and Hypotheses

Personal/Situational Factors
  Paygrade (grouped)
  Number of dependents
  Urbanization level
  Civilian housing cost
  Family's total income
  Number of times in military housing
  Relative income (within paygrade)*
  Length of marriage
Housing Choice Behavior
  Present housing type (military, civilian rental, or personally owned)
  Present housing style (single-family, duplex, apartment, etc.)
Housing Attitude
  Preference for civilian community
  Housing type preference
  Housing style preference
  Equity of present housing costs
  Housing satisfaction (present housing)*
  Importance in preference for civilian community
Career Intention/Favorability
  Career intention
  Favorability toward military career
Quality of Life*

Note: Multiple-item scales are designated by an asterisk (*). All others are based on a single item.
  Source: Compiled by the author.

A number of other items were also included in the survey but were not used in the investigation of the hypotheses and model. These items were used to obtain descriptive information such as the incidence of ownership of houses and mobile homes, sources of home financing, reasons for being on a waiting list for military housing, and other topics of interest to family housing officials.

SAMPLING STRATEGY

The sample was designed to represent the married military permanent-party population of the Continental United States (CONUS). A two-stage sampling strategy was used involving sampling of bases and of paygrade groups at the chosen bases. Bases were stratified by urbanization according to the following criteria:

Urbanization Level	Level Name	Population in Surrounding Area
1	Rural	Up to 50,000
2	Urban	50,000 to 200,000
3	Metropolitan	200,000 or more

Although the population of military families is concentrated most heavily in the "metropolitan" areas of 200,000 or more, it was desired to have equal sample sizes from each of the three urbanization levels to permit separate analysis of each level. Within each urbanization level individual bases were selected randomly, with a probability proportionate to their size and branch of service. A total of 35 bases was selected. At each base a systematic sample of families was drawn for each of the following paygrade groupings: E1-3, E4-6, E7-9, W-1-0-3, 0-4-5, and 0-6.

Since these sampling procedures resulted in different sampling ratios for each paygrade group and urbanization level, it was necessary to weight the responses received to achieve a more accurate representation of the population. Useable responses were received from a total of 16,961 military personnel and 13,625 spouses, representing 55 percent and 46 percent, respectively, of the original sample. Weighting by urbanization level and paygrade group resulted in weighted n's of approximately 22,000 military and 22,000 spouse responses, constituting about 3 percent of the target population of military families stationed in CONUS.

METHOD OF ANALYSIS

To test the model described earlier, two sets of stepwise multiple regressions were performed—one using career intention as the criterion variable and one using perceived quality of life as the criterion. Any variable included in the multiple regression equation had to meet the dual requirements of (1) producing a significant increase (at the .01 level) in the multiple correlation (R) and (2) an R^2 change of .01 or greater. In some instances, one single variable was virtually as effective as a combination of variables in accounting for variance on the criterion variable.

Individual bivariate correlations (Pearson r) and means were also examined in the analysis. The alpha level of .01 was adopted for significance tests involving correlations and differences between means.

RESULTS AND DISCUSSION

The findings of this study are predominantly consistent with the results of previous studies conducted among both the civilian and military populations. The spouse responses were generally very similar to the military responses. Consequently, the spouse correlations and multiple regressions are not mentioned in the text unless they differ from the military data.

Investigation of Urbanization
Level Similarities

The study was designed with the expectation that attitudes would be related to the degree of urbanization (city size) of the community surrounding a military base. A comparison of separate correlation matrices for rural, urban, and metropolitan respondents revealed no significant correlational differences. In view of these similarities, all three urbanization levels were subsequently analyzed together.

The similarity among rural, urban, and metropolitan respondents indicates that conclusions can be based upon the total sample without regard to urbanization level. This is not to say, however, that attitudes were identical at every base. Some variations occurred among individual bases, especially in attitudes toward the cost of housing, but they could not be explained on the basis of city size alone.

Housing Preferences

Respondents were asked to indicate the one kind of housing they
would most like to occupy at their present duty station, considering
their family's income, the local community, and the housing they
presently occupied. Single-family housing was by far the most popular style. Respondents having the highest paygrades were the most
likely to occupy and to express a preference for single-family housing.
However, at all paygrade levels (for both military personnel and
spouses), there was a substantial gap between the proportion desiring
single-family housing and the proportion actually occupying such
housing. The strong preference of both military personnel and
spouses at all paygrade levels for single-family housing is consistent
with the preferences of civilian families in the United States.

Both government single-family quarters and personally owned
single-family homes were frequently desired, but rented civilian
single-family housing appealed to a much smaller number of families.
This relative lack of interest in rented civilian homes is understandable, since they offer neither the benefits of ownership, nor the low
price of government single-family housing. The desire for ownership is strongly influenced by retirement planning and the long-term
financial advantages of ownership. The desire for government single-
family quarters seems to be motivated both by certain nonmonetary
advantages of government quarters and by their relatively low short-
term cost. Current pricing policies, in effect, provide a financial
subsidy to the families occupying government quarters. Single-
family quarters offer an especially attractive inducement, since for
any given family the cost is no greater than the cost of multiple-
family quarters, and it is generally far less than the cost of rented
civilian single-family housing.

An analysis was also performed combining preferences for single-
and multiple-family housing into the broad categories of government
quarters, rented civilian, and owned civilian housing (excluding
mobile homes). Paygrade was not significantly associated with a
preference for government over civilian housing—rather, interest
in government quarters was about the same at every paygrade level.
However, the preference for ownership over rental of civilian housing
increased as paygrade increased (with a corresponding decrease in
preference for civilian rentals).

The fact that preference for ownership over rental was directly
related to paygrade is consistent with the civilian literature and
probably reflects the inability of most families in the lower paygrades
to afford home ownership. The finding that preference for government quarters was unrelated to paygrade is somewhat surprising,
however. Prior studies of military families (Dupuy 1965; U.S.

Department of the Army 1966) found that families in the higher paygrades were more likely to prefer military housing than those in the
lower paygrades. The 1966 study, however, is not directly comparable with this one because it did not include the option of home ownership.

Factors other than satisfaction with the quarters themselves
appeared to contribute to a preference for government quarters over
civilian rental housing. One such factor is the previously mentioned
lower cost of government quarters compared with the cost of similar
civilian housing. Other related factors were their greater convenience to the place of duty and military facilities and the opportunity
to live in a neighborhood with rules, regulations, and other military
families, which are consistent with the findings of previous research
(Blockberger 1970; U.S. Department of the Army 1966; Knight et al.
1974).

Satisfaction with Housing
and Neighborhood Aspects

Respondents were asked to indicate how satisfied they were
with 24 different aspects of their present housing and neighborhood,
using the previously described 7-point scale ranging from "terrible"
to "delighted." Those in civilian housing, especially those owning
their own homes, were more satisfied than the military housing occupants with their chance to get away from the military atmosphere at
their residences. The home owners were more satisfied than either
the renters or the military housing occupants with the aspects of
privacy and residential appearance. The occupants of various housing
types did not differ as much on the remaining 21 aspects of their
housing.

There was no strong relationship between paygrade and satisfaction with various aspects of housing and neighborhood. Military
respondents and spouses showed very similar mean levels of satisfaction with most of these aspects. Their mean satisfaction ratings
did differ significantly, however, on availability of playgrounds
(spouses less satisfied than military respondents) and amount of
their housing allowance (military respondents less satisfied than
spouses) ($p < .01$).

Importance of Housing and
Neighborhood Aspects

Respondents were also requested to rate 15 different housing
and neighborhood aspects on a 7-point importance scale, ranging

from "of no importance" to "one of the most important." For both
respondent groups, availability of good schools was the most important aspect, while having other military families in the neighborhood
and having maintenance and yard work taken care of were the least
important aspects. Significant differences were found between military and spouse mean ratings for six aspects ($p < .01$). Military
personnel attributed more importance than their spouses to getting
away from the military atmosphere, while spouses gave more importance than military respondents to: convenience to military facilities,
community rules and regulations, having maintenance and yard work
taken care of, having other military families in the neighborhood,
and having a fenced-in yard.

Importance of Military Benefits
and Facilities

In order to assess the relative importance of seven different
benefits and facilities, respondents rated each one on the 7-point
scale, ranging from "of no importance" to "one of the most important." Military respondents and spouses were in fairly close agreement as to both the relative and absolute importance of these items.
Both rated medical benefits and facilities the highest in importance,
followed by comissary privileges, exchange privileges, government
family quarters, and recreation facilities, with base club facilities
and the opportunity to live in foreign countries rated as least important. Although the relative importance of these benefits was similar
for both groups, the spouses rated commissary privileges and the
opportunity to live in foreign countries higher in absolute importance
than did their military partners ($p < .01$).

It was anticipated that respondents preferring civilian housing
would differ from those preferring government quarters as to the
importance they attributed to military benefits and to different aspects
of housing and neighborhoods. Correlation coefficients (Pearson r)
were computed between each importance rating and the respondent's
score on preference for civilian community (PCC). Those importance items having correlations greater than $\pm .15$ with the PCC
score were averaged (and reversed where applicable) to constitute
a variable referred to as "importance in preference for civilian
community" (IPCC). The importance ratings for items such as having
military neighbors or getting away from the military atmosphere were
more highly correlated with the preference for government over
civilian housing than were those concerning military benefits and
facilities. While the items on recreation facilities and base club
facilities (and for military respondents, exchange privileges) were

included in the IPCC scale, their relationship to preference for government quarters over civilian housing was relatively weak.

Satisfaction with Quality of Life Aspects

Respondents were asked to indicate their feelings about nine aspects of life and about their life as a whole, using the 7-point satisfaction scale, ranging from "terrible" to "delighted." These aspects were selected in part from the work done by Andrews and Withey (1974) in measuring perceived quality of life among a broad crosssection of the civilian population. Two aspects dealing specifically with military life were added—"military pay and allowances" and "the military aspects of your life."

For both military respondents and spouses the mean response to "life as a whole" was strongly positive, the mean response to seven of the specific aspects was moderately positive, and the mean response to "total family income" and "military pay and allowances" was approximately neutral. For military respondents the mean satisfaction rating for "the military aspects of life" was lower than the mean ratings for "life as a whole," "the way you spend your spare time," and "your present house or apartment." For spouses the mean rating for "military aspects of life" was lower than for all of the other aspects except "family income" and "military pay and allowances." In several instances the spouses' mean ratings differed significantly from those of the military respondents ($p < .01$). These are noted in Table 1.2.

Test of the Model and Hypotheses

Military respondents were asked to indicate their career intention; officers were asked whether they planned to remain in the service for a career (at least 20 years) and enlisted personnel, whether they planned to reenlist. Excluding those who were already eligible for retirement, the mean response for officers and enlisted personnel combined was 3.062 on a scale ranging from 1 to 4. This corresponds to a response of "undecided but probably yes." Spouses' attitudes were obtained from an item measuring their favorability toward a military career for their partner. On a scale of 1 to 5, their mean response was 3.827, which is closest to "somewhat in favor"—not markedly different from the military mean.

The career intention item for military personnel and the favorability toward military career item for spouses were both positively correlated with the following variables: quality of life (military r = .34); number of times in military housing (military r = .27); and

TABLE 1.2

Military and Spouse Mean Satisfaction Ratings
for Quality of Life Aspects

Aspect	Military Mean	Spouse Mean
Life as a whole	5.398	5.423
Way you spend your spare time	5.092	4.888*
Present house/apartment	4.935	4.975
Military aspects of life	4.698	4.596
Standard of living	4.637	4.842*
Freedom from being bothered or annoyed	4.599	4.941*
Independence, chance to do what you want	4.495	4.852*
Amount of spare time available	4.457	4.742*
Family's total income	3.926	4.076*
Military pay and allowances	3.907	4.044
Sample size (weighted)	22,263	22,147

*Spouse mean differed significantly from military mean ($p < .01$).
Note: Rating scale ranged from 1 (terrible) to 7 (delighted).
Source: Compiled by the author.

number of dependents (military $r = .24$). For spouses, length of marriage was also positively correlated with favorability toward military career (spouse $r = .29$). This variable was not analyzed for military personnel. Two variables were negatively correlated with the career intention/favorability items for both military personnel and spouses—importance in preference for civilian community (military $r = -.25$) and preference for civilian community (military $r = -.21$).

All of the quality-of-life items except "house/apartment" were averaged together to produce a multi-item quality-of-life scale. This scale was positively correlated with the following variables for both military personnel and spouses: housing satisfaction (military $r = .53$); career intention (military $r = .34$); family's total income (military $r = .30$); and paygrade (military $r = .23$).

Fair market rental value of present housing (spouse $r = .23$) significantly correlated with the quality-of-life scale for spouses only, while relative income within paygrade (military $r = .21$) significantly correlated with the scale for military personnel only. The remaining predictor variables were not significantly correlated with the quality-of-life scale.

FIGURE 1.2

Test of the Model, Indicating Relationships
between Housing Variables, Demographic
Variables, Quality of Life, and
Career Intentions

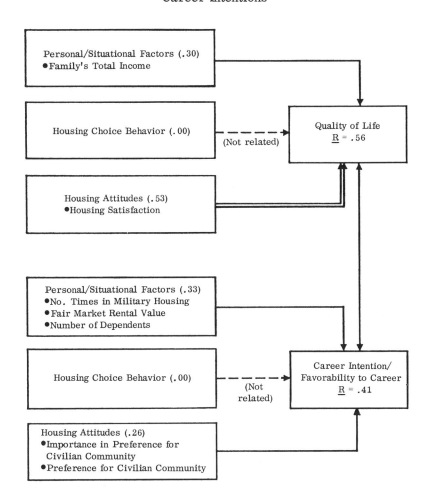

Note: Arrows point to the dependent variable in a stepwise multiple regression. Single and double lines convey the strength of relations relative to others in the diagram. The double line relation is at least double the magnitude of any single line relation (determined by r^2 values); the number in each box represents the direction and magnitude of the bivariate or multiple correlation resulting from the regression.

Source: Compiled by the author.

The results of the regression analyses are presented in Figure 1.2. Inspection of the diagram reveals that 31 percent ($.56^2$) of the variance in quality of life and 17 percent ($.41^2$) of the variance in career intention can be accounted for by the model described earlier. The weakest of the predictor categories was housing-choice behavior, which made no significant contribution to accounting for the variance in either criterion.

When considered alone, the predictor category of personal/ situational factors accounted for about 9 percent ($.30^2$ or $.33^2$) of the variance in both the quality-of-life and career intent criteria. For the quality-of-life criterion, family total income was the only variable from the personal/situational factor category needed to account for the 9 percent. For the career intent criterion, three quite different variables—number of times in military housing, fair market rental value of present housing, and number of dependents— contributed to the variance in the criterion.

Housing attitudes were the most criterion specific of the predictor categories. The variables in this category relating to the two criteria were not only different but also were related to the criteria in different directions and magnitude. Concerning quality of life, housing satisfaction alone accounted for 28 percent ($.53^2$) of the variance. This is a large percentage, considering that the whole model accounted for 31 percent ($.56^2$). Relevant to career intention, the housing attitudes category accounted for only 6 percent ($.26^2$) of the variance. The contributing variables were "importance in preference for civilian community" (IPCC) and "preference for civilian community" (PCC), both of which were inversely associated with career intention/ favorability.

The model and its hypotheses were generally supported by the data. Since the study did not include predictor variables that were related to job duties or other aspects of military work life, it was not expected that the model would account for a major share of the variance in quality of life or career intention. It was more successful in accounting for variance in perceived quality of life (military $\underline{R}$ = .56) than in accounting for career intention differences (military $\underline{R}$ = .41). The greater predictability of quality of life as compared with career intention was mainly due to the relatively high correlation between quality of life and housing satisfaction (military $\underline{r}$ = .53)— the highest correlation formed among the attitudinal variables analyzed in the study.

2 Marital Satisfaction, Job Satisfaction, and Retention in the Army

John C. Woelfel
Joel M. Savell

Problems of the army family have received relatively little attention in past military research efforts. Possibly one reason for the lack of research on the army family has been the relatively small percentage of married army personnel in past years. In 1952 only 36 percent of army personnel were married. By 1963 only 43 percent of army personnel were married (Bennett et al. 1974). However, by November 1975 more than half (57.2) of all army personnel were married. The percentages married, for officer and enlisted paygrades for November 1975, are presented in Table 2.1.

The fact that many soldiers now have family responsibilities, in addition to their army responsibilities, suggests that promotion and maintenance of family harmony among army families should act to promote job satisfaction and high levels of job performance among the soldiers from these families. Bennett et al. (1974) have suggested that family harmony is positively associated with a desire to remain in the army. While this proposition seems intuitively obvious, it has not received sufficient empirical testing, although there is some evidence that family problems are related to both AWOL status and desertion from the army (Bell and Houston 1976; Hartnagel 1974). In addition, several family-related variables have been shown to affect the intention of soldiers to remain in the army. Among these variables are frequency of permanent change of station (PCS) moves, separation from family, medical benefits, and wives' opinions of the army (U.S. Department of the Army 1971b).

The question has been posed as to whether family harmony is related to job satisfaction or performance. Although studies suggest that family life is a factor in certain army attitudes and behavior (for example, retention and delinquency), there is apparently no evidence that family harmony is related to job satisfaction or to the performance of routine duties required by the soldiers' specialty (MOS). A second question we are raising is: What aspects of army life actually produce family disharmony or promote family harmony?

TABLE 2.1

Percent Married in U.S. Army, by Paygrade

| Paygrade | Rank | | |
	Commissioned Officer	Warrant Officer	Enlisted
1	40.6	–	14.1
2	60.6	–	20.2
3	83.7	–	25.4
4	91.0	–	43.3
5	92.8	–	71.3
6	95.2	–	86.2
7	–	–	91.6
8	–	–	93.8
9	–	–	95.4
Total	81.2	90.2	53.1

Source: Data obtained from MILPERCEN Master Tape File November 1975. Data were not available for general officers, or for warrant officers by paygrade.

This question has received some attention (U.S. Department of the Army 1969; Vineberg and Taylor 1972), and several factors have been delineated which are related to family functioning, such as medical and dental care, separation from family, frequent PCS moves, and housing.

One limitation of the studies completed to date is that they have used forced-choice items to determine family problems. That is, they presented the respondents with a list of areas of army life and asked respondents to rate these areas as either satisfying or dissatisfying. This technique, however, restricts responses to areas of army life which have been specifically identified as satisfying or dissatisfying.

Still a third question concerning army families which this chapter will focus on is: How does the simultaneous experience of living both within the context of the family and simultaneously within the army experience affect a soldier's job performance and job satisfaction? These questions regarding the army family are first represented pictorially (see Figure 2.1).

Essentially, question one addresses path (c) shown in Figure 2.1, the relationship between family life and satisfaction with and performance of army duties. Question two seeks to determine path (a) by

FIGURE 2.1

Pictorial Representation of Questions
Regarding Army Families

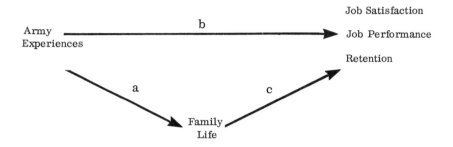

Source: Compiled by the authors.

identifying the particular aspects of army experience which have
perceptible impact on family life and by measuring the strength of
the impact. Question three looks at the interaction effects of army
experience and family life on job satisfaction and performance (paths
a x c), as well as the direct effect of army experience on satisfaction
and performance (path b).

First, we shall provide some preliminary data bearing on the
model in Figure 2.1. The data presented here derive from two studies.
The first study was designed to identify those aspects of army life
which soldiers report are either satisfying or dissatisfying to them
vis-a-vis their family life. The second study was designed to measure
the relationships among army experiences, marital satisfaction,
satisfaction with military duties, and intention to remain in the army.

METHOD FOR DETERMINING SATISFYING
AND DISSATISFYING ASPECTS OF
ARMY LIFE

The sample for this study consisted of 116 army personnel who
were either currently married or previously married while in the
army. The respondents were from Fort Lewis, Fort Dix, and Fort

Polk. An attempt was made to select respondents to include equal numbers of males and females, officers and enlisted, and whites and nonwhites. However, due to the limited number of married females at these installations, particularly nonwhite females, we were unable to obtain equal numbers of males and females or whites and nonwhites. Thus, the sample actually consisted of 77 males and 35 females, 72 white and 42 nonwhite, and 63 officers and 53 enlisted.*

The data were gathered by means of personal interviews conducted with the respondents during September 1975. The interviewers were specially trained army personnel, matched to the respondents on the basis of rank, sex, and race.

The interview schedule consisted of three parts: (a) open-ended section requiring respondents to name any problems or advantages they believed the army held for them in terms of their relationships with their spouses and in terms of raising their children (if they had any); (b) a request that respondents comment on certain aspects of army life, suggested in previous literature, which they believed to be either disruptive or beneficial to family life (for example, separation from family, PCS moves, recreational facilities, medical and dental care, and financial benefits); and (c) a section which asked respondents to list the three most beneficial and the three most detrimental aspects of army life, in terms of their relationships with their spouses and children.

The ten areas of army life which the respondents most frequently listed as either beneficial or disruptive to family life, based upon the open-ended questions from the first study, are shown in Table 2.2. The MOS-related factors were the most frequently mentioned area of disruption. The majority of complaints about MOS centered around duty hours, with respondents reporting that their hours were too long, and/or too irregular, and/or too uncertain. They frequently claimed that problems centering around duty hours either prevented them from making plans with their families or interrupted plans which had already been scheduled.

Separation from family and PCS moves were the next most frequently mentioned disruptive factors. Interestingly, one person saw benefits to separation. He felt that his separation from his wife afforded her the opportunity to be independent, a trait he valued in her. Results showed that PCS moves were listed as disruptive and beneficial by equal numbers of respondents. Some respondents listed PCS moves as both beneficial and disruptive. The principal benefits attached to PCS moves were the ability to travel and see new geo-

------

*Due to missing data, number of males and females, and whites and nonwhites do not total 116.

TABLE 2.2

Aspects of Army Life Believed to Be Disruptive
or Beneficial to Family Harmony

Variable	Percent Disruptive (N = 116)	Percent Beneficial (N = 116)
MOS-related[a]	59.5	
Separation	50.9	0.9
PCS	25.9	24.1
Financial[b]	11.2	62.9
Housing	11.2	10.3
Mandatory social events	9.5	
Medical and dental care	6.9	44.8
Child care	4.3	
Recreational facilities	2.6	9.5
Treatment of females by the opposite sex	2.6	

[a]This category included comments such as "extra duties," "needless or meaningless work," "uncertain work schedule," and "long duty hours."

[b]This category included responses such as "base pay," "retirement benefits," "PX and commissary privileges," "benefits," "job security," and "economic considerations."

Source: Compiled by the authors.

graphical locations and the opportunity to meet new people, particularly those of different social and ethnic backgrounds. The primary liability accruing from PCS moves was reported to be the disruption caused to spouse and children by uprooting them and moving to a new location.

The single most satisfying aspect of the army experience (in terms of frequency of endorsement) was financial. The majority of respondents who were satisfied with the financial aspect named factors such as job security, number and size of fringe benefits, and/or base pay as the satisfying portions of the financial conditions derived from the army. However, a few respondents were dissatisfied with their financial condition in the army, and their two primary financial concerns were declining benefits and low base pay.

The area of housing, viewed as both good and bad by almost equal numbers of respondents, included lack of on-post facilities, lack of privacy associated with on-post housing, the high cost of off-post housing, and the inadequacy of BAQ (basic allowance for quarters) to help defer these costs.

The five factors, mandatory social events, medical and dental care, child care, recreational facilities and treatment of females by males, received some mention as dissatisfying or disruptive to family life, although less than 10 percent of the sample felt adversely affected by these problems (see Table 2.2). Medical and dental care was also listed by almost half the respondents (44.8 percent) as a satisfying aspect of army life, and over half (62.9 percent) perceived the financial aspect as a satisfying part of army life. Specific complaints about army health care included long waits (up to four hours) for emergency and regular care, insensitivity of the medical staff to patient problems, and the elimination of dental benefits to dependents. Many of the satisfying and dissatisfying aspects of army life uncovered here are similar to those obtained in previous research, and, thus, offer a measure of reliability for these findings. For example, a 1969 U.S. Department of the Army study found that both officers and enlisted personnel named separations from family as the most dissatisfying aspect of army life. With regard to PCS moves, a Ladycom (1973) study of military wives also found a split in opinion; 62 percent of the wives said that the best thing about army life was mobility, while 38 percent said that moving was the primary stress on marriages.

Concerning medical and dental care, a 1972 study concluded that "actions in the health care category rank among the top MVA/VOLAR actions in terms of impact on overall attitudes and on retention. The retention impact of action in the health care category is considerably greater for married personnel than for single personnel" (Systems Development Corporation). A U.S. Department of the Army study (1971a) identified inadequate or nonexistent child care facilities a deterrent to wives of military personnel in seeking employment to relieve financial pressures on the family.

ARMY EXPERIENCES, MARITAL SATIS-
FACTION, JOB SATISFACTION,
AND RETENTION

Although the preceding data illuminate the problems and benefits army personnel see accruing to them and their families from their army experience, the data do not show to what extent these army experiences actually promote or disrupt family harmony. To accomplish this, a questionnaire was designed to assess soldiers' experiences in the same ten areas of army life listed in Table 2.2, in

FIGURE 2.2

Basic Model

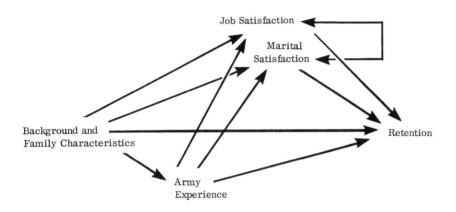

Source: Compiled by the authors.

addition to an assessment of job satisfaction, marital satisfaction, and intention to remain in the army. The questionnaire was administered to 215 soldiers at Fort Hood and Fort Riley in February and March 1976. The sample consisted of 112 males and 100 females,* of whom 83 were commissioned officers, 14 were warrant officers, and 117 were enlisted personnel. With regard to race, 158 were white, 35 black, and 15 were of other racial/ethnic origins. All respondents were either currently married, or had previously been married at some point in their army career.

The data gathered by this effort allowed further opportunity to provide some specification of the model presented in Figure 2.1 and the testing of a second (see Figure 2.2) which presents selected background and family characteristics in relation to their effect on the serviceperson's army experience, marital and job satisfaction, and intention to remain in the military service. In the model, army experiences are also depicted as influencing job satisfaction, marital satisfaction, and retention. Job and marital satisfaction, moreover, are shown as being related to one another, with no causal ordering

*Totals do not add up due to missing data.

predicted. Both these variables, job and marital satisfaction, are posited to affect intention to remain in the army.

VARIABLES IN THE MODEL

We shall not discuss in detail how each variable was operationally defined. Rather, we shall merely enumerate the various background and army experience variables, which included: sex, rank, length of marriage, number of children, MOS-related factors, hours worked per week, knowledge of duty hours, separation from family, PCS moves, economic factors, housing, mandatory social events, medical and dental care, child care, recreational facilities, and treatment of females.

Before proceeding further, however, perhaps we should define the three primary endogenous variables: marital satisfaction, job satisfaction, and intention to remain in the army. Marital satisfaction (MARSAT) was the sum of a 7-item scale obtained from Campbell, Converse, and Rogers (1975), with low scores reflecting low marital satisfaction. Job satisfaction (JOBSAT) was the sum of 11 items comprising the Military Work Role Scale (Bauer, Stout, and Holz 1977). Low scores on this scale reflect low job satisfaction. Intention to remain in the army (RETENTION) was scored one, if the respondent planned to leave army after current tour; two, if the respondent planned to stay at least one more tour; and three, if the respondent planned to stay in the army until retirement. Respondents who were undecided about their future career plans were excluded from the analysis.

SOLUTIONS TO THE MODEL

Theoretically, all the potentially satisfying and dissatisfying aspects of army life can be seen as being related to marital and job satisfaction and retention. Arguments can also be made for linking the four demographic and background characteristics to each of the army experience variables and the primary endogenous variables. In order to delineate the more important variables, a stepwise multiple regression analysis was performed to estimate each of the experience variables (excluding child care and recreation),* regressed on

---

*Child care was excluded from the analysis since fewer than 100 persons expressed an opinion about the quality of child care facilities. The recreation scale was excluded due to its low reliability.

all of the background and experience variables. Table 2.3 presents the means, standard deviations, and intercorrelations of the variables subjected to the stepwise regression.

In order to estimate the equations, complete data were required on all variables in the equations; therefore, 80 cases were eliminated, reducing the sample size to 135. Thus, the sample for this model consisted of 78 males and 57 females, and included 59 commissioned officers, 10 warrant officers, and 66 enlisted. With regard to racial/ ethnic composition, 106 were white, 17 black, and 12 were from other racial/ethnic backgrounds. The median number of years married was in the 3-6 year category.

The variables which were significant in each equation at or below the .10 level were retained, and the resulting equations were estimated using standard path analytic techniques. The variables in these equations which were insignificant were then deleted, and the equations reestimated. Figure 2.3 contains the significant paths among the variables.

Note which variables were totally eliminated—the PCS moves and mandatory social events. A glance at the correlation matrix in Table 2.3 shows that mandatory social events were strongly related to rank (r = .60), indicating that officers, more than enlisted personnel, feel pressure to attend these social events. However, required attendance at these functions does not perceptibly alter marital satisfaction, job satisfaction, or intention to remain in the army. It may seem surprising that PCS moves were eliminated, but it should be recalled that PCS moves were listed as both satisfying and dissatisfying by equal numbers of respondents in the first study mentioned in this chapter. Consequently, it is possible that if we divided our sample into those who enjoy PCS moves and those who dislike PCS moves, PCS moves might have a positive impact on the primary endogenous variables for the former group and a negative impact for the latter group. However, our limited sample size precluded such an analysis.

Of more importance than the excluded variables is the fact that none of the army experience variables or background variables exhibited any impact (positive or negative) on marital satisfaction, or at least upon the respondents' perception of marital satisfaction. Marital satisfaction, in turn, had no significant impact on job satisfaction or retention. These findings were in contrast to our prior expectations that family harmony would be related to those two variables.

Turning now to job satisfaction, we found that seven of the experience variables were related to job satisfaction, as well as to one background variable, sex. Women reported they were more satisfied with their jobs than the satisfaction reported by the men.

TABLE 2.3

Means, Standard Deviations, and Intercorrelations of the Variables in the Stepwise Regression

	y_1	y_2	y_3	x_1	x_2	x_3	x_4	x_5
y_1 MARSAT	—							
y_2 JOBSAT	.10	—						
y_3 RETENTION	.05	.40	—					
x_1 SEX	-.04	.07	-.35	—				
x_2 RANK	-.12	-.20	-.23	.02	—			
x_3 YRSMARR	-.00	.05	.40	-.43	-.10	—		
x_4 #CHIL	-.02	.10	.35	-.42	-.01	.48	—	
x_5 PMOS	.17	.20	.21	.21	-.04	.11	.07	—
x_6 #HOURS	.11	.07	.32	.43	-.10	.22	.32	.00
x_7 KNOWHRS	.02	.19	.20	.22	-.28	.07	-.11	.21
x_8 SEP	-.10	-.16	-.08	.03	.07	-.03	-.10	-.07
x_9 PCS	-.06	-.07	.04	-.21	-.07	.17	.05	-.06
x_{10} ECONOMIC	.13	.21	.13	.01	-.15	.09	.05	.11
x_{11} HOUSING	.07	.22	.08	.11	-.08	-.06	-.06	-.00
x_{12} SOCIAL	-.01	-.10	-.26	.17	-.60	-.16	-.15	-.05
x_{13} HEALTH	.10	.21	.04	.14	-.07	-.07	-.15	.02
x_{16} TREATOPPSEX	-.14	-.18	-.28	.43	.30	-.16	-.30	-.00
Mean	19.30	25.01	.86	.42	1.05	2.67	1.18	.61
sd	4.46	9.48	.86	.50	.96	1.40	1.19	.49

		x_6	x_7	x_8	x_9	x_{10}	x_{11}	x_{12}	x_{13}	x_{16}
y_1	MARSAT									
y_2	JOBSAT									
y_3	RETENTION									
x_1	SEX									
x_2	RANK									
x_3	YRSMARR									
x_4	#CHIL									
x_5	PMOS									
x_6	#HOURS	—								
x_7	KNOWHRS	-.17	—							
x_8	SEP	.06	.12	—						
x_9	PCS	.09	.01	.31	—					
x_{10}	ECONOMIC	-.04	.24	-.13	-.15	—				
x_{11}	HOUSING	-.09	-.04	-.10	-.05	.17	—			
x_{12}	SOCIAL	-.10	-.22	.04	-.08	.09	-.01	—		
x_{13}	HEALTH	-.18	.27	-.06	-.00	.11	.17	-.01	—	
x_{16}	TREATOPPSEX	-.13	.12	-.01	-.02	.02	-.02	.17	-.02	—
	Mean	4.21	.90	.53	.31	1.88	2.61	5.45	2.05	.66
	sd	1.69	.72	.57	.34	.77	.98	2.36	.72	1.06

Source: Compiled by the authors.

27

FIGURE 2.3 Solution to Path Model

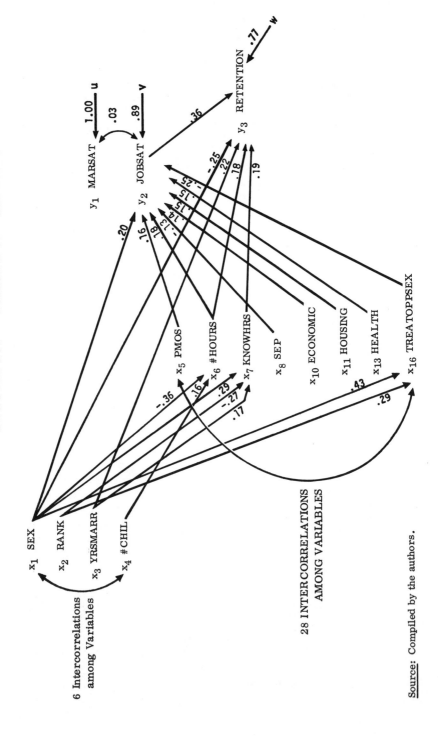

Source: Compiled by the authors.

28

This finding is somewhat paradoxical since women also report they are less likely to remain in the army than men. Women also perceived a great deal of verbal abuse directed at them by men, and this abusive treatment by the opposite sex appeared to be the strongest single factor influencing job satisfaction in a negative direction. Thus, although women are more satisfied with their jobs than men, perceived verbal abuse from men seemed to reduce their job satisfaction, which, in turn, reduced their desire to remain in the army. There may be other factors which cause women to leave the army more frequently than men, and these factors will be discussed later.

Among the army experience variables, two MOS-related factors affected job satisfaction. Respondents who were actually working in their primary MOS were more satisfied with their jobs than those who were not working in their primary MOS. Also, the number of hours a soldier worked was positively related to job satisfaction—the more hours worked, the higher the satisfaction. The fact that soldiers who work in their primary MOS are more satisfied with their jobs is not surprising, since, in most cases, the job they hoped to perform in the army is the job they were specially trained for. However, it was unexpected to find that those who worked longer hours were more satisfied with their jobs, since findings from Study 1 indicated that long work hours were a cause of dissatisfaction among the soldiers. It may be that those servicemembers who work longer hours are more committed to the army. We had intended to operationalize #HOURS as the number of hours the respondent was required to be on duty. Our speculation was that the longer a person is required to work, the more dissatisfaction there will be toward the job. However, in measuring #HOURS, we may actually have tapped the number of hours the respondents were on duty both involuntarily and voluntarily. If this were the case, it could mean that those working longer hours per week, by and large, were those doing so by choice, perhaps to improve their standing in the army. It is also possible that job satisfaction is a causal factor with respect to number of hours worked, with those who enjoy their jobs putting in more hours. In any event, since we cannot be sure that #HOURS has the meaning we intended, we cannot accurately interpret path $P_{y_2X_6}$.

Two of the experience variables which influenced job satisfaction were of a financial nature—economic index and housing quality. These relationships are consistent with common sense, as well as with evidence from national surveys of job satisfaction. Thus job satisfaction is positively related to one's satisfaction with income and housing.

Medical care is also related to job satisfaction and could perhaps be considered an economic benefit of army life since it is free to army personnel and their dependents. Separations from family, too, are related to job satisfaction. The combined effect of these eight

variables on job satisfaction accounted for 21 percent of the variance
in job satisfaction. Job satisfaction was also found to have a strong
effect on retention, as predicted. Nichols (1971), Schreiber and
Holz (1973), and Waters and Roach (1973) also found job satisfaction
related to positive intention to remain at a particular job.

In addition to job satisfaction, two background variables and two
experience variables were related to retention. The background variables are sex and years married. As noted before, men exhibit higher
levels of intention to remain in the army than women. It is not surprising to find women expressing more reluctance to remain in the
army since the army is still an organization dominated by males and
an organization in which women do not ordinarily receive equal treatment; for example, women are prohibited from taking part in combat-
related duties. In addition, women perceive that their chances for
promotion in the army are significantly less than the promotion chances
for men (U.S. Department of the Army 1974). Although years married is positively related to retention, the correlation is probably
spurious; the coefficient is probably due to the fact that years married
and retention are both related to the number of years the soldier has
been in the army.

The army experience variables related to retention are knowledge
of duty hours and number of hours worked per week. Although it was
expected that knowledge of duty hours would be related to retention
indirectly through job satisfaction, the variable appears to exert all
of its influence directly on retention. Hours worked is also related
to retention, although in an opposite direction. However, this relationship may be confounded by the relationship of hours worked to
commitment to the army, as mentioned earlier. Altogether, we are
able to account for 41 percent of the variance in retention, with the
single most important factor being job satisfaction.

SUMMARY AND CONCLUSIONS

This chapter has presented the results from two studies designed
to provide a better understanding of the relationships among army
experience, family life, job satisfaction, and intention to remain in
the army. The results from the first study indicated several areas
of army life which soldiers say impact either positively or negatively
on their family life. Among these variables were separation from
family, frequent PCS moves, financial rewards, health care, and
housing. However, when we examined those areas of army life
further, we found those experiences were not significantly related
to the soldiers' perceptions of their marital satisfaction. We cannot
completely rule out the possibility that the army experience does

affect family life in some way, since we have only looked at one indicator of family harmony, marital satisfaction. Moreover, we have not looked at the impact of the army experience on children of army personnel. We must also point out that we have measured only the soldiers' perceptions of their marital satisfaction; the findings might have differed had we measured their spouses' marital satisfaction and then related spouses' marital satisfaction to the army experience variables. Certainly, soldiers and their spouses are differentially affected by army life. The soldiers have military duties which may, in some measure, take their minds off problems in the home. They also spend a large segment of time with other soldiers with whom they can relax and discuss problems. Such interaction may act to alleviate some of the tension which the army experience produces in their families. Many spouses of army personnel, on the other hand, do not have jobs, and may not have close friends. If the spouses are not able to occupy their time with outside activities, they may tend to spend more time reflecting on their family situation and the effect the army has upon it, which could lead to a strong relationship between the army experience and marital satisfaction.

A final point to be made here is that data collection for this study took place in peacetime, whereas many prior studies of the army family have been conducted during war. With the added threat of death during wartime, we could speculate that many of the army experience variables examined would have more of a disruptive effect on the family.

Not only was marital satisfaction unrelated to any of the army experience variables, it was also unrelated to job satisfaction and retention. Our initial speculation that marital satisfaction would be related to job satisfaction and retention, then, is unsupported. Nor has the proposition that family harmony is related to job performance been proved, since we have measured job satisfaction and retention, but not job performance. Job satisfaction and job performance have been shown to be related in certain studies (Greenwood and Soar 1973; Katzell, Barrett, and Parker 1961); however, this relationship has not been found in other investigations (Kahn 1960; Martin 1969; Rosen and McCullum 1962). In the present investigation we used only one type indicator of family harmony, marital satisfaction. Although marital satisfaction was found to be unrelated to job satisfaction and retention, selected army experience variables did demonstrate effects on job satisfaction and retention, and job satisfaction emerged as the single most important factor in soldiers' intentions to remain in the army.

3

Junior Officer Retention in
the Modern Volunteer Army:
Who Leaves and Who Stays?

Donald A. Lund

The U.S. Army's Modern Volunteer Army Program, labeled "A Program for Professionals," became a subject of concern among officers in the junior grades in late fall of 1970. It was then that the official rhetoric, rumors, and political pronouncements began to indicate that change was possible throughout the institution, and this possibility sent ripples of excitement through the junior ranks. Officially, the program had as its announced objective "to expedite the development of a capably led, highly competent fighting force which attracts motivated, qualified volunteers" (U.S. Department of the Army 1971a: 1). Two directions were highlighted in the army's master plan to build a better army. Though conceptually distinct, the two, strengthening professionalism–"to build positive incentives to service," and improving army life–"to reduce the sources of dissatisfaction," certainly were related and overlapped.

Officers and noncommissioned officers at all levels were put at work to implement the Pentagon's publicly proclaimed program. Professionalism has as its explicit components willing self-discipline and a determination to do one's job with competence and commitment. Among the ways of achieving this professionalism, the army's master plan suggested the following: back to basics, exciting/meaningful training, educational development, leadership for professionals, reserve components, and focused pay.

In army terms, back to basics means returning soldiers to soldiering "by releasing them to the greatest extent possible from ancillary, nonmilitary duties" (U.S. Department of the Army 1971a: 1). Exciting/meaningful training included the objective of achieving a decentralized approach with responsibility for management in the hands of unit commanders, as well as challenging the soldier to demonstrate his ability measured against high standards by using imaginative and creative exercises, especially adventure training, as well as evaluation by testing actual performance (U.S. Department of the Army 1971a: 13). Educational development included allowing the soldier

to acquire, on duty time, civilian-recognized skills or education,
with the express purpose of, in some measure, reducing the feeling
that army service is a delay or postponement of the entry into what
the soldier considers "real life." To avoid the loss of good men who
feel that they must return to the civilian world in order to learn their
skill or profession to begin civilian careers, all levels of education
were to be emphasized.

Leadership for professionals, as made explicit in the program
included both development of army leaders and improvement of the
foundations of army leadership. The goals of the program were:
the development of leaders who could successfully accomplish their
unit mission while successfully maintaining the integrity of the officer
and NCO corps and upholding the dignity of the individual soldier; the
creation of a climate of mutual respect in which soldiers experienced
professional growth and exercised self-discipline; and the establishment of active and genuine concern for the well-being of soldiers and
the shielding of soldiers from harassment.

The foundations of leadership were felt to be improved by increasing stability of command assignments, modifying centralized management procedures to assist, rather than impede, the commander, and
upgrading and modernizing leadership instruction in NCO and officer
schools. Further, a new personnel management system providing
for ordered career progression and increased emphasis on continuing
professional education at key stages of advancement was stressed
(U.S. Department of the Army 1971a: 20). Reducing the sources of
dissatisfaction in the army's master plan included improvements in
family housing, post services, pay, barracks housing, and life style.
This chapter is a report of findings based upon data collected through
a mailed questionnaire sent to junior-grade commissioned officers
(second lieutenants, first lieutenants, and captains with less than six
years of service) and warrant officers serving in the Military District
of Washington. The purpose of the study was to determine how closely
the concerns of these officers were reflected in the goals outlined in
the army's master plan for the Modern Volunteer Army, to see if
the official plans actually addressed the perceived needs of the junior
officers, and to see what attitudes differentiated those officers willing
to make the military a career from those anxious to leave at the conclusion of their current commitment.

RESULTS

Two mailings received a response rate of 68 percent, with 121
of 178 commissioned and warrant officers responding. Of these, 99
responses were from junior commissioned officers, and it is the

responses of this latter subsample which we shall examine further. Of these 99 officers, 60.6 percent were captains with less than six years of service, 35.4 percent were first lieutenants, and 4 percent were second lieutenants. Answers were categorized regardless of current service category (that is, Obligated Volunteer, Voluntary Indefinite, Regular Army) into "stay on active duty," indicated by 49.5 percent, "leave active duty," chosen by 39.4 percent, and "undecided about future plans," which included the remaining 11.1 percent. Seventy-five percent of the Obligated Volunteers wanted to leave active service, whereas 58.5 percent of those in the Volunteer Indefinite category and 73.3 percent of those who had become Regular Army indicated that they held career aspirations.

Background Factors and Retention Plans

Junior officers who indicated intentions to end active duty at the close of current obligations were better educated and came from higher socioeconomic backgrounds. The fathers of those officers leaving active duty at the conclusion of their current tours were more likely employed in white-collar or skilled occupations (84.6 percent), as compared to the fathers of those staying on active duty (72.4 percent). Over 90 percent (92.3) of the junior officers leaving active duty had a college degree, compared to the 55.1 percent of those who indicated they were staying.

Area of upbringing and size of hometown were not significantly related to active duty plans, although slightly greater proportions of officers leaving active duty reported large or medium-sized hometowns. Geographic areas (for example, S.W. United States, N.W. United States) did not relate significantly to active duty plans.

Attitudes and Retention

Utilizing the programatic distinctions made in the army's program between strengthening professionalism and improving army life or life style, analysis of the junior officers' responses showed that over 50 percent (50.5) of the officers had no complaints about facilities or services offered. Complaints which were reported were aimed primarily at officers' clubs, which were thought to cater to senior officers' tastes, and toward unresponsive medical and dental services. Post exchange facilities, commissaries, army pay, and housing were reported to have little or no influence on whether or not the officer chose to stay or leave the service. Medical benefits, as opposed to the actual delivery of medical services, and retirement were reported to be valuable fringe benefits of army service, whereas family separations and frequent moves were cited as dissatisfactions. Between-group differences with respect to satisfaction with facilities and services, however, were not statistically significant.

Focusing next on the elements of professionalism, both convergences and divergences in thought were found among those officers planning to stay on active duty and those planning to leave. For example, 62 percent of those officers surveyed preferred a specialist role over the more typical generalist role, but differences between those electing to stay on active duty and those electing to leave were not statistically significant. Further, both groups reached substantially the same conclusion about the adequacy of their preparation for service through the branch Officer Basic Course. Of the total group, 12.9 percent felt very well prepared, 50.6 percent felt moderately well prepared, while 36.5 percent reported that their Officer Basic Course inadequately prepared them for active duty. Over 25 percent (26.3) of the officers staying on active duty, 47.2 percent of those leaving, and 36.4 percent of those undecided reported inadequate preparation. While these differences are not statistically significant, it would seem that dissatisfaction among a substantial proportion of these junior officers exists in regard to the Officer Basic Course preparation for the challenge of military service.

Officers were also asked to evaluate their preparation in a group of subareas of competence. In excess of 38 percent felt insufficiency of skill development in leadership and social/interpersonal relations, while almost half the men felt marginal or inadequate development in technical branch skills (45.9 percent), human relations skills (41.2 percent), and administrative skills (43.7 percent). Over 50 percent of the responding officers felt insufficiencies in the areas of tactics, communications (verbal, not electronic) and physical skills. Clearly, such reported developmental insufficiency may be related to problems of retention and company-level leadership. The relation of perceived insufficient skill development to weakened self-confidence among these officers, though only an hypothesized relationship, may be a significant point at which the military system could intervene to provide more "positive incentives to service," resulting in retention of more junior officers, as well as more of their subordinates.

The group staying differed significantly from the junior officers leaving or undecided for only one skill area—technical branch skill development. Almost one-fourth (24 percent) of those leaving active duty, 18.2 percent of those undecided, and 2.2 percent of those staying, reported such inadequate skill development ($p < .05$).

Factors Influencing Retention Decision

The responses of a large proportion of the officers revealed that family separation and repetitive tours in Vietnam were negative influences when they considered a military career (see Table 3.1). Retirement benefits, opportunity for leadership, promotion opportunities, the opportunity to serve in the national interest, pay and allowances, the opportunity for advanced civilian schooling, and job security were considered prime influences toward staying on active duty, confirming the validity of the program suggested in the army's master plan.

The same factor considered an influence for staying might also be reported as an influence for leaving, depending upon the retention plan of the respondent. For example, results showed that personnel and administrative practices were an influence to stay for 25.5 percent of those planning to stay, as compared to 5.7 percent of those leaving. However, that same item was an influence to leave for only 6.4 percent of those staying, but for 48.6 percent of those leaving. In other words, personnel and administrative practices influenced 25.5 percent of those staying to stay and 48.6 percent of those leaving to leave. Likewise, the opportunity for advanced military schooling was a positive influence for 56.5 percent of those planning to stay on active duty, but had a like influence on only 8.3 percent of those planning to leave active service at the completion of their current obligation.

Leadership provided by senior officers was reported as a factor which influenced 34.0 percent of those staying to stay and 37.8 percent of those leaving to leave. Interestingly, when asked the question, "If you were out in civilian life, would you hire your immediate boss as a manager," 76.6 percent of those staying answered that they would definitely hire him, while 55.9 percent of those leaving would have some reservations about hiring him, or would categorically reject him.

Public opinion of the army influenced 35.1 percent of those planning to leave active duty to do so, although it influenced only 13.0 percent of those staying to stay. Interestingly, in a comparison of their prestige within the military service relative to the civilian sphere, out of the total group, 43.8 percent believed their prestige was higher in the military. However, 53.2 percent of those staying on active duty felt that their prestige was higher in the military, while 48.7 percent of those leaving felt that they had less prestige in the military and, thus, would have greater prestige in civilian life.

TABLE 3.1

Factors Influencing Retention Decision in
A Sample of 99 Junior Officers

	Influence to Stay	Neutral	Influence to Leave
*Promotion opportunities	48.9	31.5	19.6
Unit morale	27.7	60.2	15.1
*Opportunity for leadership	57.8	36.7	5.6
Superior's interest	27.8	55.6	16.7
*Job security	44.6	52.2	3.3
*Personnel and administrative practices	16.5	61.5	22.0
*Retirement benefits	71.1	28.9	0.0
*Pay and allowances	51.1	34.8	13.5
Post exchange, army housing and commissary	34.4	61.3	4.3
*Repetitive tours in Vietnam	4.3	52.7	43.0
Opportunity to serve in national interest	52.2	44.6	3.3
Family separation	4.4	44.0	51.6
*Leadership of senior officers	19.4	60.2	20.4
*Public opinion of the army	8.7	75.0	16.3
*Civilian job opportunities	23.9	48.9	27.2
Frequency of PCS moves	8.6	52.7	38.7
*Vietnam situation	10.8	61.3	28.0
*Opportunity for advanced military schooling	34.1	63.7	2.2
*Opportunity for advanced civilian schooling	48.4	46.2	5.4
*Career development program	21.7	68.5	9.8

*Indicates significant difference between stay, leave, and undecided categories (x^2, $p < .05$ or better).

Source: Compiled by the author.

37

Wives' Attitudes and Retention

Since the influence of public opinion and prestige seemed significant in differentiating officers planning to stay on active duty and
those planning to leave active service, let us examine the perceived
attitudes of wives of these junior officers in relation to their husbands'
active duty plans. It is noteworthy that wives' attitudes have been
all but ignored in official pronouncements about the Modern Volunteer
Army. Yet, their feelings may indeed be significant in the decision-
making of their husbands.

Married officers were asked whether their wives' attitudes were
an influence to leave the service, to stay, or of neutral influence.
As shown in Table 3.2, 62.1 percent of those officers planning to
leave active service reported that their wives' attitudes influenced
their decisions. On the other hand, 61.1 percent of those planning
to stay on active duty reported that their wives' attitudes influenced
their decisions to stay on. Thus, over 60 percent of the wives in
both categories seem to have influenced their husbands' choices.
Based upon these data, it is clear that wives' attitudes are a key
factor in their husbands' active duty decisions.

Let us examine whether husband-reported attitudes of the wives
of those officers contemplating active duty careers differed significantly from those planning to leave active service. The major dissatisfactions of wives, as reported by their officer husbands, were
family separations (76.7 percent dissatisfied), housing facilities
(69.9 percent dissatisfied), and frequency of moves (71.8 percent

TABLE 3.2

Influence of Wife's Attitude on Active Duty Plans

Husband's Active Duty Plans	Wife's Attitude Toward the Army		
	Influence to Stay	Neutral Influence	Influence to Leave
Stay	61.9	26.2	11.9
Leave	6.9	31.0	62.1
Undecided	0.0	100.00	0.0
Total	36.8	32.9	30.3
	(28)	(25)	(23)

Chi Square = 39.39 P (4df) < .01.
Gamma = 0.69
Source: Compiled by the author.

TABLE 3.3

Reported Attitudes of Junior Officers' Wives
Toward Aspects of Military Service

	Wife's Feeling			
	Very Satis- fied	Satis- fied	Dissat- isfied	Very Dissat- isfied
Family separation	3.3	20.0	30.0	46.7
Pay and allowances	22.9	47.1	25.7	4.3
Housing facilities	4.8	25.4	30.2	39.7
Medical care	30.0	32.9	17.1	20.0
Frequency of moves	10.9	27.3	23.6	38.2
Military social life and protocol	23.1	41.5	12.3	23.1
Social status	23.4	54.7	17.2	4.7

Source: Compiled by the author.

dissatisfied), as shown in Table 3.3. These data indicate a clear
need to consider wives in any retention program. Wives of officers
electing to stay on active duty were reported to have greater dissatisfactions with housing facilities than wives of officers electing to leave
at the conclusion of their current obligation. In fact, greater dissatisfaction was reported for "leaving" wives in all categories, and particularly in regard to military social life and protocol and current
social status as junior officer's wives. Over 70 percent (71.4) of
leaving wives were reported as being "very dissatisfied" with family
separation, while only 28.6 percent of the wives whose husbands
were staying on active duty were reported as having this degree of
dissatisfaction. Likewise, 39.1 percent of the leaving wives, as
compared to 15.8 percent of the staying wives were reported to be
very dissatisfied with military social life and protocol. How much
these dissatisfactions influenced career choice or were influenced
by career choice remains unclear.

In response to the question about how the Modern Volunteer Army
could better address the needs of their wives, the largest proportions
of officers cited elimination of formality as most effective, followed
by stabilization of tours and improved delivery of medical and dental
care. That senior officers' wives frequently wear their husband's
rank is a common part of military lore. It is evident that this factor
affects the new army wife's adjustment and comfort as an "army wife"
and could be a crucial element in the retention of junior officers.

SUMMARY AND CONCLUSIONS

Several points are raised by these data. Recall that life-style problems were reported less important than those of professionalism and leadership in junior officers' decisions regarding retention. Officer branch skill development was reported to be inadequate in preparing the junior officer to meet the challenge of company level duties. Dissatisfaction with administrative and personnel practices were reported by a large number of the officers queried. These concerns could most likely be addressed without difficulty. However, other frequently cited problems (for example, leadership of senior officers and the public's opinion of the army) may be more difficult to address. The findings of this study show that significant differences in attitudes existed between those junior officers planning to stay on active duty and those leaving active service. What is unclear is whether these attitudes were formed before or after the decision was made. Do they contribute to, or are they the result of a decision about future career plans? These are questions for further inquiry. Clearly, though, the junior officer's wife plays an important role in his career decision. Her needs have not been addressed by the Modern Volunteer Army program. A good junior officer retention program must include efforts aimed specifically at the junior officers' wives.

A very real concern remains—one which has been raised in many previous reports (Lund 1971; Moskos 1970; King 1971; Gates 1970; Marmion 1971). Marmion has posed the question, "Where will the officer corps come from," and expressed his concern about the future quality of the officer corps under a volunteer system. "If the desired numbers can be found, will they be of sufficiently high quality? Unfortunately, under a volunteer system it seems more likely that many will become officers for other motives than aptitude for work: because they feel inadequate to compete in the civilian economy or even because they like to wear uniforms, carry weapons, and achieve instant machismo" (1971: 54). To Marmion's point, we contribute our data which show that better educated officers leave the service at the completion of their current obligation. The results also indicate, in answer to an open-ended question about the "reasons" for a career choice, that frequently mentioned reasons for staying on active duty included a desire for an army career or a bad civilian job market; reasons for leaving active duty included better civilian opportunities, a desire to continue civilian education, and a feeling of disillusionment. It is noteworthy that in response to the question, "In your opinion, how many officers on active duty would like to get out but are hesitant to give up the security and face the uncertainties of civilian life," 2.1 percent answered "none," 43.8 percent answered "a few," while the remaining 54.2 percent answered "many" or "most." Thus, an unanswered question remains, "What kind of officers are being retained, and what will the effect of their retention be on the U.S. Army?" As Marmion concluded:

> . . . America will draw its military leaders from a narrow, inbred group, not as well-educated, not coming from a broad cross-section of American higher educational institutions, and not as close to the mainstream of its democratic institution. Thus, there will arise an isolated elite in the officer corps at the top and an equally isolated group, socially and economically, in the enlisted ranks below. Such a military can hardly be viewed as a solid foundation for a democratic society." (1971: 55-56).

Perhaps we should be more concerned about the new military of volunteers.

4 Wives' Attitudes and the Retention of Navy Enlisted Personnel

Gloria Lauer Grace
Mary B. Steiner

Navy wives' attitudes are indeed a factor in influencing retention of military personnel. The investigation reported in this chapter was conducted as part of a larger program of research on retention and personnel satisfaction of navy enlisted personnel (Grace et al. 1976; Holoter et al. 1974; Holoter et al. 1973). Although wives' attitudes have generally been considered to be a factor influencing retention in past studies, investigations tended to focus on the husbands' reports of the wives' attitudes. The approach used in this study, however, was to obtain evidence directly from wives. Parallel surveys were administered both to navy wives and husbands in order to determine the extent to which wives' attitudes matched husbands' reports of wives' attitudes.

Results were compared and a number of significant differences were found. For example, in contrast with husbands' perceptions of their wives' attitudes, navy wives reported themselves to be much more willing for their husbands to reenlist.

In a study using actual reenlistment behavior as the criterion (Grace, Holoter, and Soderquist 1976), results indicated that the family was an important factor influencing retention. Comparison of results with navy retention statistics and Navy Human Resources Management Survey data also yielded supportive findings. The lives of military wives tend to be strongly influenced by their husbands' career choices because of demands of the job, including family separation, frequent moves, and within the navy, sea duty. Housing,

This study was performed under the Navy Manpower R&D Program of the Office of Naval Research under Contract N00014-75-C-0311, NR 170-791. The authors are indebted to Dr. Bert T. King of that office for his support and suggestions throughout this program of research.

educational opportunities for children, and living conditions in general
may be less than satisfactory. This is particularly true for younger
wives since their husbands' incomes are usually more limited. Other
factors negatively impacting on wives during the recent time frame
of this study include increased workloads of husbands due to personnel
shortages, inflation, and the perceived erosion of military benefits.
Although in the peacetime military, husbands sometimes perform
dangerous jobs, in wartime husbands called into combat must face
an even greater hazard—the loss of their lives. The role of wives
whose husbands work in civilian organizations has been investigated
by Renshaw (1975), Battalia and Tarrant (1973), Seidenberg (1973),
Culbert and Renshaw (1972), and Burger (1968). Except for those
specific areas discussed above, findings for the civilian community
tend to support results obtained from the military community, including those obtained by Muldrow (1971) and through the Ladycom Survey
of Navy Wives (1973). Taken together, the evidence tends to support
the hypothesis that wives' attitudes are a factor influencing retention
of navy personnel.

The research reported in this chapter was designed to investigate
the nature of these attitudes. More specifically, research objectives
were: (1) to verify findings about wives' attitudes toward navy life,
(2) to study their attitudes toward issues of specific interest to the
navy, and (3) to determine the potential of navy wives as an influence
to improve personnel satisfaction and increase retention of navy
enlisted personnel.

METHOD AND PROCEDURE

An initial sample of 442 navy wives living in the San Diego,
Norfolk, and Pearl Harbor areas was surveyed in 1973 using an
86-item questionnaire paralleling an instrument designed for use
with navy enlisted personnel. Topics included: demography;
retention/reenlistment; incentives; economic and social conditions;
information; the Navy Career Counseling Program; work environment;
organizational climate; attitudes toward navy life; housing; family
separation; location; and personal factors. In 1976 a second sample
of 584 wives from these locations was surveyed using a 91-item
questionnaire expanded to include the possibility of navy women serving at sea and the economic recession. Data were analyzed using
the two-way ANOVA and Chi-square techniques. Criteria of classification were career status and willingness of wives for husbands to
reenlist. Descriptive statistics were computed, and a comparison
was made of the two samples of navy wives.

RESULTS

In general for both time frames wives tended to have favorable attitudes toward their husbands' reenlisting in the navy. However, as shown in Table 4.1 wives' attitudes in the initial survey conducted in 1973 were found to be more favorable. In the second survey conducted in 1976, 10 percent fewer wives reported that they were willing for their husbands to reenlist, and 8.3 percent fewer reported they would encourage their husbands to reenlist if the decision had to be made "today." The second survey was more representative in that it sampled fewer wives of career personnel—50.4 percent as compared with 78.0 percent in the initial survey. Also, concern about the perceived erosion of benefits was widespread among navy wives in 1976. These factors may also have contributed to the finding that wives' attitudes and opinions tended to be slightly less favorable in the second survey. However, the patterning of responses tended to be similar in the two surveys. In order to focus on the more recent time frame, results that follow are drawn from the 1976 survey.

Wives' willingness for husbands to reenlist tended to vary according to the career status of their husbands. Noncareer status included those whose husbands were committed for less than eight years of navy service. Career status indicated husbands who were committed for more than eight, but less than $19\frac{1}{2}$ years. Over-career status indicated husbands who were committed for more than $19\frac{1}{2}$ years and thus were eligible for Fleet Reserve retirement. As shown in Table

TABLE 4.1

Comparison of Navy Wives' Attitudes toward
Husband's Reenlistment between Initial
and Second Surveys
(in percent)

| | | Survey | |
| | | Initial | Second |
Question	Response	(1973)	(1976)
Willing for husband to	Yes	63.4	53.4
reenlist at end of term	Undecided	16.8	24.6
	No	19.8	22.6
Would encourage reenlistment if	Yes	69.9	61.6
decision had to be made today	No	30.1	38.4

Source: Compiled by the authors.

TABLE 4.2

Willingness of Wives for Husbands to Reenlist
Based on Data Obtained in 1976
(in percent)

Career	Reenlistment Intent			
Status	N	Yes	Undecided	No
Noncareer	112	38.4	25.9	35.7
Career	293	60.8	24.9	14.3
Over-career	147	51.7	23.1	25.2
Totals	581	53.4	24.6	22.0

Source: Compiled by the authors.

4.2, the career and over-career wives were more willing for their husbands to reenlist. An interesting finding was that almost two out of five of the noncareer wives (38.4 percent) were willing for their husbands to reenlist, while slightly more than one in four (25.9 percent) were undecided. However, over twice as many noncareer wives (35.7 percent) were unwilling for their husbands to reenlist as compared with career wives (14.3 percent).

For nine survey items, differences significant at the .01 level of confidence were obtained across reenlistment intent for all three career status groups. These cluster into four general areas: the navy-work setting, expectations, the recession, and navy life in general. Ratings were obtained using a 5-point Likert-type scale. Of the nine items for which significant differences were obtained, seven were bipolar and two, unipolar. With regard to the navy-work setting, as shown in Table 4.3, willingness of wives for husbands to reenlist varied directly with wives' satisfaction with husbands' present jobs in the navy. Willingness also varied directly with favorableness toward navy reenlistment programs. Wives' attitudes tended to be favorable in this area. For example, mean ratings for all wives who were willing, all over-career wives, and undecided career wives fell above the midpoint on the scale for husband's present navy job. Reactions toward navy reenlistment programs followed the same pattern except that mean ratings for undecided career wives and unwilling over-career wives fell below the midpoint on the scale for that item. It appears that those wives who perceived that their husbands were happy, liked their present jobs, and were experiencing career satisfaction tended to be more likely to be willing for their husbands to reenlist.

TABLE 4.3

Relationship between Career Status and
Reenlistment Intent for the Navy Work
Setting Area

Question (Polarity)	Willing for Husbands to Reenlist	Mean Rating by Career Status Groups[*]		
		Non-career (N=112)	Career (N=293)	Over-career (N=147)
How do you feel about your husband's present navy job? (Bipolar)	Yes	3.26	3.66	3.84
	Undecided	2.86	3.04	3.26
	No	2.28	2.71	3.11
What is your reaction to navy programs or navy personnel that encourage your husband to reenlist? (Bipolar)	Yes	3.30	3.42	3.71
	Undecided	2.86	2.99	3.26
	No	2.10	2.68	2.94

[*]Midpoint on the scale was 3.00.
Source: Compiled by the authors.

For the expectations area, as shown in Table 4.4, willingness of wives for husbands to reenlist varied directly with the favorableness toward navy rules and regulations, which reflect expectations of others, and with the degree to which wives' expectations about navy life were realized. Attitudes in this area tended to be less favorable. Only the over-career wives who were willing for husbands to reenlist found navy life better than expected. Further study is needed in order to determine the nature of wives' expectations at the time when they first entered navy life.

For the recession, as shown in Table 4.5, wives who were willing for their husbands to reenlist and undecided over-career wives tended to be influenced in a favorable direction by the recession. In contrast the recession appeared to have little influence on wives who were unwilling. Also, willing wives tended to be of the opinion that the end of recession might encourage their husbands to reenlist. This finding was interesting in view of the fact that undecided noncareer and career, and all wives who were unwilling tended, as a group, to be of the opposite opinion. These findings indicate that the national economic condition appears to be a factor influencing wives' attitudes toward reenlistment. In discussions held after completion of the survey, many wives reported concern about their husbands' trying to start a new career during a recession. Wives in general seemed to prefer to hold on to the security of navy life and were reluctant to consider other possibilities at the recession's end. This tendency needs further study to determine the extent to which it exists during periods when the national economy is robust.

For the navy life area, as shown in Table 4.6, willingness for husbands to reenlist varied directly with favorableness of attitudes toward navy life and with being proud to be associated with the navy. Recent attitudes toward the navy tended to be less favorable than attitudes toward navy life in general. Only the unwilling or undecided noncareer wives and unwilling career wives had mean ratings below the midpoint on the scale.

The navy was also interested in obtaining information about wives' attitudes and opinions about the possibility of navy women serving at sea. Therefore, these attitudes were surveyed in this study and are presented in Table 4.7. Over one-third (36.0 percent) of the navy wives sampled reported they would discourage their husbands from reenlisting if the law were changed to permit navy women to serve

TABLE 4.4

Relationship between Career Status and
Reenlistment Intent for the Expectations Area

| | | Mean Rating by Career Status Groups* | | |
Question (Polarity)	Willing for Husbands to Reenlist	Non-career (N=112)	Career (N=293)	Over-career (N=147)
How do you feel about having to live by a set of navy rules and regulations? (Bipolar)	Yes	2.62	2.89	3.12
	Undecided	2.24	2.62	2.56
	No	1.97	2.34	2.73
To what extent has navy life met the expectations you had when you became a navy wife? (Bipolar)	Yes	2.91	3.21	3.50
	Undecided	2.45	2.79	3.00
	No	2.24	2.20	2.70

*Midpoint on the scale was 3.00.
Source: Compiled by the authors.

TABLE 4.5

Relationship between Career Status and
Reenlistment Intent for the Recession Area

Question (Polarity)	Willing for Husbands to Reenlist	Mean Rating by Career Status Groups*		
		Non-career (N=112)	Career (N=293)	Over-career (N=147)
How has the <u>recession</u> in the national economy influenced your feelings about your husband's reenlisting in the navy? (Unipolar)	Yes	3.33	3.57	3.45
	Undecided	2.86	2.75	3.18
	No	1.68	2.24	2.22
In your opinion, what influence will the end of the recession have on your husband's decision to reenlist in the navy? (Bipolar)	Yes	3.22	3.39	3.33
	Undecided	2.69	2.59	3.00
	No	2.13	2.31	2.63

*Midpoint on the scale was 3.00.
<u>Source:</u> Compiled by the authors.

at sea. The navy should perhaps keep this finding in mind in making contingency plans in preparation for the possible legal change with regard to the sea-duty status of navy women.

The navy was also interested in finding out how wives obtained information about benefits, entitlements, services, and career opportunities. Frequency and perceived accuracy of a number of potential sources of information were investigated. First choice as the most frequent source of information was the husband, with almost two-thirds of wives sampled (62.0 percent) reporting this resource. Except for the <u>Navy Times</u> (14.2 percent) and other navy wives (9.9 percent), additional sources tended to be seldom chosen. With regard to perceived accuracy of information, husbands (45.7 percent), the <u>Navy Times</u> (26.2 percent), and navy personnel (10.5 percent) were most often chosen first. These findings emphasize that the two major sources of wives' information about the navy are word-of-mouth and the printed page. Results of other studies in this program of research indicated both navy personnel and wives tend to be inaccurate sources

TABLE 4.6

Relationship between Career Status and
Reenlistment Intent for the Navy Life
in General Area

Question (Polarity)	Willing for Husbands to Reenlist	Mean Rating by Career Status Group*		
		Non-career (N=112)	Career (N=293)	Over-career (N=147)
How do you like the navy way of life? (Unipolar)	Yes	3.12	3.99	4.30
	Undecided	2.93	3.17	3.55
	No	1.97	2.69	3.43
How would you rate your attitude toward the navy in the past six months? (Bipolar	Yes	3.10	3.21	3.73
	Undecided	2.59	2.77	2.62
	No	1.93	1.98	2.64
Are you proud to be associated with the navy? (Bipolar)	Yes	3.60	4.25	4.49
	Undecided	3.03	3.50	4.06
	No	2.50	3.24	3.81

*Midpoint on the scale was 3.00.
Source: Compiled by the authors.

TABLE 4.7

Effect of Permitting Navy Women to Serve
at Sea on Wives' Attitudes

Effect	Percent (N=578)
Encourage husband to reenlist	6.4
No effect	57.6
Discourage husband from reenlisting	36.0

Source: Compiled by the authors.

of information about navy benefits, entitlements, services, and career opportunities. In order to assist in counteracting this tendency, a Navy Wives Contact Model was developed.

NAVY WIVES' CONTACT MODEL

The Navy Wives' Contact Model was designed to increase the flow of accurate information about the navy and to provide a means by which wives' attitudes toward the Navy could be improved. Information obtained from navy agencies, from interviews conducted with knowledgeable navy wives, and other research results were used to develop this model which is presented in Figure 4.1. Central to the model was the Housing Office at the new navy location because it appeared to be a dependable place through which to establish early contact with navy families who were about to move. The dependability of the Housing Office as an initial point of contact was later questioned by knowledgeable navy personnel; however, a better contact point is yet to be determined.

According to the model, the navy wife to be relocated was to receive information about the Housing Office at the future location soon after her husband received transfer orders. Directions about how to reach the Housing Office, including a map and telephone number, and brochures describing the new location were to be included. Letters of personal welcome were also to be sent by a navy wife from the new command and by the head of the local Navy Wives Information School. When the husband reported to his new navy location, he was to be encouraged to sign an appropriate Privacy Act Statement permitting navy personnel to contact his wife directly. Unless such a signature is obtained, information about the navy and how to obtain assistance, if needed, cannot be provided to wives according to current navy regulations. Also, both husband and wife were to be given information about other agencies shown in Figure 4.1 and alerted that except for the Wives' Ombudsman, wives would be contacted in the near future—unless the husband or wife refused the offer. Special attention was to be given to ensuring that the hesitant or timid wife was contacted as soon as possible in order to forestall difficulties and help alleviate any problem that might not surface otherwise.

Important features of the model were an honest appraisal of living conditions, exposure to husband's work environment, career counseling for navy wives, and planned follow-up by the agencies included in the model. For example, the Housing Office was to discuss real or commonly perceived inequities in housing in the area and to provide valid reasons during initial contact with the family. Experience has shown that if wives find out about such inequities later—by word of

FIGURE 4.1

Elements and Direction of Initial Flow of
Communication in the Navy Wives'
Contact Model

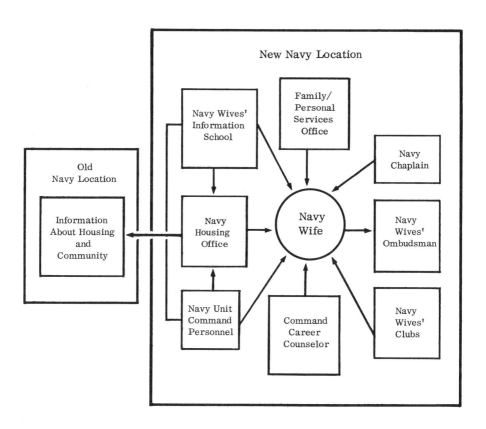

Source: Compiled by the authors.

mouth or through experience—dissatisfaction with navy housing and
distrust of other information provided by the navy tends to be stimulated. Commands were to arrange for wives to visit their husbands'
specific work locations as soon as possible. If this were impossible
for security or other reasons, at least a general tour of the premises
was to be arranged. The purpose was to provide wives a better understanding of their husbands' jobs and to give commands the opportunity
to advise wives of the importance of their husbands' jobs—both to the
navy and to our nation's defense. Wives were also to meet a career
counselor during the visit. Later, this counselor was to contact the
wife personally and arrange for her to be counseled concerning her
husband's career, with the preferred method a joint husband-wife
session. Counseling of wives in groups was also to be arranged.

The navy has developed a slide presentation for use with wives,
and other types of wives' presentations which encourage group discussion have been developed at various navy locations. Even though the
wife had previously been counseled at another navy location, she was
to be encouraged to attend and update her information about the navy,
as navy programs change and information needs to be updated in order
to remain accurate. Also, the head of the Navy Wives' Information
School was again to contact the new wife and invite her to attend the
school's next session. Provisions for baby-sitting and transportation
were to be made in order to encourage the wife to attend.

The function and role of the Navy Wives' Ombudsman was to be
explained during the wife's first visit to the Housing Office. Information about how to reach the Wives' Ombudsman was also to be provided
because under current navy policy, initiative for follow-up rests with
the wife. The other agencies shown in Figure 4.1 were to contact the
arriving wife according to a coordinated follow-up plan. For example,
the Navy Wives' Clubs of America, local enlisted and ship's wives'
clubs, and Wifeline were to acquaint the new wife with their organizations as soon as possible and to invite her to accompany a member to
a club meeting. Although the navy wife may not choose to participate
further in club activities, our research has shown that most navy
wives were interested in obtaining more information about such clubs.
A visit to a meeting is a good way to obtain information, and it also
provides an opportunity to meet other navy wives. Similarly, the
Navy Chaplain was to provide information about religious activities
at the new location and to invite the family to attend if they so desired.
At a slightly later time, Family/Personal Services Office, which
serves as a contact point to direct wives to needed resources such
as Navy Relief, was to follow up in order to determine how well family
needs were being met at the new location. In short, the Navy Wives'
Contact Model was designed to ensure that all wives arriving at a new
navy location are recognized and treated as persons worthy of respect.

Although the model has not as yet been implemented by the navy, it has generated interest and helped to stimulate development of plans designed to increase the satisfaction of navy wives and their families.

DISCUSSION

Navy wives' attitudes are recognized as a factor influencing the retention of enlisted personnel. Wives generally were found to have favorable attitudes toward the navy. However, noncareer wives tended to be less favorable than other wives. This finding is important for retention because a large part of the navy is comprised of noncareer personnel who are also least likely to reenlist. Although the navy is not structured to accommodate retention of all noncareer personnel, of critical importance is the retention of quality personnel in the specialities experiencing a critical shortage of manpower.

With regard to wives' attitudes toward reenlistment, a little more than half of those sampled were willing for their husbands to reenlist; less than one-fourth were unwilling; and about one-fourth were undecided. Wives' satisfaction tended to vary directly with willingness for husbands to reenlist. Undecided wives appeared to be experiencing a certain ambivalence with regard to the navy. This ambivalence could be expected to make them susceptible to change. A strategy designed to increase satisfaction of undecided navy wives might also tend to make them more favorable to their husbands' reenlistment. Based on results of the study reported in this chapter, such a strategy should be centered on the navy work setting of the husbands and expectations of wives about the navy. The strategy should also be directed toward improving the job satisfaction of navy enlisted personnel because husbands talk to wives about their work situations. If husbands' attitudes are unfavorable, wives are likely to develop similar negative attitudes. The strategy should also ensure that good rapport is established between wives and the navy retention program.

With regard to expectations, the strategy should be two-pronged. First, it should be directed toward what the navy expects of wives—and their husbands—in terms of rules and regulations. Second, it should be directed toward creating realistic expectations about navy life on the part of wives new to the navy. Other factors that need to be taken into consideration in developing such a strategy include the condition of the national economy and the possibility that navy women may someday serve at sea.

In order to implement such a strategy, techniques to increase the flow of information about the navy to the navy wife and to improve the accuracy of information she receives need to be developed. The Navy Wives' Contact Model is an example of such a technique. By

increasing the flow and improving the accuracy of information, wives
will become more knowledgeable about their husbands' jobs, and
about navy-career and other opportunities. This appears to be of
potential benefit to the navy and well worth the cost. Increased understanding of husbands' jobs and the navy work setting will equip families
to take better advantage of navy opportunities and benefits, which will
improve the quality of navy life experienced by these families. Also,
their expectations will be brought into balance within real-world conditions. Apart from humanitarian considerations, these improvements
are in the best interest of the navy because they are designed to improve the satisfaction of navy wives, whose attitudes influence the
reenlistment decisions of their husbands.

PART II

THE CHANGING
MILITARY FAMILY

"Over the last decade, the military has shown itself to
be increasingly subject to the same trends and pressures
as the society-at-large. With the decline in an insulated
environment, changes in social values, laws, and family
norms are being felt more and more by the military
personnel."

Dennis K. Orthner and
Richard J. Brown

5 The Effectively Coping Black Family

Robert Hayles
Wade Nobles

The amount of attention recently being directed at the family might suggest that the institution called the family is in jeopardy. From newspaper reports and scholarly reviews to political editorials, a common opinion expressed is that the family as we know it is rapidly changing and soon will no longer exist. Many experts in the field (Bronfenbrenner 1977; Etzioni 1977) share this negative viewpoint. As is typical among experts, many also disagree with the sounding of the death note for the family. Experts like Libman and Lawson (1976) and several authors in the 1977 spring issue of <u>Daedalus</u> argue that the family is still a strong resilient force. Even though there is "scientific" evidence for both opinions, the common belief is that the condition of the American family is less than optimal.

Although most writers choose to talk about the overall condition of the American family and the difficulties it faces, it is readily recognized that some segments of the population are experiencing more difficulties than others and have, due to their condition or circumstance, a unique set of problems. This segment includes two easily identifiable populations, black people and military personnel. Both groups have disproportionate numbers of persons in less than ideal circumstances. Members of military families have to cope with hazardous duty (fathers, sons, brothers, and other males viewed as members of immediate or extended families) and separation (parents and children, husbands and wives). The periods of hazardous duty and/or separation may be planned and of a specific duration, as in normal duty assignments, or unplanned and for an unknown or unspecified period of time, as in the cases of prisoners of war (POWs) and personnel missing in action (MIAs). Writers McCubbin, Hunter, and Metres (1974) present a discussion of family adaptation to the POW and MIA experience. Black families must struggle to survive in a modern postindustrial society with an endless variety of forms of discrimination and racism. They must cope with planned and unplanned separation of family members for reasons such as employ-

ment, unemployment, and a welfare system that still reinforces the
absence of men from households. Even in the 1970s being black in
the United States is hazardous duty (recall the violence perpetuated
on peaceful demonstrators in Boston, racial violence on U.S. Marine
Corps bases, cross burnings in Maryland and Mississippi, grossly
disproportionate numbers of black prison inmates on death row, and
inner city life in general).

What seems clear is that, in spite of the long history of racial
atrocities, black people as a group are more married and family-
oriented than the majority of society. While the wider society has
slowly moved to a point of predicting its own demise, the black family
has continued to refine its coping skills for surviving in a hostile and
generally unpleasant society. The questions to be dealt with here are
how black families cope with adverse life situations, and what can be
learned from such coping that may be of value to military families
and families in general?

BRIEF HISTORY OF BLACK FAMILY RESEARCH

Billingsley (1968) presents four stages in the history of family
research, most of which has been done in a field called family sociology. The beginning of family sociology was in the late nineteenth
century during the period when Social Darwinism was being advocated.
The focus during this first stage was on earlier primitive family life
forms, with the assumption that current forms were evolutionary
descendants of earlier forms. The object was to trace the evolutionary process while focusing on patriarchy, matriarchy, polygamy,
and other such issues. During this time the black family was not a
topic of interest and was viewed as not existing as an institution.

The second phase of family research (late 1800s and early 1900s)
was stimulated by conditions of poverty and focused on the conditions
of life being faced by contemporary families. Typical of this phase
were surveys conducted to document the conditions of working-class
people living in urban areas. The black family in the United States
was still ignored and not viewed as a contemporary family. The one
notable exception was the work of DuBois (1909).

The third phase of family research began in the 1920s when the
focus shifted to middle-class families. The topics most frequently
studied during this phase included adjustment (personal, sexual,
psychological) and individual happiness. Typical of this period were
the works of George H. Mead and Ernest W. Burgess. Again the
black family was all but totally ignored.

The fourth phase, from 1930 to 1940, included some of the best
studies of black family life available. The impetus in this phase came

from both a general situation and the emergence of specific scholars. Society as a whole began to recognize that the black family was in trouble and in need of both close examination and remedial action. It was during this period that a number of black scholars (with support from white institutions and occasional collaboration with white scholars) produced some of the classic studies of black family life (Davis and Dollard 1940; Drake and Cayton 1945; Frazier 1939; Johnson 1941; Reid 1940).

Billingsley (1968) described the period from 1940 to 1960 as being essentially void of family research. That period was filled with concerns such as war, industrialization, and child-rearing practices. It was a resurging interest in poverty in the 1960s that rekindled the interest in the family. That resurgence was aided by an increase in the number of scholars and the pressing need to examine such juxtapositions as war/humanitarianism, equal opportunity/uneven distribution of resources, and racism/melting pot. The disproportionately large representation of minorities among the victims of the above juxtapositions prompted the growing number of black scholars to examine the troubled black family within the broader context of society in general.

Beginning in the late 1960s, more and more black scholars began to recognize the need to be critical of the treatment of blacks in the social sciences (Billingsley 1968; Hill 1972; Ladner 1973; and Staples 1971a). As a result of these critical assessments, black scholars and a few white scholars recognized that the study of the black family had been primarily a comparative analysis of black family experiences as if they were identical to white family experiences. Given the ever-present state of racism in this society and, on the positive side, the recent appreciation of its multi-cultural fabric, there are not, nor were there ever, grounds for an assumption of homogeneity across American family life conditions. Nevertheless, the prevailing theories (based for the most part on studies of a small minority of black families) argued that the black family was a deviant or pathological form of social organization. The simple recognition that the conclusions about black family life were based on a minority of black families alone overturned the accepted scientific opinion. Even such notables as Erikson (1966) had to ask why so much was said about the absent father and so little about present fathers, even though the majority of fathers are present. He further questioned the lack of focus on the mothers who are present and achieve many successes against staggering odds. The magnificent strength of low-income black mothers was surely a primary agent in the prevention of family disintegration. Erikson went on to conclude his query with a note about the excessive focus on the weaknesses of low-income families and the absence of interest in their strengths.

Billingsley, as discussed earlier, reiterated this point in 1968.
A particularly succinct summary of the research on the black family
was presented by Staples (1971a: 133). Staples noted:

In an overall assessment of theories and research on black
family life, their value is diminished by the weak methodology employed; the superficial analysis that ensues from
the use of poor research designs; biased and low samples;
and inadequate research instruments. While data must be
theory-oriented and theory must be confirmed by data collection (Merton 1959), the inferences drawn from data to
theory on the black family are unjustified on the basis of
the research evidence presented by most investigators of
black family life. Much research on black family patterns
seems to have been based on preconceived notions about
the pathological character and malfunctioning of the black
family—notions that frequently derive from the use of white,
middle-class models as an evaluative measure for families
subject to an entirely different set of social forces which
determine its structure and dynamics (Rodman 1959).

Several years after Rodman (1959) and Merton (1959), Handel
(1967) argued that there were no methods for studying whole families.
A brief summary of the methods used in research on the black family
substantiates a similar finding.* The present authors examined the
1909 study by DuBois, along with 49 randomly selected other studies
that were reported between 1939 and 1974. Although the categories
and number of data collection methods utilized are not mutually exclusive, the results were as follows:

Interviews (17)
Questionnaires (6)
Case histories, essentially from clinical records (7)
Observation, participant and unobtrusive (11)
Use of census data (10)
Opinions backed with literature reviews (15)
Social systems approaches (1)

---

*Black family research has been reviewed and more than ade-
quately critiqued by several black scholars (Billingsley 1968; Staples
1971a, 1971b; Ladner 1973; The Black Scholar, June 1974; Nobles
1976; Journal of Afro-American Issues, 1976; and The Western
Journal of Black Studies, June 1977). A bibliography on the black
family is presented in the December 1971 issue of The Black Scholar.

Willie, Kramer and Brown (1973) recrystalized the obvious and placed the resilient strengths and coping skills of black people into a perspective which has value for any people struggling under adverse conditions. They noted that:

> What has not been recognized by professionals and the
> public is the extraordinary way in which many blacks and
> members of other racial minority groups have coped with
> adversity. How they have strengthened themselves to
> overcome the obstacles of racism is worthy of careful
> studies. Such investigations would make significant con-
> tributions to the accumulated body of knowledge and clinical
> practice in mental health. Well-documented life styles
> of effectively coping individuals and families could serve
> as models for dealing with danger and difficulty (p. 582).

Fortunately, the current family research trends include more rigorous data collection and analysis procedures, more structured interviews, increased use of standardized scales, inclusion of more than one ethnic group in each study, less exclusive reliance on participant observation, and a small movement in the direction of studying the effectively coping whole family.

A FOCUS ON THE POSITIVE

Let us first examine the slowly growing trend toward looking at successful families and individuals or at least comparing the successful with the unsuccessful. There have been a number of isolated efforts to move in that direction, perhaps beginning with Frazier (1939). In that work he described the model stable black family and supported that description with detailed case studies. Many years later Willie and Weinandy (1963) compared the structure and composition of "problem" and "stable" low-income families in St. Paul, Minnesota. The results of that study showed that stable families had a slight edge in education and employment status. The major difference between stable and problem families was seen as a difference in family structure. Problem families were more often structured differently from the societal norm of male-headed, two-parent households. Stable families tended to consist slightly more often of

---

See the spring 1977 issue of Daedalus and the May 1977 issue of Psychology Today for a quick update on research concerning the family in general.

partners in their first marriage, with fathers and mothers being slightly older than those in problem families. Willie and Weinandy concluded that problem families lack the knowledge, understanding, and orientation necessary for individual and collective survival. Low-income problem families are therefore "inadequately socialized."

Billingsley (1968) took the view that researchers who do not view the black family within its own unique historical milieu distort the context enough to collect inappropriate data, distort interpretations, and draw faulty conclusions. It is obvious that such an error can easily lead one to overlook positive aspects of black family life. However, rather than focus on effectively coping whole families, Billingsley took on the task of trying to present the appropriate context, both historical and current, for black family research. Without question, this singular choice of direction helped set the stage for later research and scholarship.

In the late 1960s and early 1970s black scholars and others studying minority families, following the lead of Billingsley, began to refute much of what white scholars were saying about the black family. Grier and Cobbs (1968), both black psychiatrists, collected a large volume of case-history data while practicing psychiatry with black clients. Based on their psychiatric experience and analyses of their case-history data they concluded that the bond between men and women is the prime ingredient making it possible for minority families to form, function, and grow. In 1969 the Joint Commission on Mental Health of Children expressed an opinion, that despite the many difficulties imposed on family stability by discrimination and poverty, the minority family has been a primary contributor to the mental health of children. The strength and love of black mothers is considered legendary. The Japanese family is credited with being a key factor in motivating its children to avoid delinquency and to seek educational and economic success. The commission also noted a general trend for American Indian and Latino families to resist sending their children to institutions outside of their ethnic communities. Willie's (1970) edited book of readings on black family life did not show a strong emphasis on effectively coping whole families but was one of the first documents to include several studies dealing with middle- and lower-class families from both pathological and nonpathological perspectives. Scanzoni (1971), in the introduction to his book on the black family, discussed the negative stereotypes that flourish about black families in general but only approach validation for considerably fewer than one-third of all black families. Scanzoni's book, however, focused on the two-thirds majority to which such stereotypes do not apply.

The response of Hill (1972) to the ever-increasing need to refute much of what white scholars were saying about the black family was noteworthy. This black scholar's analyses revealed five functional characteristics of black families: (1) strong kinship bonds; (2) strong work orientation; (3) adaptability of family roles; (4) strong achievement orientation; and (5) strong religious orientation. Another black scholar, Staples (1974), also sought to determine what contributed to the survival of the black family. He identified three key factors: (1) a group of very strong and supportive women; (2) an extended kinship system; and (3) children with a great deal of flexibility and resilience.

In reporting on research which began in the mid-1960s, Stack (1974), a white woman, examined the survival strategies used in a poor black community. Her data consisted of taped conversations, field notes, participant observations and structured interviews. Collaboration with black colleagues and community members was extensive. The black kinship network was revealed as a major force contributing to the survival of black individuals and families in a typical poor black community. Two paragraphs from her conclusion are particularly informative:

> Black families in The Flats and the non-kin they regard as kin have evolved patterns of co-residence, kinship-based exchange networks linking multiple domestic units, elastic household boundaries, lifelong bonds to three-generation households, social controls against the formation of marriages that could endanger the network of kin, the domestic authority of women, and limitations on the role of the husband or male friend within a woman's kin network. These highly adaptive structural features of urban black families comprise a resilient response to the social-economic conditions of poverty, the inexorable unemployment of black women and men, and the access to scarce economic resources of a mother and her children as AFDC recipients (p. 124).

> Distinctively negative features attributed to poor families, that they are fatherless, matrifocal, unstable, and disorganized, are not general characteristics of black families living substantially below economic subsistence in urban America. The black urban family, embedded in cooperative domestic exchange, proves to be an organized tenacious, active, lifelong network (p. 124).

McQueen (1977) reported his research dealing with the inner-city poor and near-poor. He sought to analyze family functioning, paying special attention to the strategies used to cope with the inner-city environment, pursue family life with long-term viability and satisfac-

tion, and attempt to raise children for a better tomorrow. He also
dealt with erroneous interpretations and stereotypes of black family
life and pointed out the underlying reasons for many negative aspects
of such life. The following three reasons were proposed as prime
causes for troubled families: (1) economic distress, (2) shortages
of black males, and (3) changing norms for marriage and family life.
From a sample of 100 poor and near-poor families, McQueen identified 34 effectively coping (future-oriented) families and 23 ineffectively
coping families and compared them along a number of dimensions.
The future-oriented families were found to be stronger than the ineffectively coping families on the strength of their family orientation.
They also expressed higher and more clearly articulated mobility
aspirations, a stronger quest for respectability, greater planning/
action to improve the family situation, and tendencies toward greater
self-reliance. In general, there was more evidence of discipline
and sacrifice among effectively coping families.

The above series of studies is representative of the slowly
developing trend in black family research. While this presentation
is not exhaustive, there are in fact very few published works similar
to those just described.

Fortunately, more and more researchers have begun to use
improved methodologies (McCubbin et al. 1976; McQueen 1977),
develop conceptual frameworks which take into account the system
within which the black family existed and now exists (Harris 1976;
Nobles 1976), collaborate more closely with persons within the
studied communities (Cromwell, Vaughan, and Mindell 1975), and
discuss effective coping behavior in and of families (Blaydon and
Stack 1977; Hareven 1977; Hayles 1977; McCubbin et al. 1976;
McQueen 1977; and Snyder 1977). Unfortunately, there is still a
paucity of empirically sound research being conducted, and even less
being reported.

Without question, even the few citations mentioned previously
would be absent if not for the work of black scholars like Staples,
Hill, and Billingsley. Hill's work, for instance, stands alone as
the landmark attempt to document and identify strengths in the black
family. Some have viewed the research conducted on the black family
by Nobles (1974) as "strengths in the black family" research, and
the "sense of Africanity" as another item in the developing list of
black family strengths. This is not totally accurate, and although
this work will be discussed in more detail later, a point of clarifica-
tion should be made at the outset. The sense of Africanity as a concept in black family research is much like the power source which
energizes the system. Africanity is best viewed as a cultural attitude
which acts as a motive force and predisposes the system to act in a
particular way. In terms of family life and/or dynamics, the sense

of Africanity predisposes the system to express certain features
(that is, child-centeredness, elasticity, or spirituality). Hence,
rather than viewed as a strength item, the sense of Africanity should
be viewed as the explanatory power which determines in part the
expression of those attributes or characteristics which many writers
have defined as strengths.

NOBLES' RESEARCH ON THE BLACK FAMILY– THE ISSUE OF AFRICANITY

Conceptual Framework

Before describing Nobles' research it is necessary to present
the conceptual framework behind the investigation. It begins with
the observation that many scholars and researchers have erroneously
analyzed black family life. The black family has mistakenly been
depicted as a dark-skinned white family with many negative characteristics. At least three orientations have characterized that depiction:

1. Poverty-Acculturated Studies. Both early black researchers
reflecting this orientation (DuBois 1909; Frazier 1932, 1939) and
whites using and advocating it (Bernard 1966; Chilman 1966; Jeffers
1967) viewed the disorganization of black families as a direct result
of slavery, racism, and poverty. It was felt that black families,
when thrust into such conditions, lost all the cultural stability they
may have had as Africans in African milieus.

2. Pathologically-Oriented Studies. This view, touted by such
persons as Moynihan (1965), Aldous (1969), and Rainwater (1970),
focused on the supposedly negative structural and functional features
of black families. These studies assumed that cultural stability did
not exist in African or early Afro-American life, and that the above
negative features of black families lead to overrepresentation of
blacks among those who are poor, uneducated in the formal sense,
and incarcerated.

3. Victim-Oriented Studies. Victim-oriented researchers
(Liebow 1966; Rodman 1963; Scanzoni 1971; Willie 1970) typically
argued that black families would be identical to white families if the
experiences of both in the United States were identical. Racism and
discrimination were posited as the prime causative agents for the
far less than optimal situation of the black family today.

The consequence of adopting the above simplistic orientations is
that research on the black family, like much of the research on black
people in general, gets consistently reviewed vis-a-vis the white
experience. To avoid that error, one must scientifically ground
research in a culturally and/or ethnically consistent analytical frame-

work. Such a framework is briefly described in the following paragraphs. A more detailed description can be found in Nobles (1976).

For black family research, the first axiom of this analytical
framework or grounding is that "an African cultural spectrum forms
the foundation of the black cultural sphere." The second axiom states
that the "wider (Anglo-American) cultural milieu serves as the medium in which the black cultural spectrum must operate." These
axioms represent the position that black culture in the United States
is the result of an admixture of the continuation of an African world-
view or cultural perspective operating within an environment dominated by an Anglo-American world-view of cultural reality. It is
called a "cultural continuity" approach because it assumes that the
cultural essence of the African world-view was not destroyed by the
Middle Passage or New World slavery. An understanding of the
residuals of this world-view is seen as necessary to explain the
dynamics of black culture and family life, in particular. Such an
axiomatic position calls for the following research assumption: It is
the combined continuation of African value systems and their reactions
to the cultural imperatives of the dominant Anglo-American dominated
culture which form the root of the special features observable in
black family life. The framework is completed by an interpretive
ruling stating that the observable behavior of black families must be
interpreted in terms of understanding (a) the African cultural residual
of continuity which serves as the basis for behavior, and (b) the
American conditions which influence their development and/or expression.

While the above framework may at first glance seem quite different from the majority of research on the family, its uniqueness is
only in its explicit declaration of a specific culturally relevant analytic
grounding. Most family research does reflect an analytic grounding
that is heavily influenced by culture, usually Anglo-European culture.
The idea that the world outside of the individual researcher's mind
influences the conduct of research is not new. Mannheim (1936)
argued cogently that the nature of society influences the kind of knowledge that people are exposed to. Kuhn (1970) added the recognition
that what we can know is already limited by what we do know. In
some cases, such as in the study of Anglo-European families, the
dominant but seldom explicitly declared framework may be appropriate. But since black social reality is obviously different from
Anglo-European social reality, the errors caused by using research
models and conceptualizations based on nonblack world-views demand
the use of models and conceptualizations based on black social realities when black people are the subjects of the research.

In relation to the family, it has been argued (Nobles 1976) that
it is important to comprehend the particular philosophical, ontological, and cosmological understanding of the universe belonging to the

people under examination. For black family research, one must accordingly understand the significance of the African world-view as manifested in contemporary black reality. Briefly, the traditional African world-view understood everything in the universe to be endowed with the Supreme Force (Forde 1954; Tempels 1959). Thomas (1961) also pointed out that Africans traditionally believed that the very nature of existence was the Supreme Force. It was believed that this force was vitalistic and that all things in the universe are interconnected or interdependent (Thomas 1961). While the African world-view has not been fully explicated with respect to the family, it has been argued that the African understanding of the universe determines the structure, functions, nature, and definition of "family" (Mbiti 1970; Nobles 1976).

In terms of the notion of family, the implicit African cosmological (Oneness of Being) and ontological (Nature of Being is Force, Spirit) understanding, along with the way in which "time" and "space" are defined within those cosmological and ontological dimensions, suggest that the family constitutes the center of the universe, that is, the center of one's being or existence. The individual is an integral part of the collective unity—the family. The family is the reference point wherein one's existence is perceived as being interconnected to the existence of all else. The individual owes his/her very existence to all the members of the family, tribe, or clan (Mbiti 1970). The family includes the dead, the living, and the yet-to-be-born (Busia 1954). Mbiti further describes the African belief system as congruent with the notion that "I am because We are, and because We are, therefore I am." The "We," when considered in the context of a belief in "Oneness of Being," seems clearly to refer to the family.

Existence is at the level of the family. That is, family existence is more important than individual existence. The simple and logical belief is that the begetter is always more powerful than the offspring and the family entity constitutes more power or force than the individual entity. Accordingly, the family existence is "paramount" to individual existence and to paraphrase Sartre, the family essence precedes the individual essence. The family, again including the dead, living, and unborn, is therefore the focal point wherein the essence of the community, tribe, or clan is kept alive.

The Nobles' Study*

In discussing some of the findings of Nobles' research, we shall point out the implications his findings have for military families and

---

*The study reported on in this chapter was part of a larger research project supported in part by an Office of Child Develop-

families in general. It is believed that the coping strategies evolving out of the African heritage of black people and developing in the historically racist milieu of American society are of value to all families which must survive in a hostile nonsupportive environment. As witnessed by the reported demise of the white American family, the hostile nonsupportive conditions seem to have spread to many American families. The investigation conducted by the Nobles team was carried out with special efforts made to respect the special integrity of black family life styles.

Subjects

The subjects for this study were 52 predominately black families in the San Francisco Bay area. These families were randomly selected from lists of black families compiled from various agencies and/or people who work with black families—as in churches, hospitals, YMCAs. Most households had young parents (26–35 years old), two to three children, and an income of approximately $7,800 (median). Most rented their homes, were Protestant, and considered their cultural heritage to be either African (46 percent), American (28 percent), or an admixture of Indian, Spanish, Asian (26 percent). The majority of the informants (64 percent) grew up in the South. Of those not growing up in the South, California was the most favored single state in which the adults spent their childhoods (39 percent). Sixty-six percent had lived in the state of California, with 60 percent having lived in the San Francisco Bay area for more than ten years. Thirty-two percent of the respondents were married, and 28 percent were divorced at the time of the study. The 52 families included 140 children, 131 being biological children of the respondents, and nine being extended family members. Sixty-six percent of the mothers and 46 percent of the fathers had some form of college education which was not matched by an equally high occupational distribution. Among these families, 30 percent were in the top-level occupations (teachers, managers, or professionals), and 20 percent were in unskilled positions (cleaning services, food services, or health care services).

Instrumentation

Several instruments were developed for use in this study: (1) The Westside Black Family Interview Schedule, Forms P and C;

---

ment Grant (#90-C-255), Department of H. E. W. and the Research Department of the Westside Community Mental Health Center, Inc., San Francisco, California.

(2) The Black Family Research Project Demographic Data Form; and (3) The Westside Black Family Observational Checklist. The interview schedules went through several modifications based on pretesting and the previously described analytical grounding and conceptual framework. The final version of the data collection battery resulted in a document which had several features that should be noted. The items on the schedules were designed to address one or both of the theoretical family components (structure and/or function) and one or several of the relevant analytical variables (social organization, role definition, organizational purpose, and interpersonal relations). The children's schedule was age-graded so that some items were asked only of older children. Both interview schedules (Forms P and C) included a project-developed, "extended-family grid," which was especially designed to determine the structural features of the family. In addition to the interview schedules, an observational checklist form was also developed. This form consisted of a physical environment and social interaction checklist, as well as a rating scale section which allowed the interviewers to state both their objective and subjective opinions about each family session.

Procedure

In addition to being trained in interviewer/observation techniques, each interviewer was also involved in the theoretical and conceptual development of the instruments from item generation to final item selection. Families were contacted by letter, phone, and finally visited by a member of the staff. During the first interview session, the payment procedure for participating in the study was fully explained. Respondents were told that all collected information would be strictly confidential and were given a detailed explanation of exactly how the information would be used. The actual interviews were conducted individually except when impossible. On the average, the time necessary to interview an entire household was about eight hours. This was accomplished in a single visit or several visits. The data were reviewed for accuracy, inspected for completion, and then placed on electromagnetic tape.

Results

As previously noted, it is generally recognized that because of racism and discrimination, black families must constantly struggle to survive in a modern postindustrial U.S. society with the same intensity that was required for survival during slavery and Reconstruction. The dominant condition influencing the expression of black family dynamics is, without question, racism. The difficulties and degradation caused by it are indeed well-documented. The data in this study add to that historical documentation. The data, for instance, revealed that the high educational level of the sample was not matched by equally high-status occupations or high family income. Similarly, stories reported to our respondents and retold to us as part of the interview indicated again and again the preponderance of racism as a prevailing condition or characteristic of the larger U.S. society. Similarly, our respondents indicated or felt that racial discrimination in the educational system and in the employment arena made it extremely difficult for their families to make it. Interestingly enough, the higher the educational level of the respondents, the more likely they were to mention education as the one thing which made it easier for their families to succeed. The majority of respondents, educated and uneducated alike, however, saw absolutely <u>nothing</u> in this society which made it <u>easy</u> for them to succeed. The fundamental truth which seemed evident to the majority of our respondents was that racism and discrimination resulted in families living in less than ideal circumstances.

What is of interest in this chapter, however, is the particular way in which black families responded to these societal conditions, or more specifically, how black families effectively cope with adverse life situations. Parenthetically, it must be restated that the response styles learned from such coping may be of value to military families and families in general.

The results of Nobles' research are quite extensive and can only be sampled within the boundaries of this chapter. Nevertheless, a brief presentation of results in three areas which are particularly relevant to this discussion follows.

Meaning of Family

In general, the data suggested that the criteria for family membership were fluid, and psychological functions were more strongly emphasized than structural features (most prevalent among lower-income subjects). More subjects saw their families as being "extended" than viewed the family as including only "immediate" members. The concept of family was synonymous with closeness, strength, togetherness, sharing, and mutual responsibility. The family was thought to provide emotional support, a feeling of completeness, and "roots." Specific major family functions were the provision of material needs and the marital or man/woman relationship.

It should be rather evident that if any living system is to survive it must "see" value in its being. In terms of the family system this translates as the family giving meaning to its members. The more

important entity is the family entity and not the individual member.
In a technological society where the general opinion is that the family
is a burden and obstacle in the individual's quest for personal achievement, a systemic model wherein the family's mission is to protect
and nourish its members seems to be necessary if the personal
aspirations of people are ever to be actualized in today's materialistic
nonsupportive society. The kind of personal support stemming from
the nature of the black family was evident in its functioning and interpersonal dynamics.

Family Functioning and Interpersonal Relations

In terms of the social organization of the black family, this study
suggested that its organization was inclusive and elastic, with an
active family network involving both blood and nonblood family members. In terms of the organizational purpose of the family, the data
suggested that the primary function of the family is to have and rear
children. The dominant secondary purpose seemed to be to provide
a buffer against the racism of society. In terms of family dynamics
and interpersonal relations, an index of perceived interfamilial
closeness was developed and indicated that 22 percent or less of the
respondents viewed family relationships as distant for both blood
relatives and in-laws. Lack of acquaintance or inability to visit or
communicate by telephone were the main reasons given for distant
relationships. Only 4.5 percent of the subjects mentioned differences
in value orientation or goals as reasons for lack of closeness. Children tended to have much stronger interrelations than adults. Education, occupation, and income did not relate significantly to familial
relationships. Perception of heritage did relate to perceived closeness. Interestingly enough, persons viewing their heritage as African,
rather than American, had significantly higher scores on the index
of perceived closeness. In terms of family dynamics, the mother-
in-law (no distinction made between the wife's mother and the husband's mother by the subjects) played an important or central role
in the family's set of interpersonal relationships. When the mother-
in-law was absent, her role was often filled by another woman in the
family network.

In terms of family functioning it was not unusual for children to
visit other relatives and sometimes to stay with those relatives for
long periods of time as "members" of their relatives' immediate
households. These interfamilial consensual adoptions and/or multiple
parentages expose children to a variety of adult roles and role per-
formances. This situation appears to instill greater role flexibility
in children. It would be expected that within-family interpersonal
relationships influence interpersonal relationships in general.

The older members of black families are a critical source of psychological support, especially in dealing with crises and family transitions. They were most often the storytellers in the family, who naturally possessed the longest living histories and largest body of family heritage information. One may be young and intelligent, but being wise is traditionally true of only the old.

These data suggest that the ease and/or difficulty experienced by black family members in their interaction with society at large may be partially explained by the disparity between the nature of families and the nature of the wider society. To the extent that success in the wider society is based on domination rather than closeness or harmony, the black person finds it difficult to succeed. However, given the recognition of a rapidly developing interdependent world community, this society in general, and the military in particular, would do well to model its contact with the world community after the black family pattern of flexible and fluid relations.

Family Functioning and Value Transmission

The general values stressed by the parents in order of decreasing frequency were: (1) respect for self and others, (2) morality, (3) education, (4) cooperation, and (5) responsibility. Although achievement was stressed, it was within a cooperative framework and not in terms of competition or individualism. Such values were not emphasized. As suggested earlier, children are highly valued in black family life. Eighty percent of the subjects considered the education of their children to be most important. Seventy-one percent viewed "establishing a home" as very important, with the presence of children and their welfare as dominant reasons for having a home. Events viewed as important and as motivators for bringing the family together were crises such as funerals, illness, or trouble, (over 85 percent) and rituals such as reunions, births, and parties (over 90 percent). Older siblings, blood and extended kin were mentioned as key figures in value transmission.

The black family has provided a kind of sanctuary for its members and children. It has spiritually nourished its children, encouraged respect for elders, and instilled a survival-oriented black value system (see Hayles 1977, for a discussion on the survival value of this system). Both the results of Nobles' (1976) study and the descriptions of successful blacks in other literature (biographies, autobiographies, history) bear out the assertion that the individual success*

---

*It is extremely important that we highlight the point that our discussion of success and strength in black families is not, or should

of most black persons has been heavily influenced and supported by the family from which they came and continued to belong. The family nurtured the strength and commitment to struggle—so necessary for individual success. One key to the development of such strengths is the noncontingent nature of black love. While black parents do punish their children, seldom did the black parents in Nobles' (1976) and other studies use expressions of their love for a child as reinforcement contingencies for the emission of appropriate behaviors. This may be a very powerful element of the supportive nature of the black family.

IMPLICATIONS AND RECOMMENDATIONS FOR MILITARY FAMILIES AND FAMILIES IN GENERAL

The most important implications of the studies discussed in this chapter are those dealing with strengths and skills necessary to handle a variety of less than optimal situations. Many such skills and strengths are developed and nurtured by and/or within families.

Let us briefly discuss one major problem faced by families, child rearing in the absence of a parent. Black families have been shown to deal with parental absence through using a variety of resources. If one parent is absent the other may be adaptable/flexible enough to fill, at least partially, the role of the absent parent. This support is supplemented and added to by the active participation of extended family, blood and nonblood kin. The extended family provides a broader range of role models and exposure to both sexes and persons of all ages. Military families and families in general typically deal with parental absence by expanding the duties and roles of the parent who is present. It is less common for the typical military or civilian family to draw systematically upon an extended family to fill the full range of possible roles. The benefits to children of having exposure to a broad range of others were noted earlier. The adults within an extended family also benefit, both by being recipients of an expansive range of assistance and by participating in mutually rewarding family networks. Recognizing those benefits, encouraging partial families to meet their needs through expansion/extension, and adopting selected coping behaviors exhibited by effectively func-

---

not, be interpreted to mean that all is well with black family life. Research on the black family should not be directed solely toward identifying inner strengths. Attention should not be focused away from the debilitating conditions imposed on black families by an oppressive and racist society.

tioning black families is advocated. More specifically, research directions and additional family supports for military families are indicated as follows. Research emphasis should (a) address the question of how children can receive what they need as members of families which temporarily or permanently lack one parent; (b) continue to examine the dynamics and the process through which families cope and prosper; (c) explore the impacts of encouraging competition more than cooperation, and individualism more than the family as a whole; (d) examine the long- and short-term effects of learning and teaching in an environment where unconditional or non-contingent love exists; and (e) recognize and study the role of culture and values in family functioning.

Within the military family additional help/supports would be available if planners and policy makers would (a) encourage and reward persons who "fill-in" for absent parents; (b) provide the same support for fathers without partners as is recognized as needed for mothers without partners (for example, day care, leave policies, work schedules); and (c) provide opportunities for senior citizens to share their experiences and participate in educational, social, recreational, and parental activities.

In other words, it appears evident that the military could learn from black family life through (a) the use of the extended kinship network typically found in black communities as one model of an effectively functioning and coping system; and (b) the adoption of selected values typical of the effectively coping black families (that is, values for the group/nation as a whole, cooperation, internal development, interdependence, children, and harmony).

CONCLUSION

This chapter has not attempted to deal with all the problems faced by the family. Hence, its listing of recommendations is by no means comprehensive. It is meant to stimulate future research and suggest actions in selected areas that may contribute in a positive way to the family, both civilian and military, and to its individual members.

6 The Legal Struggle For a Military Woman's Right to Have Children

Nancy K. York

Traditionally, the military family has been composed of a military husband, a dependent wife, and their dependent children. Although this pattern varied occasionally when the couple remained childless or the family lost its mother, the one essential component of the military family–the military man–remained constant. Without the husband's military status, the family would lack any military connection and would consequently possess no military identity.

Almost by definition, the traditional military family did not consist of a military woman, her husband, and children. This is not surprising since the applicable regulations of all the armed forces prior to 1 June 1974 provided for the mandatory involuntary separation of any servicewoman who became pregnant or otherwise assumed parental status. For years these regulations, based on some very rigid ideas about women and their roles in raising a family, went unchallenged. A great many servicewomen submissively gave up their military jobs and careers to marry and have children or decided to forego marriage and/or family life in favor of a military career.

The origin of these regulations may be traced back to Executive Order 10240* issued by President Harry S. Truman on 27 April 1951. This order prescribed permissible grounds for the discharge of any woman who belonged to one of the five enumerated categories dealing with parenthood, child custody or pregnancy. Specifically, if a woman were the parent, by birth or adoption, of a child under a certain age (to be determined by the secretary of the military department concerned) or had, while serving in the military, given birth to a living child, she was subject to discharge. If a woman had personal custody of a child under such minimum age or were the step-parent of a child under such minimum age, and the child was within her household for a period of more than 30 days a year, she was subject to discharge.

---

*16 F. R. 3689 (27 Apr. 1951).

And, of course, if a servicewoman were pregnant, she could be
separated from the service with an administrative discharge under
honorable conditions.

However, the implementing regulations stretched the limits of
the Executive Order's mandate. By the use of the word "may" in the
phrase ". . . such women may be totally separated from the service
by administrative action . . . ," the order established permissible
grounds for the discharge of servicewomen rather than mandatory
grounds. It was the implementing regulations which substituted the
word "shall" for the word "may" and set the minimum age for children quite high. Each of the secretaries of the military departments
made 18 the minimum age with no distinction between dependent and
emancipated children.

That the secretaries went beyond the intent of the Order can be
demonstrated by referring to the authorizing legislation for the Executive Order. This legislation, the Army-Navy Nurses Act of 1947*
and the Women's Armed Services Integration Act of 1948,† contains
language which indirectly shows a congressional acknowledgement
that women with dependent children are fit to serve on active duty.

No doubt one of the reasons that the implementing regulations
were so harsh was the laudatory desire of the drafters to establish
procedures which would facilitate efficient personnel management.
Therefore, they drew up regulations which applied across the board
and assumed that all women subject to these regulations had certain
characteristics in common. This foreclosed the possibility of a
case-by-case determination of the fitness of each woman to serve.
As was noted in Stanley v. Illinois, ‡ "[p]rocedure by presumption
is always cheaper and easier than individualized determination."§

However, the regulations were by no means uniform throughout
the services. During the transition period of the early 1970s, a
military woman's chances of remaining in the service were dependent
upon which armed force she joined and when she became pregnant or
assumed parental status. In addition to the variation of regulations
among the services existing from the start, each service revised
certain of its regulations at irregular intervals and instituted a
waiver procedure which it administered in its own inimitable style.

For example, until three years ago regulations provided that
pregnant navy and Marine Corps women would be discharged unless
they could demonstrate that they merited a waiver. This included

---

*61 Stat. 41.
†62 Stat. 356.
‡405 U.S. 645 (1972).
§ Id. at 656-657.

proving to the satisfaction of headquarters that they could care for their children and still work fulltime. Navy women and women marines whose pregnancies were terminated prior to their separation from the service would nevertheless be discharged unless their request for a waiver were approved.

The army rules were reminiscent of those examined in Doe v. Osteopathic Hospital of Wichita, Inc.* Army women who requested a waiver had to be married to have their babies while on active duty. Unwed pregnant soldiers were not considered suitable for retention. However, if such a woman lost her baby before birth by any means, she would be allowed to stay in the army if she could prove herself to be of good moral character.

Compared to the other services, the air force appeared to be the most liberal. While it still adhered to the basic policy of involuntarily discharging pregnant members, the air force allowed both married and unmarried pregnant servicewomen to request waivers. Should a pregnancy be terminated before a final determination had been made on the waiver request, discharge action would be cancelled.

In seeking relief from these regulations, a few servicewomen turned to the federal courts believing that ". . . the military is not a system apart but lives under a Constitution. . . ."† They were encouraged by the general agreement among the cases that a person entering military service does not leave all his constitutional rights behind him though his rights are subject to a certain amount of curtailment necessary to the accomplishment of the military mission.

These women found the due process clause of the Fifth Amendment to be a promising grounds for complaint and were encouraged by the much-quoted words of Circuit Judge Maris in United States ex rel. Innis v. Haitt:‡

> An individual does not cease to be a person within the protection of the Fifth Amendment of the Constitution because he has joined the nation's armed forces and has taken the oath to support that Constitution with his life, if need be. The guarantee of the Fifth Amendment that "no person shall . . . be deprived of life, liberty, or property, without due process of law," makes no exception in the case of persons who are in the armed forces. The fact that the framers of the amendment did specifically except

---

*333 F Supp. 1357 (D. Kan. 1971).

†Secretary of the Navy v. Avrech, 418 U.S. 676, 680 (1974) (Douglas, J., dissenting).

‡141 F. 2d 664 (3rd Cir. 1944).

such persons from the guarantee of the right to a present-
ment or indictment by a grand jury which is contained in
the earlier part of the amendment makes it even clearer
that persons in the armed forces were intended to have
the benefit of the due process clause.*

The difficulty arose when a serviceperson asked a federal court
to enforce his right to due process or to protect some fundamental
interest from encroachment by the military. He was then met with
the historical reluctance of federal courts to interfere in the operation of the military.   The general feeling on the propriety of reviewing
military affairs was expressed by the Supreme Court in Orloff v.
Willoughby.† In delivering the opinion of the Court, Justice Jackson
wrote:

> The military constitutes a specialized community governed
> by a separate discipline from that of the civilian. Orderly
> government requires that the judiciary be as scrupulous not
> to interfere with legitimate army matters as the army must
> be scrupulous not to intervene in judicial matters.‡

Concerned that the exercise of jurisdiction ". . . would be a
disruptive force as to affairs peculiarly within the jurisdiction of
the military authorities,"§ Justice Jackson observed:

> We know that from top to bottom of the army the complaint
> is often made, and sometimes with justification, that there
> is discrimination, favoritism, or other objectionable
> handling of men. But judges are not given the task of
> running the Army. ‖

However, the judicial reluctance to become involved in areas
within the primary responsibility of the military was undergoing a
reevaluation. While the courts were still deferring to military judgment on uniquely military affairs as demonstrated by the U.S. Supreme Court case of Parker v. Levy,⊥ they were displaying more
confidence in their ability to handle matters which had their counter-

---

*Id. at 666.
†345 U.S. 83 (1952).
‡Id. at 94.
§Id.
‖345 U.S. 83, 93 (1952).
⊥417 U.S. 733 (1974).

parts in civilian life, and did not require the courts to become en-
meshed in the day-to-day operations of the military as shown by the
U.S. Supreme Court case of Frontiero v. Richardson.*

One of the most striking examples of military procedures paralleling civilian practices involves the policy of terminating the employment
of pregnant women. A comparison between the civilian cases and the
military cases reveals that many of the same arguments were used
against both military and civilian women. Not surprisingly, civilian
women have led the way in demolishing these arguments. Their
victories have encouraged military women in their more difficult
struggle.

The battle waged by pregnant servicewomen is more arduous
because they must overcome two additional obstacles. The first is
the reluctance of federal courts to review military decisions. This
reluctance has a tendency to affect the decision on the merits. The
second obstacle is proving that military readiness need not be adversely affected by pregnant women. This obstacle is at the very
crux of the problem since it is difficult to argue that military readiness is not a compelling governmental interest.

The first military cases to be heard after the landmark decision
in Reed v. Reed† were brought separately by three air force women,
Captain Susan R. Struck, First Lieutenant Mary S. Gutierrez and
Airman First Class Gloria D. Robinson. Their cases, ‡ which involved no disputed questions of fact, exhibited many similarities
beginning with the fact that each woman became pregnant while unmarried and ending with the final disposition of each case a few months
apart in 1973 when the air force relented and finally granted each
woman a waiver while appeals were pending.

Although the regulations were undergoing modification while
their cases were being prepared, they were all fighting a rule which
basically provided for the immediate discharge of any woman who
became pregnant. Each applied for a waiver when that opportunity
was offered to her, and each was initially turned down. Then each
applied for and received a temporary injunction from federal court
to keep from being discharged before her case could be heard.

The court which heard Captain Struck's case emphasized the
terrible consequences which might befall her, her unborn child, her

---

*411 U.S. 677 (1973).

†404 U.S. 71 (1971).

‡Struck v. Secretary of Defense, 460 F. 2d 1372 (9th Cir. 1971),
vacated and remanded for consideration of the issue of mootness,
409 U.S. 1071 (1972); Gutierrez v. Laird, 346 F. Supp. 289 (D.D.C.
1972); Robinson v. Rand, 340 F. Supp. 37 (D. Colo. 1972).

patients and the air force should the hospital in which she was serving in Vietnam be shelled. The anticipated result was that she would be injured or suffer shock which would lead to a miscarriage. Then, naturally, she would become a burden to the air force since she would be a patient instead of a nurse. Any objections to this scenario were dismissed as irrelevant.

It is obvious, however, that this eventuality did not really form one of the bases for the regulations dealing with pregnant women. Any military organization prevented by a court from discharging a pregnant woman could reassign her to nonhazardous duties with a minimum of inconvenience. A vulnerable serviceperson, male or female, would not be left in a combat zone.

However, while using more restrained language than the Struck court, the other courts agreed that the regulations could be sustained under a passive standard of review. They found that the regulations served to promote the immediate availability and physical capability of military personnel to serve anywhere in the world. The courts further agreed that these legitimate governmental interests would be thwarted by allowing pregnant women to remain on active duty since they might not be available for all authorized assignments at all times.

The courts were able to reach this conclusion because they looked at the issue in terms of whether the air force had a rational basis for treating pregnant air force women differently from those members with no disability. The courts appeared to be aware that they were comparing apples and oranges, but passed on to other points. If they had examined this problem more closely, they might have asked some of the following questions. Is it the military's policy to discharge involuntarily all personnel whose physical ability is temporarily impaired? Is there a uniform practice of involuntarily discharging military personnel whose temporary disability was incurred voluntarily or negligently? Does pregnancy result in a certain impairment of physical ability? If so, is this disability of a temporary nature?

After answering "no" to the first two questions and "yes" to the last two, the judges could ask themselves why the regulations treat pregnancy differently from other transitory disabilities. The answer might be that pregnancy is the only medical condition which changes the status quo ante when the affected person returns to normal. This is because the natural result of a pregnancy is the birth of a child.

Then the judges might inquire whether military people are allowed to have children. The answer would have to be that only male personnel can have children and remain in uniform as a matter of course. When the basis for this disparate treatment of the sexes is explored, it becomes apparent that it is based upon certain outmoded expectations about women's exclusive responsibility for child care. Supposedly, a woman with children must devote her time to making a home for them to the exclusion of remunerative work.

This line of reasoning might be objected to on the basis that the issues of pregnancy and child care should not be mixed since they are separate grounds for discharge. In addition, a pregnant woman might get an abortion or put her baby up for adoption so that she would have no child care responsibilities. Nonetheless, when these regulations were first written, abortion was illegal as a general rule, and a military woman could not be forced to give up her child for adoption (as is still the case). It stands to reason, therefore, that it was really a concern for the performance level and assignability of women with children which led the services to discharge pregnant servicewomen.

The decision in the Struck case, which held that the mandatory discharge rule for pregnant servicewomen was constitutional, was ultimately vacated and remanded for consideration of the issue of mootness by the U.S. Supreme Court after the air force ordered Captain Struck's retention in the air force.

The Gutierrez court was in agreement with the Struck court's handling of the suspect classification and fundamental interest arguments. Following the Struck court's lead, it also quoted a passage from Greunwald v. Gardner* for the proposition that discriminations based on sex are valid. However, like the Struck court, the Gutierrez court did not appreciate the fact that Gruenwald, a case dealing with the more favorable treatment accorded women over men in the Social Security Act, interpreted that legislation as "affirmative action" rather than as "protective" in nature.

As characterized by Frontiero v. Richardson, protective legislation is a discrimination ". . . rationalized by an attitude of 'romantic paternalism' which, in practical effect, put women not on a pedestal, but in a cage." This concept is diametrically opposed to the idea of "affirmative action" as developed in Gruenwald and Kahn v. Shevin.† This concept is best explained by a passage from Bastardo v. Warren.‡

> It may be that when the particular racial or sexual classi-
> fication is "benign," that is, when its purpose and effect
> is to redress oppression or disadvantage previously suffered
> by a certain racial or sexual group in a certain context

---

*390 F. 2d 591 (2nd Cir. 1968).
†416 U.S. 351 (1974).
‡332 F. Supp. 501 (W.D. Wis. 1971).

such as employment or housing or educational opportunity,
then the compelling state interest may be more easily
demonstrated than it may be when the classification is
not benign. *

As happened in the <u>Struck</u> case, the judgment in <u>Gutierrez</u> was
vacated as moot after the air force ordered the retention of Lieutenant
Gutierrez in service following her appeal to the court of appeals.

The Robinson court skinned over the problem of sex as a suspect
classification, but conscientiously presented a review of the nature
of the "fundamental" and "compelling" interests involved and attempted
to reconcile them. After noting that ". . . courts have been demanding men and women be afforded equal treatment,"† the court concluded
its discussion of sex discrimination by declaring that ". . . the
accused air force regulation does operate discriminately, may well
be based on outmoded stereotypes, and does force a woman to choose
between important private rights and her career."‡

The court then proceeded to find that the air force regulation,
which it found neither wholly arbitrary nor irrational, interfered
with the petitioner's fundamental right to bear a child. Viewing the
regulation upon procreation with the strict scrutiny demanded by
<u>Skinner</u> v. <u>Oklahoma</u>, § the court determined that it was intolerable.
Instead, the military would have to use a "'. . . less drastic means
for achieving the same basic purpose.' "‖

The government appealed this decision. But before the appeal
could be decided by the Tenth Circuit, the air force granted Airman
First Class Robinson a waiver. This rendered the issue moot.

Two factors distinguish the following two Marine Corps cases
from the three preceding air force cases. The first factor, which
was more favorable to the petitioners in the Marine Corps cases,
was time. <u>Crawford</u> v. <u>Cushman</u>⊥ and <u>Downen</u> v. <u>Warner</u>, ** the
Marine Corps cases, were decided in 1976 and 1974, respectively,
as opposed to 1972 when the air force cases were tried and 1973
when they were finally settled. During that interim period, many
important cases relevant to this inquiry, such as the Supreme Court's

---

*<u>Id</u>. at 503
†340 F. Supp. 37, 38 (D. Colo. 1972).
‡<u>Id</u>.
§315 U.S. 535 (1972).
‖Shelton v. Tucker, 364 U.S. 479, 488 (1960) quoted at 340 F.
Supp. 37, 38 (D. Colo. 1972).
⊥378 F. Supp. 717 (D. Ver. 1974).
**No. 70-410 (S.D. Cal. 1974).

Frontiero v. Richardson, Cleveland Board of Education v. LaFleur,*
and Parker v. Levy, were decided.

The second factor, which involved the position of the petitioners,
was less favorable. While the air force cases concerned women who
were fighting to stay in the service, the Marine Corps cases dealt
with the efforts of two women to get back into the military after having
been separated for parental status. This difference in position caused
additional difficulties for the former women marines. Not only did
they have to prove that the motherhood regulations were infirm, but
they had to contend with exhaustion-of-remedies arguments and the
rules which deny enlistment or reenlistment to women with children
under the age of 18.

The situation in which Corporal Stephanie V. Crawford found
herself in 1970 was no different from those in which Captain Struck,
Lieutenant Gutierrez, or Airman First Class Robinson found themselves at approximately the same time. All were unmarried and
facing an "automatic discharge" because of pregnancy. However,
Corporal Crawford did not object to her discharge. Instead, she had
her baby as a civilian and tried to reenlist after she gave her baby
up for adoption. When reenlistment was denied on the grounds that
she had a parental relationship with a living child under 18 years of
age, Crawford filed suit charging the Commandant of the Marine Corps
with sex discrimination.

In the district court opinion in Crawford v. Cushman, Chief Judge
Holden noted the Supreme Court's decision in Cleveland Board of
Education v. LaFleur. However, he quickly dismissed it by differentiating civilian employment from military service. In addition to the
standard "readiness and mobility" rationale, he concentrated on the
Levy case theme that ". . . the military is, by necessity, a specialized society separate from civilian society."†

The fundamental interest in bearing and raising children was
dealt with as if Crawford had waived that right when she signed her
enlistment contract. Moreover, the district court was persuaded
that there was even ". . . an undertaking on her part that she would
not become subject to the debilitating consequence of pregnancy!"‡

The only good thing that can be said about the lower court opinion
is that it did not perpetuate the unsupported assumptions about the
ability of pregnant women to work. Nor did it give undue prominence
to the symptoms associated with the last trimester of pregnancy as

---

*414 U.S. 632 (1974).
†417 U.S. 733, 743 (1974).
‡378 F. Supp. 717, 726 (D. Ver. 1974).

did the court in <u>Schattman</u> v. <u>Texas Employment Commission</u>.*
Instead, it joined the Supreme Court in recognizing that ". . . the
ability of any particular pregnant woman to continue at work past
any fixed time in her pregnancy is very much an individual matter."†

Actually, Chief Judge Holden's opinion aided in understanding
the problem of the motherhood discharge in one way. It cast light
on why the military chose to separate women as soon as their pregnancy was confirmed. Obviously, it was not because the servicewoman became useless at that point. Nor was she any more vulnerable
to injury during her first few months than usual. Rather, the opinion
lent support to the theory that pregnant women were discharged from
the service because of fears about the performance of women with
children and because of old-fashioned stereotypes about the proper
role of women.

It mattered not at all to the judge that Crawford had already
placed her baby in a foster home and that other servicewomen could
request a hardship discharge if they were unable to make suitable
arrangements for the care of their children.

On 23 February 1976, the United States Court of Appeals for the
Second Circuit reversed the district court decision in <u>Crawford</u> v.
<u>Cushman</u>‡ and held the regulation mandating discharges for pregnancy
invalid as a denial of equal protection and due process. The court
summarized the basic dispute by stating that:

> The question here is not whether it is rational to classify
> personnel under the temporary disability of pregnancy as
> subject to mandatory discharge, while not classifying those
> personnel free from disability similarly. The questions
> are, rather, whether it is rational to classify pregnant
> personnel differently from personnel with other temporary
> disabilities, and whether there is "some ground of differ-
> ence" between the two classifications which bears a
> substantial relation to the purposes of mobility, readi-
> ness, and administrative convenience. §

The court then answered its questions by finding the Marine
Corps' differentiation between the disability of pregnancy and all
other temporary disabilities irrational. This finding was based on

---

*459 F. 2d 32 (5th Cir. 1972).
†<u>Cleveland Board of Education</u> v. <u>LaFleur</u>, 414 U.S. 632, 645
(1974).
‡531 F. 2d 1114 (2d Cir. 1976).
§<u>Id</u>. at 1122.

a showing that the subject discharge regulation was applied in both a demonstrably underinclusive and overinclusive fashion.

The regulation was deemed to be underinclusive since it did not apply to personnel suffering from any other temporary disability which inhibited mobility and readiness. The regulation also was irrationally overinclusive since it required the automatic separation of pregnant marines without any individualized determination of their fitness to serve. In so doing, the regulation established an irrebuttable presumption that a pregnant servicewoman was permanently unfit for duty. This presumption constituted an impermissible burden on the constitutionally protected right to procreate.

The case of Downen v. Warner involved a woman marine who would have had little trouble making appropriate arrangements for the care of her children. Captain Gail Waugh Downen's case is unique among those examined here since she received a motherhood discharge although she was not pregnant. Her case is also the most outrageous because the government lost the services of a perfectly fit, well-trained officer who desired to continue serving in the military.

After having served seven and one-half years in the Marine Corps, the captain married a man who had custody of his two children, aged 15 and 13 years. Then she and her new family took up residence together. Subsequently, the Marine Corps initiated administrative discharge proceedings which resulted in the termination of her commission. The grounds relied upon authorized such action when it was reported that a woman marine was ". . . the step-parent of a child under the age of 18 years, and the child is within the household of the woman member for a period of more than 30 days a year.*

The reason for this action appears to be stated in a letter† written to Captain Downen denying her request for a waiver. Paragraph four of this letter explains the motherhood discharge by stating that it ". . . is based on the fact that a woman who is the parent of a child should devote herself to the responsibilities of her household and children."‡

Needless to say, competing family obligations are not grounds for the involuntary discharge of male marines. The government attempted to justify this discrimination by arguing that the military would be reduced, to the detriment of national security.

---

*MCO 1900.16, para. 2103.3c, 32 CFR 730.61(c)(2)(i).
†CMC ltr DMA-msb dtd 10 Dec. 1968 included in Clerk's Record at 78.
‡Id. at para. 4.

However, women are also an integral part of the military establishment. To discharge a willing and able servicewoman involuntarily is surely as much of a blow to military preparedness as separating her male counterpart. Regardless, the main ingredient of military readiness is the predictability of personnel strengths. Since pregnancy is a condition of predictable duration, and child custody arrangements necessitate preparation, military planners can make their calculations accordingly.

Notwithstanding the government's arguments, Downen won her case. Unfortunately, the case was not reported, but the decision was based on the due process clause of the Fifth Amendment.

In the final analysis, the military women whose cases have been discussed in this chapter were attempting to lead modern lives in one of the last bastions of male dominance and traditionalism. Even though the military establishment has come more and more to display the characteristics of any large-scale organization, many senior officers still view every member of their command in terms of his ability to fight on the front lines. It is natural, therefore, that these decision makers continue to see servicewomen in World War II terms as auxiliary personnel rather than permanent members.

Instead of recognizing that modern women may desire a career as well as a family, they cling to the belief that with proper guidance, servicewomen will retire to their homes as soon as they get married and become pregnant. In their view, it would serve no purpose to put up with any inconvenience caused by a pregnant woman who will be leaving the military soon anyway.

However, women are no longer willing to have their lives controlled by such stereotyped notions. While Captain Struck could have pursued her calling as a nurse in a civilian hospital, and Corporal Crawford could have used her clerk-typist skills in industry, each felt strongly enough about her military career to seek protection from the courts.

Presumably because of the current trend in court decisions enforcing womens' rights to procreate and to enjoy due process and equal protection on the job, the Department of Defense made the determination on 1 June 1974 that its policies permitting involuntary separation of women for pregnancy and parenthood were no longer viable. * The policy that the separation of women who were pregnant or became parents should be voluntary, with involuntary separations

---

*Memo for Assistant Secretary of the Army (M&RA) from Vice Admiral John G. Finneran, USN, Deputy Assistant Secretary of Defense dtd 25 Nov. 1974 entitled "Involuntary Separation of Women for Pregnancy and Parenthood."

of mothers to be based on nonperformance of duties, was transmitted to the military departments for implementation.

Based upon a comprehensive set of suggested administrative policies and procedures issued by the Department of Defense, the military departments began to develop coordinated procedures for implementation by 15 May 1975.*

The revised policies published in 1975 were a disappointment in that the old ad hoc waiver procedure was simply elaborated. Upon certification of pregnancy, the woman must request retention or release from active duty. If she desires to stay in the military, she must satisfy the designated authorities that among other things, suitable arrangements have been made for the care of the infant. Needless to say, male service members do not have to demonstrate their ability to provide care for their offspring prior to their birth.

However, changing attitudes toward women, favorable court decisions in recent years, and the military's need for qualified personnel bode well for the future. Since the armed forces are experiencing some difficulty in attracting sufficient numbers of acceptable male recruits, they are making plans to increase the number of women in the military for a potential trade-off with men. It is anticipated that the increased representation of women in the services will lead to an abandonment of paternal regulations which discriminate against women on the basis of sex.

---

*Memo for Assistant Secretary of the Army (M&RA) and Assistant Secretary of the Navy (M&RA) from John F. Ahearne, Acting Assistant Secretary of Defense dtd 11 April 1975 entitled "Involuntary Separation of Women for Pregnancy and Parenthood."

7

Single-Parent Fathers: Implications For the Military Family

Dennis K. Orthner
Richard J. Brown, III

In 1975 a male marine sergeant stationed at Cherry Point, North Carolina was granted a divorce and exclusive custody of his 11-year-old boy. His former wife had been dissatisfied with her husband's military career and left the family to return to her parents. Several months later she sued him for divorce and sought custody of her son. The father argued that he was a better parent for the child, and the court agreed.

In 1976 a male navy petty officer stationed at Norfolk, Virginia gained exclusive custody of his two school-age sons after a lengthy court process. His former wife had attempted to prove that a military career would limit the father's capability for being an effective parent. But in this case, the judge was persuaded more by the greater demonstrated interest in the children by the father than by the "tender years" doctrine which usually results in custody being granted to the mother.

In a different type of case, a male army captain stationed overseas in 1972 had cohabited with a foreign national. When his tour of duty there ended, the couple decided that their child would be in a better position with the father. Paternity was established and legal custody granted to the father. Today, both father and child live together in the United States, although the father is no longer in active military service.

These cases, each somewhat unique, represent a growing trend in the U.S. family, in and outside the military. There is little question that single-parent fatherhood is on the increase and that social and legal processes are at work affecting child custody arrangements throughout U.S. society. In 1976 in the United States, there were approximately one-half million fathers rearing 710,000 dependent children.

About one out of every ten U.S. households headed by a single parent had a father as the head. Seven percent of all children in single-parent households were being reared by their fathers, and 1 percent of all the children in the United States lived exclusively with their fathers.

Comparable data for military families are presently not available or under analysis, but it is possible to estimate the number of single-parent fathers in one of the services. Air Force data currently indicate that there are 487 widowed fathers rearing 886 dependent children. There are also approximately 16,000 divorced and separated men in that service, and these men support over 12,000 child dependents. If we conservatively estimate that 5 percent of these children are under the custody of their fathers, nearly 1,000 children are involved. Add to this the number of single fathers with dependent children (over 1,500), some of whom they have adopted or are rearing, and we see that there are potentially well over 2,000 children that have single-parent fathers in the air force alone.

If the trends we are to discuss continue, it is apparent that this phenomenon of single-parent fatherhood cannot be ignored by the military. In the past, there has been somewhat of a barrier between the military community and the remainder of society. The fence surrounding the military compound was more than a fence—it also represented a different subculture milieu. Now, in a sense, the fence is coming down. There is more cross-fertilization of values; more military persons are living, shopping, receiving medical care, and attending church in the civilian community, especially those stationed in the United States.

Over the last decade, the military has shown itself to be increasingly subject to the same trends and pressures as the society-at-large. With the decline in an insulated environment, changes in social values, laws, and family norms are being felt more and more by the military personnel. Therefore, it is important to look at the way in which changes in parental roles and custody arrangements may influence the military family.

In this chapter, we shall examine the specific situations of those men who are not only taking more seriously their parental responsibilities, but who also are the primary parent of their children. We shall also explore the trends that are increasing father participation in the family and how these trends may be influencing military men as well. Evidence regarding the capabilities of fathers to be the primary parent of dependent children will then be examined in light of the need for information regarding the supports necessary to maintain these family units satisfactorily. Finally, we shall consider several important implications for military policy that should be addressed if more military men adopt the role of single-parent fathers.

TRENDS INFLUENCING SINGLE-PARENT
FATHERHOOD

There are several trends that appear to be converging which
influence the potential for more single-parent fathers in the near
future. These include changes in the concept of fatherhood and
motherhood, a rise in divorce rates and a decline in legal impediments to father custody, increasing possibilities for adoptions by
men, and the increase in child-support services for single parents.
Each of these trends is occurring within the military, as well as in
civilian communities and should have an impact on the number of
men who become single parents.

Concepts of Parenthood

One of the major changes in the family today is the redefinition
of parenthood. The concept of father has traditionally been limited
to the economic support and provider roles of the family. A "good"
father was a "good" provider. Even recently, Lopata (1971) found
that most housewives considered their husbands' most important
contribution to the family to be that of breadwinner. But the concept
of a nurturing father is now increasing in prevalence. Perhaps because it is more difficult for many men to satisfy all their personal
needs on the job, or perhaps because they are beginning to see important needs they can meet in their children, many are coming "back
home" to assert their parental presence.

The number of popular books and magazine articles reinforcing
this nurturing father is mounting. Men are being encouraged to
invest more of their time, energy, and other resources into their
parental responsibilities. And this encouragement is reflected in
the growing number of preparation for parenthood classes before the
child is even born, in father-coached delivery programs such as
Lamaze, and in the increased reinforcement for fathers to participate
actively with their children throughout their development. These
trends are affecting men across the entire social and occupational
spectrums, and military fathers are increasingly being affected as
well.

Coupled with the greater participation of fathers inside the household, however, is a trend toward mothers moving outside the household. Over 35 percent of the mothers in the United States are now
employed, and the rate of female employment is increasing rapidly.
In a sense, we find ourselves in the midst of a role-value revolution
in which support for traditional motherhood roles is declining while
support for new fatherhood roles is increasing. In an intact family,

this crossover should result in greater coparticipation in parental roles. But if the marriage should dissolve, the conditions are also ripe for the father to demand his rights to the children and perhaps to seek full custody of them.

Custody Arrangements

The opportunity for fathers to have their day in court and be assured of a reasonable hearing for their custody desires is now occurring. Until quite recently, few fathers sought custody, and those who did so, found they must prove the mother "unfit" for parenthood. The courts have rarely weighed the relative capabilities of both parents, depending more on a legal "presumption" of motherhood fitness. This presumption followed normal role differentiation in the family and eased the process of making custody decisions in the context of a rising backlog of divorce judgments. Legal support for this right of the mother came from the tender years doctrine which emerged out of case law—a doctrine which discouraged many fathers from seeking custody of children younger than adolescents.

Two major trends in state laws are now removing the legal restraints on fatherhood custody. First, more and more states are allowing no-fault divorce arrangements. Most of these no-fault laws permit the couple to decide for themselves who should have custody of the children. Thus, the necessity of an adversary court proceeding in which the court will make a judgment as to the placement of a child is eliminated. It should be noted, however, that in most no-fault states, if the father and mother do not agree on custody, they become subject to the judgment of the court, and this will likely be biased toward the mother.

A second trend in state laws is now removing the traditional bias toward the mother, even in contested divorces. With the addition of North Carolina in 1977, there are now 13 states which have legally eliminated the presumptive tender years doctrine. This increases the likelihood that fathers in these states, which include Virginia and California and their major military installations, will gain custody of their children. It is important to understand that these changes affect military as well as civilian families. Divorces, even in the service, are granted by the state in which the couple resides, and as these state laws relax their provisions for limiting father custody, we can expect more judgments in favor of military fathers as well. Also, even when fathers do not request custody, the obligation of the court to consider equally the relative capabilities of the mother and father may lead many men to become single-parent fathers if the judgment of the caseworker so recommends. Not surprisingly, many fathers find that due to desertion, alcoholism, mental illness, or other reasons, they become single parents by allocation, not request (Orthner, Brown, and Ferguson 1976).

Adoption

The legal right of single men to adopt children is also increasing. This is certainly a minor factor in the overall scope of single parenthood today but may be particularly important to military men, especially those who go overseas and adopt foreign nationals. In this country, most men are usually restricted to adopting older, mixed-race, or other hard-to-place children, and yet the number of those adoptions is increasing steadily (Kadushin 1970). The United States Supreme Court in the case of Stanley v. Illinois also eliminated prohibitions against single men adopting their own child, thus providing an avenue by which some men may gain custody of a child that their unmarried partner rejects. With increases of nonmarital cohabitation in all segments of society, including the military, the potential for single men adopting their own children should also increase.

Support Services

Although not a factor directly influencing the incidence of single-parent fatherhood, the increasing availability of support services for single parents has indirectly given men more opportunities to seek and maintain single-parent status effectively. This is particularly true in the area of child-care services. Before the advent of public and private child care, men had a more difficult time finding adequate substitutionary child-care facilities. Rarely did they receive child support or alimony so it was assured that they had to continue employment, despite the age of the child. But without adequate child-care arrangements, all but the most affluent fathers often found it difficult to demonstrate that they were capable of insuring a healthy and secure environment for their children.

Organizations such as Parents Without Partners and Solo Parents have also helped ease the transition of some men into single parenthood. These and other supportive organizations provide opportunities for men to share some of their frustrations and gain tools to help them in their parental experience. Classes in personal growth, child rearing, Parent Effectiveness Training, and other such topics are increasingly available to men and help supplant their lack of parental socialization. Even groups such as Men's International and various divorce counseling agencies are affecting single-parent fatherhood by making men more aware of their legal rights to child custody, thus increasing their chances for continuing in their parental roles.

CAPABILITIES OF SINGLE-PARENT FATHERS

One question we must address is this: How do single-parent fathers fare as the primary parents of dependent children? This is an important question since it is important to have evidence regarding demonstrated capabilities before we suggest altering regulations and developing support services to facilitate the emerging trend. Certainly, there is a need to understand the strengths and strains experienced by single-parent fathers so that more appropriate military family policies can be established. As part of a larger study of 212 male and female single parents, lengthy semistructured interviews were conducted with 20 single-parent fathers in the Greensboro, North Carolina area. The proportion of fathers in the sample is similar to the national average, but the respondents were not randomly selected, and they should not be considered necessarily representative of all single-parent fathers. Attempts were made, however, to provide a broad cross-section of men and women in the sample from which the subsample was drawn and not to limit the respondents to divorced persons. Each of the single parents in the study had custody of children under 19 years of age who were living with them at the time. Ten of the fathers had at least one preschool child; the other ten had only school-age children. Nine of the fathers had one child, nine had two children, and one had three children. The youngest father was 25 years of age, the oldest 64. Some comparable data between the single-parent mothers and fathers in the study are reported in Table 7.1.

The overall higher economic status of the single-parent fathers compared to the mothers in the study appears to come partly from the higher perception of competency required by the courts in the case of fathers. Proof of such competency is more easily demonstrated if financial resources are more than adequate. As the resource level of the fathers dropped, however, the men who did receive custody of their children were more likely to have received it because the mother did not want or was not considered capable of caring for the children. In general, the higher income fathers were the ones most likely to have sought and received custody through the court process.

Parental Responsibilities

A common theme in much of the literature on single parenthood, particularly in popular books and magazine articles, is the fear that

TABLE 7.1

Differences between Men and Women
Single Parents

Single-Parent Status	Men		Women	
	Number	Percent	Number	Percent
Separated	8	40	58	31
Divorced	7	35	61	32
Widowed	3	15	11	6
Never married	2	10	57	30
Mean number of children	1.75		1.9	
Employed part or full time		85		72
Income (percent over $12,000 per year)		45		8

Source: Compiled by the authors.

single-parent fathers may not make very good parents. This fear
has been the basis for the legal presumption of motherhood competency, and we find some encouragement for this even in professional
publications (Biller and Meredith 1975; Goode 1956; Weiss 1975).
But in our study we did not find the single-parent fathers to be particularly anxious about their ability to be parents. Nor were they fearful
of any resulting harm to their children from the experience. Eighty-
four percent of the fathers described the relationship between themselves and their children as very close. This was quite similar to
the 82 percent of the mothers who felt this way. The fathers did not
report as affectionate a relationship, however. Only 25 percent
reported their family very affectionate, compared to 44 percent of
mothers.

The fathers in the study spent a great deal of time with their
children, nearly as much as the mothers. There is little evidence
in the data to support the contention that single-parent fathers shift
their children over to other parent substitutes. In contrast almost
all the fathers seemed to go out of their way to be with their children
and to take them on weekend outings and to evening activities. Some
95 percent at times took their children with them on dates; a figure
higher than the 74 percent of the single-parent mothers who did this.
The fathers also seemed to depend less on television as a sitter for
their children than did the mothers in the study. On a "typical" week,
the fathers reported that the children watched television an average
of 21 hours, compared to 27 hours for the mothers.

Nevertheless, there are areas of parental concern among single-parent fathers that must be recognized. While the professional litera-ture increasingly supports the idea that one-parent families are not necessarily dysfunctional child rearing environments, 63 percent of the fathers in the study felt that a two-parent situation is usually best (only 37 percent of single-parent mothers felt this way). This percep-tion of strain is also evident in the greater wish of the divorced and separated fathers that their marriages had not failed. Somewhat surprisingly, 73 percent reported they sometimes or frequently felt this regret compared to only 43 percent of the mothers.

Fathers who were rearing daughters expressed some concern over providing appropriate role models for them. Similar concerns were expressed by mothers for their sons, but fathers were consider-ably more adamant about differences in sex-role socialization between boys and girls. The two fathers whose daughters were going through puberty felt they were not as competent in handling questions about menstruation or sexual development. But these concerns should not be taken to mean that the fathers doubted their ability to rear daugh-ters. Quite the contrary, the same developmental problems men-tioned by the fathers were also mentioned by mothers, and overall, there was little difference in the feelings of parental competence between the fathers with sons and those with daughters.

All factors considered, the fathers felt they were quite adequately rearing their children. Two-thirds expressed the belief that their children were having the same kinds of experiences as other children their age. Still, when they were asked what their principal difficulty was in being a single parent, the most common response centered around meeting the needs of their children. This could be taken to mean that the children were a significant source of strain. But in the context of questioning, what this really meant was that the fathers were more secure in their personal, occupational, and financial con-cerns. Thus, their principal concern was for the children. In con-trast, the single-parent mothers were most likely to mention finances as their greatest problem, and personal problems were almost as frequently mentioned as child-oriented problems.

Work-Family Responsibilities

One of the major concerns of employers has been the ability of employees to reconcile their occupational and family responsibilities. Therefore, much of the attention in this area has been focused on employed mothers and their ability to maintain household, child-rearing, and occupational roles. It has been assumed that the husband-father owed his primary allegiance to the job and that the family would adjust to his occupational demands. But in the case of the single-parent father, there is no proverbial wife-mother at home to handle the "kinder and kitchen." Thus, he, too, faces many of the same potential strains so frequently mentioned in employed-mother literature.

The advantage we found that the single-parent fathers enjoyed over their female counterparts, however, was in their career longevity. None of the fathers had interrupted their career to be a parent so they were generally more advanced on their ladders of success. Twelve of the 20 men interviewed were in professional or managerial positions, and one other was in sales. There were only five blue-collar men in the sample, along with one student and one unemployed former manager.

Nonetheless, the unemployed manager is a case in point. His new parental responsibilities clearly resulted in the loss of his job. His position had required long hours and at times he was forced to reduce his work load to care for the children. Interruptions to meet with teachers, schedule medical checkups, and other normal parental responsibilities also resulted in less favorable evaluation of his productivity. In a tight economy, he was fired.

For the majority of fathers, however, child rearing was not considered a major deterrent to their occupational goals. Many of the fathers complained that they did not feel they spent enough time with their children or that they had insufficient patience with them, but the tenor of these complaints was similar to that reported by employed mothers (Hoffman and Nye 1974). When asked if child-care problems had interfered with their work, 88 percent of the fathers said no.

Overall, most of the fathers appeared to have arrived at a satisfactory adjustment in their work-family responsibilities after the first year of single parenthood. The first year was considered the most critical period of adjustment by most of the fathers, with many reporting a rearrangement of their work priorities at that time. For those fathers with preschool or early school children, the ability to find quality child-care arrangements was deemed a particularly important step in their feeling comfortable about their children while at work.

Somewhat surprisingly, kinship supports were often recognized as very important in the first year's adjustment period. Rarely did the fathers depend on their parents for regular child care or household help, but a majority relied on them for periodic extended care while involved in job-related endeavors, such as attending conventions, meetings, or searching for other positions. Kin support was more important to the men than the women in the study, with 53 percent of the fathers feeling that their parents definitely supported them compared to 34 percent of the mothers. But most important, this vanguard of interpersonal support was most frequently mentioned as the factor that eased their transition into single parenthood and facilitated early work-family adjustments.

Personal-Family Responsibilities

One of the genuine surprises of the survey was the sense in which the single-parent fathers appeared to be quite satisfied with their life situations. On a 12-item scale of life satisfaction, each with possible scores ranging from 1 to 7, the fathers demonstrated a mean scale score of 4.9 (for mothers, 4.6). Even more revealing was the lack of a strong motivation to remarry. We had assumed that the additional roles acquired by the fathers would create role strain accompanied by a greater desire to remarry and reduce the strain. But that is the picture that emerged more for the single-parent mothers than for the fathers. Some 90 percent of the fathers who had been previously married reported no plans to marry again, compared to 52 percent of the previously married mothers. While the possibility of remarriage was recognized, the single-parent fathers interviewed had been in their situations for an average of three years, and it was clear that they were quite comfortable with their present life style.

Among those men who were divorced or separated, most indicated rather cordial and mutually supportive relationships with their former wives. Approximately 80 percent of these former wives visited their children at least monthly. This was almost twice as high as the frequency of fathers visiting with their children when the wife had custody (50 percent). The fathers reported that their responsibility for coordinating these contacts between mother and children had considerable value for the family and relieved some of the strain on them as well. Interestingly, single-parent fathers indicated much better relationships with their former wives than single-parent mothers did with their former husbands. Perhaps the lack of financial dependencies when the father had custody of the children explains this difference.

Parental roles were mentioned as having a negative effect on the personal life of the fathers in one area—evening and weekend activities in which children were to be excluded. All but one of the fathers were dating, and there were numerous other occasions when meetings or dinners required their presence without children. Some of the fathers complained about their inability to make short-term decisions, to finish work at the office, or to go out after work "with the guys" without a carefully planned schedule.

The major source of this anxiety centered around an assumption
by most persons that fathers have a wife at home to care for the
children coupled with the reality of inadequate evening and weekend
child care. Baby-sitters had to be reserved days in advance, and
there were few places or events that provided for children. Meetings,
even of Parents Without Partners, rarely offered child care, so they
often did not go. Few of the fathers liked to rely on girlfriends for
this service out of the fear that this would lead to a personal obligation (pressure to marry) or a dependency of the child on that person.
This plea for more child-care services after school, in evenings,
and on Saturdays was also echoed by the single-parent mothers in
the investigation.

IMPLICATIONS FOR MILITARY POLICY

There are several trends presently juxtaposing which suggest a
growing need for policies related to the role of the single-parent
father in the military community. First, there is the impact of the
present national commitment to an all-volunteer military. Without
the draft, the military services must successfully compete for employment with the private sector which is often more understanding
of personal circumstances. This increases the need for military
policy which is sensitive to the personal needs of its members.

Traditionally, the purpose of the military is to perform a specific
mission or set of missions. As such, the military has demonstrated
very little tolerance toward any human constraints upon the satisfactory performance of the mission. However, in recent years the
military community has demonstrated increasing awareness of, and
support for, human factors. In an all-volunteer force this is quite
important since the individual question of remaining in the military
will often be decided more on the basis of personal considerations.

As social trends increase the number of single-parent fathers
in the civilian community, these same trends are bound to have a
comparable effect within the military community. A voluntary military increases the need for the military community to be more sensitive to general trends of society, since it is out of this pool that the
military services must attract and enlist its personnel. This is also
important in relation to the retention of career personnel since characteristics of life in the military community become determinants in
the decision to reenlist or not.

The need for the military structure to become sensitive to those
characteristics which affect the quality of life of its members becomes even more critical in the light of reductions in strength within
all branches of the military. When a person is being asked to increase

his work output to compensate for strength reductions, it is to be expected that other aspects of his life in the military will increase in importance as he weighs the pros and cons of reenlisting or pursuing a military career. In short, there is a need for the military structure to recognize that some highly desirable and qualified personnel are going to be getting out of the service if they have become or are contemplating becoming single-parent fathers and do not feel any understanding or support from the military.

Another trend affecting the single-parent father in the military is the rising rate of divorce. Increasing divorce rates mean increasing custody suits which mean increasing opportunities for fathers to win custody. Given the national trends of increasing parental involvement among fathers and growing awareness of the importance of the father in child development, military fathers are going to be perceiving themselves as more capable of providing primary parental care for their children. With this trend, it is likely that increasing numbers of military fathers are going to be seeking custody of their children.

A third trend would be the growing resource capabilities of military personnel. Not only have military incomes been rising, especially those of enlisted personnel, in an effort to maintain an all-volunteer force, but support services and benefits have become more comprehensive. All this is likely to create a more favorable impression in the court's assessment of the military father's capability for providing primary care for his children.

Acceptance of Single-Parent Fatherhood

It is only in recent years that fathers have been seen as capable of providing for the primary care of children. It is understandable, therefore, that the single-parent father's life style has traditionally been looked upon with skepticism and suspicion. This attitude has been heightened by the strong, stereotypic masculine image perpetuated in the military services. It would not be untypical for a military commander to suspect that a man interested in caring for his children probably would not be able to function as "a good soldier."

In light of this situation, it would be both appropriate and essential for military leaders to reexamine their attitudes and the position of their branch of service regarding the support and advocacy of single-parent fatherhood. This should not be taken to mean that the military should find itself encouraging marital dissolution or father custody among less competent men, but rather, the military should positively place itself in the position of supporting those fathers who on their own initiative seek and/or acquire custody of children.

Commanders and supervisors at all levels need to recognize and
support the growing importance of responsible father involvement
in child rearing. This need is only heightened when the father is
the primary parent.

It is hoped that those personnel who effect the daily implementation of military policy will see the single-parent father as pursuing
an acceptable life style. To encourage this, the following are recommended.

1. A study of single-parent fatherhood in the military services
should be undertaken. The limited data cited above indicate our weak
understanding of how this phenomenon is currently affecting military
personnel and effective policies demand a more accurate picture.

2. Commanders should have and be able to make available to
supervising personnel information on the extent and characteristics
of single parents within their command. This will facilitate a clearer
understanding of the degree to which the single-parent phenomenon
may be affecting their sections.

3. Workshops should be provided for supervising personnel on
the general characteristics and needs of single parents, particularly
fathers.

4. Members of the military community should be made more
aware of the redefinition of sex roles taking place in society and the
effect this is having on parenthood and parent roles.

5. There is a need for more broad-based support of father
involvement in child rearing. Evidence is mounting that nurturant
fatherhood behaviors have a positive impact on children (Lynn 1974)
and the encouragement of father-child activities should enhance the
opportunity for men to realize their parental potential.

6. The military community should increase its already evidenced
sensitivity to family-life concerns and issues among its personnel.
This needs to come from within the system in order to complement
the growing concern over the family in the society at large.

Examination of Military Regulations

In addition to the need for personal support on the part of commanders and supervisors, there is a growing need for official recognition of the single-parent father within the military. This will
require appropriate military directives to those agencies and sections
within the military community having the greatest opportunity to
affect single-parent fathers. Regulations in certain important areas
are likely to particularly affect these men, including those related
to type of work assignment, work schedules and extended duty hours,

availability of on-base family housing or housing supplements, sub-
sistence allowances, and permanent and temporary change of duty
station.

Given the potential for military regulations to influence the
parental capabilities and functioning of single-parent fathers, it is
recommended that a thorough examination be made of the regulations
in each branch of military service to determine the extent to which
implicit and explicit policies affect the parental roles of single-parent
fathers. It is understood that the basic purpose of military regulations is to execute the mission satisfactorily, but, it is hoped that
by identifying potential points of conflict, appropriate modifications
can be effected in such a way that human concerns are accounted for
in a manner that supports the mission rather than detracts from it.

Provisions for Support Services

Another area in which military policy could have an important
effect on single-parent fathers would be through establishing and
extending supportive services to these men. The data presented
earlier clearly indicate that those fathers who received interpersonal
and parent-child support more successfully adjusted to their new
parental roles. Given the concern of the military for maintaining
the operational effectiveness of its personnel, it should be obvious
that providing such support will not only reduce personal trauma but
increase individual effectiveness and mission capabilities.

Single parents, in particular single-parent fathers, have been
shown to benefit from involvement in support systems of friends,
kin, and other single parents. There is a tendency for many single-
parent fathers to feel somewhat isolated and unprepared for their
experience. But opportunities to get help or support may even be
limited by a lack of adequate child care. Because of this apparent
need for supportive services and the benefits that can be derived
for the personnel involved as well as the military, the following are
recommended.

- A chapter of Parents Without Partners or other similar organizations should be formed on those bases with a sufficient number of
  single parents. This should provide an adjustive environment
  and educational programs to increase effective parenting.
- Provisions should be made for child-care services or the extension
  of present child care to cover the working hours of single parents.
  This should also be made available for evening and weekend activities.

- Psychological and personal adjustment services should be examined to be certain that they are equipped to meet the needs of single-parent fathers and recognized as a viable source of information and support.
- Divorce and legal counseling needs to be available to military personnel so that they are properly informed of their rights under state laws to child custody and the inherent obligations implied in parenthood.

8 Dual-Career Military Families

John W. Williams, Jr.

The dual-career family is one in which both husband and wife follow independent careers and simultaneously carry on a viable family life together. The dual-career family is not one in which the husband pursues a career and the wife takes a full- or part-time job merely to increase the family income. Commitment of both spouses to a career is necessary before they may be defined as a dual-career family. For example, families in which the husband is a practicing attorney and the wife a physician is a dual-career family; however, where the husband is a tenured professor and the wife a secretary or sales clerk then that couple is not a dual-career family. Rather, it is a "dual-worker" family (Rappaport and Rappaport 1971). The key is probably the fact that the wife has an independent career of her own; however, in U.S. society this is not an easy task. According to Lynda Holmstrom (1972), author of a recent book on dual-career families, there are many barriers these couples must face in order to successfully combine career and family. These impediments include frequent pressures to move geographically for career advancement, the expectation that certain jobs held by men demand that wives devote time and energy to entertaining, the single-minded devotion to work that a career requires, and the subsequent difficulties in raising children when both spouses work. Any one of these factors are major obstacles, but when taken together, they present an almost impossible barrier to successful dual-career family success.

Although the idea of two-career families is not new to U.S. society there has been much recent interest, probably because of the intensified concern for the roles of women. Additionally, it appears that the two-career style of life is gaining in popularity, especially among newly married couples (Hunt and Hunt 1977). There are many reasons why this increase in dual-career families has occurred. The rising inflation rate, loss of buying power of the dollar, and the dramatic increase in the cost-of-living index

have probably forced many professional women out of the home and
into the occupational world to enable the family to maintain an acceptable standard of living. Although the typical woman may be dedicated
to her home and family, she also recognizes that one way of serving
her family is by earning additional money (Kellian 1971). Doors are
beginning to open for women in many areas formerly closed to them;
society is more accepting of women in the work world than in previous
years. Further, the recent growth and acceptance of day-care centers give working mothers a safe, reliable place to leave their children during working hours.

LITERATURE ON DUAL-CAREER FAMILIES

There is a paucity of information on dual-career families, probably due to the fact that only during the past few years has the population of these couples been large enough to generate strong interest
among social scientists. The book by the Rappaports, Dual Career
Families, published in 1971, is perhaps the best known and most often
quoted. That book reports the case studies of five couples in which
both spouses pursued independent careers and simultaneously lead
active family lives. A second book, entitled the Two-Career Family,
by Holmstrom (1972) reports on the problems, successes and failures
of 54 couples as they attempted to follow separate careers. The
book emphasizes the difficulties associated with the dual-career
family arrangement and discusses the issues of competitiveness,
divorce, colleagueship, allocation of time, effort, and money and
the life cycle of the family. Still another noteworthy publication is
an edited volume by Constantina Safilios-Rothschild (1972), Toward
a Sociology of Women. Articles in this book provide information on
dual-career families in terms of role conflict experienced by the
professional woman, the views of the male in the dual-professional
family, and the problems of women in professional specialities.
All the publications mentioned thus far point up the special problems
faced by dual-career families and the various techniques developed
to overcome or ameliorate those problems.

THE INCREASING NUMBER OF
DUAL-CAREER FAMILIES

All three of the major services appear supportive of dual-career
families, but none actually guarantees the couple will always be given
joint assignments. Regulations for all three service branches state
that where an officer is married to an enlisted person, the assignment of the officer will take precedence.

In conversations with personnel officers from all branches of the military, the author learned that there has been a substantial increase in the number of dual-career families in recent years. We are referring to the situation where both spouses are members of the military and both plan on a full career. By a full career we mean that both husband and wife plan to serve on active duty until retirement (normally 20 or more years). The first step in examining the approach taken by each branch of the service (army, navy and air force) was an analysis of each service's personnel regulations. In every case there appears to be solid support for these couples, and each service has specific regulations governing their assignment.

The air force regulations are quite explicit and supportive; however, they do point out a few restrictions and restraints concerning couples being assigned together. For example, Air Force Regulation 36-20 states that ". . . military requirements permitting, members with a military spouse are authorized assignment to the same or adjacent location; however, since manning considerations are paramount, there is no guarantee that couples are always assigned together." The regulation goes on to point out that this policy is designed to give military couples every reasonable opportunity to establish a common household and to minimize family separation at least to the degree experienced by other married couples. The regulation also points out the fact that members must share the responsibility for minimizing family separation and must not base career development or family planning on the premise that joint assignment is guaranteed. There are indeed a number of instances where a joint assignment may not be possible, such as (a) a short tour in a remote location where the spouse could not be effectively utilized; (b) a school for training; (c) special duty (for example, Air Attaché duty); (d) a location where the spouse's Air Force Specialty Code (AFSC) is not authorized; and (e) a controlled tour (for example, one year as a White House Fellow). In many instances, however, the air force will retrain or reclassify an individual in order to facilitate joint assignment.

The army also has detailed regulations covering dual-military career couples and is, in general, supportive of joint assignments. Army Regulation 614-200 states that ". . . to the maximum degree possible, married couples in the army will be assigned to locations where they can establish a common household; further, they will not be subjected to greater family separation than other married members, except when joint assignment is impracticable." This regulation is quite similar to the air force regulation.

The navy has policy letters which cover the assignment of what they term "duty with spouse" couples. Although the navy makes an active effort to assign couples to the same location, they, too, have restrictions. For example, because women cannot be assigned aboard

navy combat ships, sea duty for the husband would not permit a "duty
with spouse" assignment. However, it may be possible for the wife
to be assigned to the shore installation servicing the husband's ship.
The navy, more so than the army or air force, places responsibility
with the couple to work out assignments to the same location. Once
the couple locates assignments where they are qualified and acceptable, the navy, in most cases, cooperates by cutting orders which
enable the couple to move concurrently to the new station. A navy
bureau of personnel spokesman* recently pointed out that there are
now over 3,000 dual-career navy couples and, thus, it is becoming
more and more difficult to assign them together, especially if they
possess dissimilar ratings.

A STUDY OF DUAL-CAREER FAMILIES

The author recently completed a pilot study to gain insight into
specific problem areas for dual-career couples. The investigation
also sought information about their perceptions of the air force as
supportive of their situation. A longitudinal study is planned to follow
these couples as they move through their air force careers. Couples
were initially contacted and questioned about their experiences as a
dual-career family. From the total group, couples were divided
into various categories: both spouses officers, both spouses enlisted,
and one spouse officer and the other an enlisted serviceperson.

Results

During the initial phase of this study, data from interviews
produced a number of noteworthy findings. One of the most surprising
findings was that almost all of these couples were adamant in their
intention not to have children. For the most part these were couples
in their late twenties, in vigorous health, and with no evidence of an
inability to have children. Two of the couples had already taken
medical steps to insure that they would not have children, and all
others were practicing birth control.

It should be noted that air force policies permit women to remain
on active duty even though they have children, but there are certain
restrictions on children accompanying the mother to all assignments.
For example, a new mother may be given up to six weeks maternity

---

*VADM James D. Watkins, in the opening address at the Military
Family Research Conference, San Diego, California, September, 1977.

leave following the birth of her child; however, if she is assigned to
a remote area where it would be impracticable for the child to accompany her, she would be required to leave the child with the husband,
friends, or relatives while she carried out that assignment. Most
women interviewed declared emphatically they believed that children
would interfere with their careers and, for that reason, did not intend
to have any. We know, however, that many dual-career couples on
active duty do have children, and couples with children will be included
in the next phase of this research effort.

When asked why they had chosen the dual-career life style, most
couples reported financial reasons. The desire for a higher standard
of living than that offered if only one partner worked was mentioned
by every couple. For most of the couples, both held the rank of
captain and, thus, had a combined income of approximately $40,000
a year, in addition to other service-related benefits such as free
medical and dental care, retirement annuity, and commissary and
base exchange (PX) privileges. Their higher than average standard
of living is obvious from the homes most owned, the type of subdivi-
sions in which they lived, the kinds of automobiles they drove, and
their general life styles in terms of entertaining, clothing, home
furnishings, and travel.

Most of the couples felt the air force was treating them fairly,
but they reported becoming quite apprehensive as the time approached
for new assignments. All couples appeared familiar with the personnel regulations and knew what their options were. Many of the wives
pointed out that they did not believe the air force takes them seriously
and assumes that they will soon get pregnant and leave the military
service. None of these wives reported having that intention. Some
of the couples had already had short, periodic separations, but none
had had lengthy separations. All reported that they would attempt to
obtain assignments in the same area as their spouses when reassigned,
but that they would tolerate lengthy separations if it meant solid career
progression for one or the other of the marital partners. Both husbands and wives reported they would take a less than desirable assignment in order to accompany their spouse if the spouse received a
career-enhancing assignment at a critical time; for example, close
to promotion-eligibility time. All the couples had a great deal of
anxiety about being able to meet the requirements for promotion into
the higher ranks while still achieving a "normal" married life. All
service branches consider breadth and depth of experience when
promoting officers into the higher ranks. An officer must move
often to gain experience in many areas. Doing so, however, imposes
extreme difficulties on couples who are pursuing separate careers
while simultaneously attempting to be assigned together.

For every couple, highly structured procedures for accomplish-
ing household tasks were found. In no case, however, did any couple
view certain tasks as "woman's work" and others as the sole responsibility of the man. All couples appeared to make special efforts to
share equally such household tasks as washing dishes, vacuuming,
or mowing the lawn. The only exceptions were three instances where
a husband refused to iron clothes and two in which wives insisted the
husbands take out the garbage.

Competition did not appear to be a serious problem for the marital partners, but most agreed that they would avoid assignments in
which one spouse was the military commander of the other. In fact,
all agreed it would be inadvisable for them to be assigned to the same
unit since they would have to compete for the higher efficiency report.

All wives in this sample of dual-career couples reported having
apprehensions about social obligations once the husband became a
commander. They did not know how they would be able to handle the
social responsibilities of being the commander's wife while aggres-
sively pursuing their own career at the same time. Although military
social obligations have changed greatly in the past decade, there still
remain certain obligations on the part of the wife in terms of social
traditions and customs. Most wives reported concerns that their
lack of full participation in the social life of their husbands' organizations would, in some way, harm his career. None of them had a
solution for this dilemma.

All couples interviewed highly recommended their life styles
and had become recruiters of others contemplating dual-career
status. In fact, two of the couples were married for a number of
years before the wife came on active duty. In both cases, it was
the husband who had convinced the wife to join. None had regrets
and felt their marriages were more exciting, rewarding, and fulfill-
ing as a result of both spouses pursuing careers. All couples in this
sample appeared exceptionally well-adjusted, happy and enthusiastic
about their somewhat unique situation. Since all of them reported
strong, healthy marriages it could be that there is less strain in
this type of marriage than in more conventional ones. Divorce rates
in relation to the dual-career status were not available, but there
is some evidence to suggest they may be lower than divorce rates in
general.

The next phase of this research will involve examining dual-
career air force families serving in world-wide locations, serving
both jointly and apart, and with and without children, as well as
examining low- and high-ranking couples and couples in unique situations.

Discussion

As more and more women enter the military, we can expect to see increasing numbers of dual-military career families. It is no longer necessary for a woman to leave service if she becomes pregnant; thus, we can predict more situations in which active duty couples have children, with the marital partners sharing in all required activities associated with the care of infants. It is no longer absurd to believe that at sometime in the future entire families—mother, father and children—may be on active duty, simultaneously performing their required duties in the military while living together as a family unit.

Military planners in all service branches are becoming concerned about the effects of dual-career couples, single-parent families, and other alternative family styles upon the operational mission. The navy, although generally supportive of dual-career couples, is finding it more difficult to assign couples jointly due to the requirement for periodic sea duty for males, the uniqueness of many navy specialities, and the limitations placed on women in combat-type jobs. In a recent Air Force Times article the author stated that the growing air force female population posed unique problems since women in service tend to find marriage partners among their peers (Staff writer 1977). At the present time, about half of the air force's women members are married, and of those married, more than three-quarters are married to members of the air force. This presents no great problem as long as both members are junior in rank; however, once they are senior-enlisted or field-grade officers (major or above), the picture changes. Concern must then be given to important considerations such as career broadening, equitable assignment selection, best match of person to job, attendance at professional military schools, graduate education, and many others which affect career progression. With each consideration, the military services' chances of finding assignments for the couple jointly at the same place and at the same time are decreased. As increasing numbers of couples decide to pursue careers in the military, military personnel systems will find it extremely difficult to satisfy these couples' desire for assignments which are both career enhancing and at the same time permit a family unit to have a normal family life together. Although the military services are now quite compassionate vis-a-vis dual-career couples, there is an awareness that any major increase in numbers of these couples will bring profound personnel problems. Humanitarian concerns are important and will receive close attention, but consideration must also be given to those servicepersonnel who would be adversely affected by the special treatment afforded dual-career couples. For example, requiring a single officer or one with a wife who is not in the active-duty military to serve an inordinate number of remote tours so that the dual-career couple can be assigned together would be terribly unfair. Service couples who choose to make the military a career must be prepared to face family separations for extended periods.

It is probably much easier for civilian couples to have dual careers than it is for military couples, although there are similar problems. Most military couples interviewed pointed out that they are aware of the hazards and potential problems, but that they sincerely believe they can have a relatively normal family life and still have a successful military career. With enough flexibility, they can perhaps succeed.

PART III

COPING WITH LIFE CHANGES

"A major aspect, or characteristic, of the [military] family is a life style punctuated by comings and goings, departures and returns, separations and reunions."

Kathryn Brown Decker

9

Coping with Sea Duty: Problems Encountered and Resources Utilized during Periods of Family Separation

Kathryn Brown Decker

A major aspect, or characteristic, of the navy family is a life style punctuated by comings and goings, departures and returns, separations and reunions. The single, inescapable fact for the navy family is that navy men go to sea. It is therefore axiomatic that a career navy man's family must function within the context of separations, actual or potential, for 20 or more years. To function within these constraints is trying at best and, at some times, traumatic. Indeed, separations are probably the most stressful periods for navy families. A knowledge of the range of family problems encountered, as well as of the types of problem-solving resources needed and the nature of the families' adjustment during separations can contribute toward initiating and coordinating preventive and corrective services. The focus for the study reported in this chapter was on the recurring separations which are an expected part of a navy career. How do wives in these families cope? What problems do they encounter? What caretaking resources (inner strengths and/or outside assistance) do they utilize? This study was an exploration of these questions using a cross-section of navy wives in the Tidewater Virginia area whose husbands were deployed during the spring of 1976.

PAST RESEARCH ON FAMILY SEPARATION

Most of the research concerned with the adaptation of military families to separation in general, and the coping patterns of wives in particular, dealt with families undergoing extended or unusual separations (one-year or longer wartime separations, POW/MIA families, and so on). Few studies can be found which are concerned with the regular and frequent family separations necessitated by the husband's choice of a naval career. Thus, this study was an attempt to look at the problems and coping responses identified in these previous studies to determine their applicability to this sample of navy wives.

Prior studies, beginning with Hill (1949), have characterized
the military family as a family under stress, and the special stresses
inherent upon military service members and their families have been
enumerated. However, as Darnauer (1976) pointed out, these potential impacts of the military system on the family can be considered
in differing ways—as "assets and liabilities, advantages and disad-
vantages, or 'stresses' and 'opportunities'. . . ." In general, past
studies have indicated that the difference between whether families
consider their situations as stresses or opportunities depends upon
the family members' perceptions of them and situational circumstances at one particular point in time. What may be perceived as
an opportunity at one period, may be a stress or a crisis at another.
Coping has been previously defined as the pattern of responses made
to stresses or crises by the family members. These responses can
be either adaptive or maladaptive for the family depending upon the
situation (Fagen et al. 1968), and that definition of coping was used
for this study.

One of the major accomplishments of recent research with
military families undergoing separation, especially the work with
prisoner-of-war families and families of servicemen missing in
action by McCubbin, Hunter, and Dahl (1975), has been the identification of specific problems which beset wives during separation. Pearlman (1970), Isay (1968), Bey and Lange (1974), Hall and Simmons
(1973), and Montalvo (1976) also identified a wide range of emotional
difficulties which may beset wives during family disruptions—from
feelings of loneliness, loss of companionship, and social isolation to
symptoms of depression. These, plus other studies which included
the children experiencing father separation noted similar difficulties
in children, in addition to difficulties in the area of mother-child
interactions (Dahl, McCubbin, and Lester 1976).

Resource knowledge and usage have been the subjects of several
previous studies, specifically those of Montalvo (1976), Lindquist
(1952) and Spellman (1976). All noted that knowledge of resources
outside the military was very limited, and even knowledge of resources
within the military system was frequently limited. A decided preference for usage of military resources, however, was found, and
Montalvo made a very strong case for the existence of a separate
and distinct military subculture to which military families ascribe
and from which they take their "identity, values, attitudes, behavior,
style of living, and preferred sources of support in maintaining the
family as a functioning unit" (1976: 149-51).

A STUDY OF NAVY WIVES DURING
FAMILY SEPARATION

The 108 women surveyed for this study were navy wives who were presently coping with the problems of family separation. They were not necessarily representative of all navy wives as these women were all members of wives' clubs. Their husbands were attached to five selected ships which were currently deployed. In a search for patterns or trends, the study was designed to elicit information about problems and resource usage during family separation. A self-administered, self-report questionnaire, the "Coping with Sea Duty Questionnaire," was designed for this study. Based upon prior research, 19 items which had been identified as possible problem areas were included under the three general categories of child-care problems and concerns, problems of home management, and problems of personal-need satisfaction. The questions were designed to determine which items were perceived by the respondents as current problems, the severity of these problems, whether or not they had occurred or increased in severity in relation to the husband's deployment, and what resources, if any, the respondents had utilized in coping with each situation. Also included in the questionnaire were measures of general resource knowledge and of the emotional symptoms wives undergoing separation could be expected to experience. In other words, the questionnaire provided information on the wives' subjective perceptions of the families' ongoing life experiences.

The survey was conducted during the period believed to require the greatest amount of adjustment for the wives, the third to fourth month after the husbands' deployment. Specific objectives of this exploratory survey were: (a) to determine the extent to which certain types of problems in the areas of child care, home management, and personal-need satisfaction occur and their perceived severity; (b) to determine the nature of the caretaking resources used; (c) to determine the pattern of caretaking use; (d) to determine the relationship, if any, between the nature and distribution of caretaking resources used and the nature of the problems encountered; (e) to lay the groundwork for subsequent research; and (f) to provide suggestions for interventive approaches to the problem of family separations.

The study was an attempt to observe whether the problems and patterns of resource usage found in earlier studies of military families are similar and therefore applicable to problems and resource usage patterns of navy wives in the Tidewater area. A second goal was to present concrete evidence of discrete patterns of resource usage and, thus, suggest possible models for resource development and dissemination of information about resources which could be used by formal military and civilian caretaking resource planners.

FINDINGS

Sample Profile

A profile drawn of the respondents from this sample of 108 cases[*] showed that the typical respondent was 28 years old and had been a navy wife for five years. Her husband was 35 (median 29) years old with eight and one-half years[†] of service, and he had attained the rank of either petty officer (E-5), if enlisted, or junior officer (0-3, Lieutenant) if of officer rank. Approximately one year before the current deployment, he had experienced one prior extended deployment. At the time of the survey, he had been deployed for three months. The couple had two children (2.25) living at home. The wife was most likely to list her occupation as housewife and was not employed outside the home. She had been born and raised within the United States in a civilian family and had completed one year of college or trade school. The family usually lived off base. The wife indicated that she, in fact, preferred living off base, and she listed her friends as being approximately half from the civilian and half from the military community. During the present deployment, the respondent and her children were living alone, with no close relatives living nearby.

Problems Encountered

To determine if there had been an increase in the number of problems[‡] or their severity during deployment, 19 items describing possible problems were covered within the three general categories of child-care problems and concerns, home-management problems,

----

[*]The figures used are the means.

[†]Eight and one-half years of service time was the mean for all 108 men, regardless of rank.

[‡]Although there is considerable exception taken to the word "problem" within the social-work profession, that word was used most frequently by navy ombudsmen, navy wives, and chaplains to describe situations which created tensions and either taxed or were beyond the scope of the wife's inner resources. Therefore, the word "problem" is used in this study to describe like situations.

and problems of personal-need satisfaction. Figure 9.1 is a rank
ordering of these items based on the frequency of responses to these
items. This figure indicates the percentage of persons who perceived
each item to be a problem of some degree. The degrees of severity
of the problems were categorized on a 4-point scale as very minor,
relatively minor, relatively serious, and very serious.

Three research questions were set forth regarding the problems
encountered: Which problems will the sample group encounter with
the greatest degree of frequency? Can the frequency of problems
encountered be attributed to the husband's deployment? Is there a
significant and quantifiable relationship between the perceived severity of a problem and the husband's deployment status?

The study confirmed the assumption that the stresses of separation are reflected in an increase of problems and/or an increase in
their perceived severity during deployment.* If a problem were
perceived to be minor, it was also usually perceived as having remained the same after the husband deployed. However, the more
serious the problem was perceived to be, the more likely it was also
to be perceived as having increased in severity subsequent to the
deployment of the husband.

The problems explored in this study are similar to those noted
in previous studies (McCubbin, Dahl, and Hunter 1976; Montalvo
1976; Duvall 1945). Lack of companionship and loneliness were the
two most frequent problems. The findings that nighttime was the
loneliest, followed by Sunday and Saturday, confirms expectations,
in that these are the times usually reserved for family- or couple-
oriented activities during the periods when the husband/father is at
home. A general feeling of social isolation has been reported in
previous studies; and 49 percent of this sample group perceived it
as a problem for them. Most wives, however, perceived it as a
relatively minor problem.

Wives were generally hesitant to discuss feeling of sexual frus-
tration or tension attributed to the husband's absence. When asked
about these feelings on the anonymous questionnaire, 81 percent
indicated that for them this was indeed a problem, and the perceived
degree of seriousness was relatively evenly spread across all four
response categories from very minor to very serious.

Most of the previous studies of the emotional problems and
symptoms present in military wives during separation have used
samples of wives who were identified psychiatric patients and then

---

*The zero-order correlation between perception of seriousness
of the problem and the likelihood of its increase due to deployment
was significant at the .001 level for most problem variables.

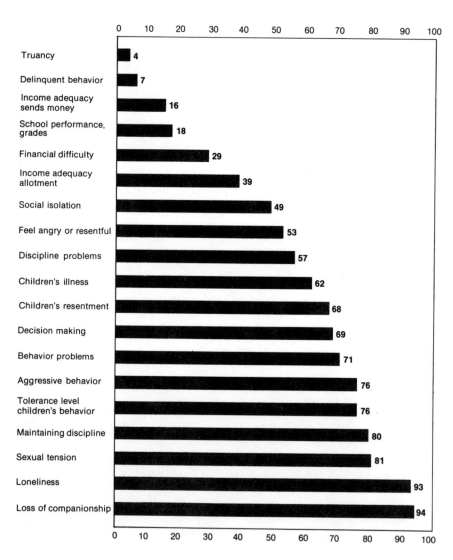

FIGURE 9.1

Problem Variables Ranked by Frequency
of Response
(in percent)

Note: Percentage of respondents indicating specific area was a problem of some degree for them. Percentages based on total sample (N=108) of whom 21% (N=23) did not have children.

Source: Compiled by the author.

proceeded to study their emotional behavior. The present study focused on symptoms and behavioral responses to separation of "normal" wives—wives not identified as having psychiatric problems. Therefore, a measure of the wives' perceptions of increases or decreases in symptomatology during the husband's deployment was included in this study.

The findings indicated that many of the wives present the symptomatology of minor depressions. This finding is not unexpected when one views the separation of one member of the family by deployment as a type of bereavement. The absent member is "lost" to the family for a given period of time. His services can only be supportive and from a distance. Communication, though possible, is often spread out over significant periods of time. He is therefore effectively removed from much meaningful participation in the many decisions that must be made in the day-to-day experience of family living.

Because of the demands of their careers, many navy men miss important milestones in the life of the family, such as births of children, birthdays, anniversaries, Christmas celebrations, and other holidays. During informal conversations, wives indicated that these are special occasions the most difficult times to be alone. One question was included which asked if the wife felt anger or resentment because of the husband's absence and toward whom or what these feelings were targeted. Over half of the respondents indicated that they felt such anger or resentment, and for 39 percent of the wives, these feelings were targeted toward the navy. There was a significant negative correlation between paygrade and the target of resentment. The wives of men in the lower paygrades were more likely to perceive the navy as the recipient of their anger ($r = -.16$, $p < .05$). Perhaps this is an area which calls for additional study. Certainly, the manner in which a wife handles her feelings of anger or resentment, directed either outward or inward, may have a significant bearing on her ability to cope with other problems and stresses of separation.

Studies by McCubbin and colleagues (1976a), Hall and Simmons (1973), and others have also observed the presence of depressive symptoms in children and other reactions to loss of the father due to separation. Further, it has been suggested that the adjustment of the mother may well be the most significant factor in the adjustment of the children. In the present study the most frequently mentioned problems and concerns in regard to the children were related both to the child's behavior and the mother's interaction with her child. The mother's perception of her lowered tolerance level for children's behavior or misbehavior was mentioned most frequently and was perhaps a reflection of the mother's own tensions. In terms of the mother's perception of the children's behavior, the children's resentment of the father's absence, aggressive behavior toward siblings and peers, and behavioral expressions of sadness, depression, and excessive crying were the most frequent problems. Poor school performance, delinquent behavior, and truancy were the least frequently mentioned problems. Serious financial problems may occur with considerable frequency among navy families, especially during deployment. Most of the problems stem from the inexperience of the wife in handling budgetary affairs, a family pattern of poor money management, or the navy man's failure to make appropriate arrangements to insure that sufficient funds would be received by his family to maintain household expenses in his absence. Financial problems of some degree were reported by 29 percent of this sample group.

Family role assignments with respect to money management and decision making both when the husband was at home and when he was at sea were also a focus of this investigation. Responses indicated that, for most families, these roles were performed jointly by husband and wife when he was at home and by the wife alone when he was deployed. These patterns tend to suggest that in these particular areas, navy families tend toward egalitarianism. In fact, it is quite possible that navy families may have, for very pragmatic reasons, tended toward more egalitarian divisions of roles within the home and the marital relationship some years before the concept of egalitarian marital roles came into focus for the general public.

Assessment of Coping

For each of the three major problem areas, child-care concerns, home-management problems and problems of personal-need satisfaction, respondents were requested to rate their own ability to cope.* These assessments were then correlated with wife's age, number of years as a navy wife, husband's paygrade, residence location (on or off base), the length of time husband had been gone on present deployment, and number of previous deployments. The length of

----

*As used here, coping was subjectively defined for the respondents as the way in which they dealt with problem situations, including the pattern or responses made to stresses or crises by family members. With the exceptions of these personal assessments, coping was measured in this study only in terms of problems encountered and resources used, and does not take into account emotional states or other factors.

time the husband had been gone on the present deployment and his previous number of deployments did not correlate significantly with any of these assessments. The wives' perceptions of their ability to cope with children's problems was positively related to higher paygrade ($p < .02$), increased age ($p < .06$), and residence in the civilian community ($p < .02$). Perception of ability to cope with home-management problems correlated positively with paygrade ($p < .04$). Perception of ability to cope with problems of personal-need satisfaction correlated positively with age ($p < .05$), number of years as a navy wife ($p < .02$), and paygrade ($p < .002$).

Previous studies have posed the question of whether or not prior experience with separation leads to more successful coping with future separations. MacIntosh (1968) suggested that there may be a relationship between both past experience and educational level and successful adjustment to separation. Fagen et al. (1968) and Dickerson (1964) observed that mothers with the greatest amount of experience with separation were less successful at coping with present separations than the less-experienced mothers. Therefore, one of the questions posed in this study was whether respondents thought coping with these kinds of problems became easier, more difficult, or remained the same with succeeding deployments. Results indicated that the wives believed that the ability to cope with separation becomes more difficult with subsequent deployments ($p < .001$). Results also indicated that the longer the time period between deployments, the more likely the wife was to perceive greater difficulties in coping with succeeding deployments ($p < .056$). There appeared to be no relationship between perceived difficulty in coping and the respondent's educational level or children's ages.

KNOWLEDGE AND UTILIZATION OF RESOURCES

For purposes of this study, caretaking resources were denoted either as informal or formal. Informal caretaking resources included the respondent's own inner resources, family members, friends, neighbors, and social clubs that provided assistance during times of need. Formal caretaking resources included military and community social-service agencies which have organizational structure, authority, and a professional or semiprofessional staff trained to assist individuals in problem-solving activity. These agents are usually financially remunerated from some source (public or private), and the caretaker and the recipient in need of service take on the formal roles of helper and client (Montalvo 1976).

Resource Knowledge

Knowledge of resources was assessed by asking each respondent to indicate her general knowledge of military and community resources. Both awareness and utilization were assessed. These results are reported in Table 9.1.

Note that identification of resources by name was far greater than actual use of or referral to those resources. Also military and quasi-military resources were much better known than resources in the civilian community. Although 63 percent of the sample knew of a ship or squadron ombudsman, only 6 percent had used, been referred to, or otherwise demonstrated knowledge of her functions. In the Tidewater area, the ombudsman functions as a central information and referral source for family problems and concerns; thus, it would appear that that objective of the local program is not being achieved. There was a low percentage of responses to knowledge of mental health services; however, most dependents in the Tidewater area who require psychiatric services are referred to private physicians and clinics under CHAMPUS funding. The Legal Aid Society was the best known of the community resources, which suggests that navy families may have frequent need of legal services.

One must conclude that navy wives' knowledge of formal resources is somewhat limited, in that the average number of resources known to these wives was only eight out of a list of 25 (32 percent), and the mean number of resources used or to which the wife had been referred was less than one. However, for those who had actually used resources, the mean was 2.7.

Resource Utilization

Tables 9.2 and 9.3 present breakdowns of the percentages of resources utilized for each of 18 problem statements of the 19 items included in the study.* Table 9.2 presents types of problems encountered by the respondents and the percentages of informal and formal resources used to cope with these problems. These problems are again presented in Table 9.3 to show the percentages of times that specific resources were used to handle the problems.

It is readily apparent that informal resources are utilized most, as they comprise 93 percent of the total resources reported. The

---

*One item, social isolation, was not included because the response categories for that particular item were not congruent with the remaining 18 problem areas.

TABLE 9.1

Knowledge and Use of Formal Resources*
(in percent)

Don't Know	Know of	Used or Re-ferred	Name of Resource
			I. Military Resources
13	75	12	Chaplains' Office
31	63	6	Ship or squadron ombudsman
44	44	12	Legal Assistance Office, NOB
64	33	3	Alcohol Rehabilitation Center, NOB
67	31	2	Fleet religious support activity
84	13	3	Counseling and Assistance Center
			II. Quasi-Military Resources
18	73	9	American Red Cross
16	67	17	Navy Relief Society
			III. Civilian Community Resources**
58	39	3	Legal Aid Society
61	37	2	Department of Social Services (all cities)
68	31	1	Tidewater Rape Information Service (TRIS)
67	29	4	Family Service/Traveler's Aid of Norfolk
70	27	3	Juvenile Court (all cities)
74	24	2	Catholic Family and Children's Service
77	21	2	Guidance counselors—public schools
80	18	2	Community Mental Health Center
82	16	2	Hampton Roads Information Service
84	16	0	INTERACT—Interagency Crisis Team of Virginia Beach
87	13	0	Child Guidance Clinic (Norfolk)
87	12	1	Jewish Family Service
89	11	0	Family Psychiatric Association of Virginia Beach
90	10	0	Child and Family Service of Portsmouth
94	6	0	Comprehensive Mental Health Services of Virginia Beach
95	5	0	Comprehensive Addictive Services Program of Norfolk
96	3	1	Other

*N = 108.

**The resources listed in Section III are not intended in any way to represent a listing of the total civilian community resources available in the Tidewater, Virginia area. Those included were selected on the basis of the investigator's familiarity with them and/or their similarity in name or program to similar agencies likely to be found in other communities.

Source: Compiled by the author.

TABLE 9.2

Utilization of Resources by Type of Problem*
(in percent)

| Problem | Resources Used | | Wives Reporting |
	Informal	Formal	Specific Problem**
Child-Care Problems and Concerns			
Children's behavior	87	13	74
Discipline problems	88	12	54
Maintaining discipline	91	8	70
Children's illness	85	15	61
Tolerance level	95	5	68
Aggressive behavior	100	0	58
School performance grades dropped	76	24	16
Truancy	37	63	7
Children's resentment	96	3	55
Delinquent behavior	40	60	9
Problems of Personal-Need Satisfaction			
Loneliness	97	3	96
Loss of companionship	95	5	100
Sexual tension	97	3	98
Anger or resentment	94	6	56
Home-Management Problems			
Financial difficulty	97	3	32
Income adequacy allotment	93	7	38
Income adequacy sends money	96	4	20
Decision making	97	3	92

*N = 108.

**Persons responding that they perceived the item as being a problem of some degree (from very minor to very serious) and for which they utilized resources in one or more of the categories listed.

Source: Compiled by the author.

TABLE 9.3

Resource Utilization by Problem
(in percent)

Item Description	Handled by Self	Talked to Friend, etc.	Talked to Ombuds-man	Talked to Chaplain	Sought Help Military Source	Sought Help Civilian Source	Total Sample
Children's behavior	54	34	1	4	4	4	74
Discipline problems	66	22	2	5	2	3	54
Maintaining discipline	69	24	1	3	1	3	70
Children's illness	68	17	3	2	9	2	61
Tolerance level	62	33	1	1	0	3	68
Aggressive behavior	86	14	0	0	0	0	58
School performance—grades	71	6	6	6	0	12	16
Truancy	37	0	13	13	13	25	7
Children's resentment	73	24	0	2	2	0	55
Delinquent behavior	30	10	10	30	0	20	9
Financial difficulties	79	18	0	0	3	0	32

(continued)

Table 9.3 (continued)

Item Description	Handled by Self	Talked to Friend, etc.	Talked to Ombuds-man	Talked to Chaplain	Sought Help Military Source	Sought Help Civilian Source	Total Sample
Income adequacy—allotment	83	10	0	0	7	0	38
Income adequacy—sends money	82	14	0	0	4	0	20
Decision making	60	37	0	0	0	3	92
Loneliness	34	63	1	2	0	0	96
Loss of companionship	25	70	1	4	0	0	100
Sexual tensions	70	27	–	2	0	1	98
Anger/resentment	29	64	2	3	0	2	56
Mean	58.0	34.8	1.2	2.5	1.7	1.9	

Informal Resources	Military Resources
93	Formal Resources
	7

Source: Compiled by the author.

category of "handled by self" was utilized twice as frequently as "talked to friend." Formal resources comprised only 7 percent of all resources used. Of the formal resources, "talked to chaplain or minister" was most frequently used (2.5 percent), followed by "sought help from a civilian source" (1.9 percent). It is interesting to note that "talked to ombudsman" was the least used of the formal resources (1.2 percent).

Most of the wives indicated that they had coped with problems during the cruise by handling the problems by themselves or by talking with a friend, neighbor, or family member. These informal resources were used 13 times, more frequently than any of the formal resources. The only two problem areas in which use of formal resources exceeded the use of informal resources were children's truancy and children's delinquent behavior; both are problem areas which would most likely come to the attention and active intervention of authorities, whether or not the family actively sought assistance. This finding tends to confirm Montalvo's statements about the importance of the informal caretaking resources as the first line of defense for families. It appears that only after the failure of these informal resources is assistance sought from formal resources.

Utilization of Formal Military and Civilian Resources

Again looking at Table 9.3, the results show that military resources were utilized by 5.4 percent versus 1.9 percent for civilian resources. Thus, it appears that military resources are preferred. Montalvo (1976) noted that because of the significance of the subculture, families in his study turned first to military resources. This finding was confirmed in the present study. Formal resources accounted for 7 percent of the resources used, of which 5.4 percent were military resources (ombudsman, chaplain, or other military source). Civilian resources accounted for only 1.9 percent of the resources used. Another possible reason for the preference for military resources may be that generally the same resources (ombudsman, chaplain, legal officer, and so on) are available at every base, and, therefore, no matter where the family lives, they know that these persons are available as resources. Since civilian resources may differ in quantity, quality, and name from city to city, civilian resources would have to be learned and located with each move the family makes. Further, it seems quite logical to assume that most families would not seek out knowledge about these resources until they had need of them. This lack of knowledge of formal resources and use of them could be improved by better use of media,

educational programs, and the location of these resources on base
where families are most likely to look for them.

It should perhaps be noted that these wives showed a strong
tendency to handle their problems by themselves or informally with
friends. Does this mean that these wives are very competent women
who need no outside assistance, or do they need it but do not know
that it is available or how to go about getting it? Only a study using
in-depth interviews could answer this question.

CONCLUDING COMMENTS

The study reported in this chapter was an exploratory survey of
problems encountered and resources used by navy wives during periods
of separation from their husbands. The 108 wives which comprised
the sample were drawn from wives' clubs and were wives of men
attached to five currently deployed surface ships. The major findings
were that there are a significant number of problems, of varying
degrees of severity, which occur with considerable frequency in
families experiencing routine separation. Problems of personal
needs or adult-need satisfaction, such as loneliness and loss of
companionship of the husband, were the most frequent problems
reported. Problems of child care were also frequent, especially
those relating to childrens' behavioral reactions to the father's loss
and to interactions with the mother. Financial problems, although
occurring within this sample population, did not occur as frequently
as other problems. The perceived severity of the problems was
found to be directly and significantly related to the husband's deployment. The conclusion is made that family separation severely taxes
the abilities and capacities of the wife and family members remaining
in the home to maintain a homeostatic balance within the family.
The physical and emotional tasks of family maintenance are continued
but frequently only at great emotional costs.

The families in the sample appeared to attempt first to cope with
these problems through utilization of their own inner resources and
the informal assistance of friends, neighbors, and other family members. When these informal methods of coping failed to satisfy fully
these needs, formal resources were then sought. The most frequently
used formal resources were those within the military system (chaplains, ombudsmen, and other military sources of assistance). Resources in the civilian community were rarely utilized. Possible
reasons for these utilization patterns are: (a) the nature of the family
system to prefer informal resources, (b) the identification with the
military subculture, (c) the lack of knowledge about the availability
of civilian resources, and (d) as noted in previous studies though not

addressed here, the perceived effects on the husband's career of using formal resources.

The findings with regard to resource knowledge and usage tend to reaffirm, in general, the conclusions of previous researchers, notably Montalvo (1976) and Spellman (1976), about the importance of informal resources and the preference shown by military families for resources perceived as coming from within the military community. These findings indicate the need for greater dissemination of information about existing resources available to military families within both the military and civilian communities. The preference for military resources reaffirms the necessity of locating needed services where families will be most likely to look for them—on base.

It was found that informal resources provide the first line of defense for families. These resources should be encouraged and should be viewed as available and viable. Another secondary but noteworthy finding was provided by an examination of the profile of navy wives' club members. From that study, it is estimated that only 20 percent of eligible wives belong to a wives' club. Noticeably absent from these rolls were the wives of very young seamen and minority wives.

It is commonly accepted that some navy wives, unlike those in the sample for the present study, have very serious problems and great difficulty coping with them. This situation can be attested to by the physicians at dependents' clinics, by chaplains, and by the staff at American Red Cross and Navy Relief Society who specialize in emergency relief to families. What separates the group of women with severe problems from those in the study? Since the study sample was drawn from persons attending navy wives' clubs meetings, perhaps club attendance may be one of the keys to successful coping, as it provides for social participation, a chance to get a "break" from home and children for a few hours of adult conversations, and an opportunity to make new friends and therefore increase one's informal resource network. It appears from this limited study that social participation and a strong network of informal resources (inner strength as well as friends and family) are important factors in differentiating coping ability. Much more remains to be learned, however, about what differentiates those wives who feel they are coping well from those who feel they are not.

10   Personal Transitions and Interpersonal Communication Among Submariners' Wives

Kathleen Reardon Boynton
W. Barnett Pearce

Since Homer portrayed the plight of poor Penelope, the stress produced by periodic, prolonged separations of military personnel and their families has been the object of attention and concern. The problems confronting modern navy wives are usually less tangible than a courtyard of boozing suitors, but just as real. Considerable evidence attests to the personal and interpersonal difficulties experienced by "waiting wives," and there is more than an idle suspicion that the prospects of repeated familial separations adversely affect retention of career personnel. "The progressive weakening of affective ties and commitment to group goals and values," or demoralization (Lang and Lang 1964: 66), is the likely consequent of prolonged separations between military persons and their spouses, particularly if they have not developed effective ways of dealing with them.

RECURRENT FATHER ABSENCE IN THE SUBMARINER FAMILY

Recurrent absences of the husband/father which are characteristic of the families of the officers and men of the submarine service produce at least three types of conditions, each of which is stressful. First, the stability of the family unit is threatened in a particularly virulent way. An abrupt change in the social structure of the family (for example, the husband's departure on patrol) creates a situation which requires some adjustment. The extent to which this adjustment to separation is successful, however, is inversely related to the ease with which the family can accommodate his return. Bey and Lange (1974: 225), Isay (1968: 650), and Bowlby (1960) report that the reintegration of the husband into the family can be disruptive of stable patterns of action in much the same way as the adjustment to his absence. The evidence clearly indicates that the perceptual transitions engendered by periodic departure and reentry of the husband is stressful.

In addition to instability, "waiting wives" must cope with aloneness. There is reason to believe that persons in our culture are not
well-equipped to handle aloneness (Winnecott 1958). There are many
social institutions designed to teach persons social skills and sociation itself provides immediate feedback on good and poor lines of
action, but there are few, if any, institutional guides for being alone,
much less for using aloneness productively (Slater 1970). A navy
wife unprepared for aloneness frequently experiences a debilitating
syndrome characterized by the belief that she is handling aloneness
badly, embarrassment because she thinks that she should be handling
it better, and the construction of a repertoire of intrapersonal ration-
alizations and interpersonal covering techniques which emerge to
conceal the bad response, the embarrassment, and the fact that
something is being concealed. The maintenance of such a complex
"presentation of self" requires considerable effort in addition to that
involved with coping with aloneness itself.

The problems of instability and aloneness are exacerbated by a
third problem, that of role ambiguity. To some extent, persons'
social behaviors are "scripted" (Schank and Abelson 1977), in that
there are recurring patterns of interaction which they identify as
part of themselves, which they know how to perform, and which
other persons recognize as legitimate for them (Jackson 1966; Biddle
and Thomas 1966). Two forms of role ambiguity can deprive a
"waiting wife" of the ego strength she needs to cope with perpetual
transition. The feminist movement has achieved a significant change
in the attitudes and life scripts which women will accept. The role
of "husband's helper" and "good navy wife" are increasingly unsatisfactory in an age when exposure to the movement is so pervasive that
its often unobtrusive effects cause role conflict. As a result, the
support services for navy wives which stress what Isay (1968: 648)
and Pearlman (1970: 73) called "navy ethos," seem irrelevant to the
personal needs and preferred roles of many women. Military wives
may, in fact, find the formal "pep talks" alienating and insulting.

A second form of role ambiguity comes from the lack of role
models for married, but alone, women in our society. A woman
knows how to act—and others know how to act toward her—if she is
single, or married and with her husband. There is a great deal of
reciprocated uncertainty, however, if she is married but alone for
significant periods of time. For her to construct and maintain a
definition of herself and develop a repertoire of persons who understand and are able to competently coenact a script which is acceptable
to her requires considerable communicative versatility. Unfortunately, this ability is frequently lacking in the woman, her acquaintances,
or both.

Women who have difficulty coping with these stresses are not
by that fact shown to be weak, or sick, and therefore contemptible.

Such an attitude, surprisingly prevalent, is the distant scion of Calvinistic theology which heavily influenced Western, particularly Anglo-Saxon, thought. A more insightful view of the problem is produced by the application of "systems thinking," one of the truly revolutionary ideas of the twentieth century. Individuals and the societies of which they are a part are inextricably mixed. In large measure, the problems manifested on an individual level have their genesis in the combination of social institutions which affect the person. These institutions may subject the person to a range of stresses and provide any amount of institutional help in coping with these stresses. As Goldschmidt (1974: 28) said, "society creates situations with which each individual must cope . . . by establishing barriers to the successful administration of the symbolic self." It is naive to expect each person to possess the resiliency, creativity, and self-knowledge to cope with any or all stresses adequately. Sometimes individuals must be helped to cope, and sometimes the coping must be done at an institutional or social level. "Increasingly, it is clear that major stresses on modern man are not amenable to individual solutions, but depend on highly organized cooperative efforts. . . ." (Mechanic 1974: 34).

"The Submariners' Wives Syndrome" (Isay 1968) is prima facie evidence that the present institutional facilitation of coping with the requirements of military family life is inadequate. This syndrome consists of four phases in which patrol schedules are paralleled by socio-emotional adjustments by wives. Several weeks before her husband is to leave, a wife is likely to dread his departure, blame the navy for her distress, and wish he were not going. As the departure nears, she may feel personally inadequate and that she will be unable to cope alone. In such cases depression and psychosomatic illnesses are common. The third stage, detachment, occurs as she adjusts to aloneness. Her husband's return at the end of the patrol creates the problem of intrusion, as she must reshuffle her life to accommodate his presence and adjust to his role as husband and father.

What are the procedures navy wives and others use to cope with the stress of transitions? Are certain of those procedures more efficacious than others? Without attempting a neurological or psychological explanation of the processes involved, it is assumed that the stress produced by transitions is real rather than imaginary; it must be lived with, rather than eliminated or avoided (Mechanic 1974: 33). Further, it is assumed that procedures used for coping with stress vary in effectiveness in some sort of regular pattern.

Transitions are endemic in modern society, as a function of three characteristics. First, change per se is positively valued. Innovations in products and life styles are to some extent adopted simply because they are new, and such changes frequently have non-obvious and far-reaching consequences (Rogers and Shoemaker 1971). Second, the structure of modern political and commercial institutions foster geographic, vocational, and social mobility which creates a society of persons who must maintain their identities and learn to interact with others with a minimum of social support (Lofland 1973; Toffler 1970). Third, transportation and communication technologies have decreased the ability of persons to ignore the fact of diversity and change (Cushman and Craig 1976). The ubiquity of transitions makes the ability to cope well with instability a survival characteristic. Those who are less able to adjust will accumulate a series of failures which preclude professional achievement and psychological health.

The wives of submarine personnel comprise a unique cadre of practiced copers. In addition to the normal stresses of society, they are confronted with the prospect of a continuing series of scheduled disruptions of their family unit. Because of their experiences, these women are an important source of information about the ways transitions can be coped with.

A STUDY OF SEPARATION IN THE
SUBMARINER FAMILY

This chapter reports on a study of family separation within the submariner community. What are the ways in which persons cope with disruptions of their normal definitions of situations and means of action? Many previous studies have examined populations experiencing both a change in their social structure and grief or anxiety when their husbands are declared prisoners of war, missing in action, or sent to combat areas (McCubbin et al. 1975; McCubbin, Hunter, and Dahl 1975; McCubbin, Dahl, Lester, Benson and Robertson 1976; Bey and Lange 1974). In contrast, the present study looked at women experiencing routine separations. Of interest to the investigators were those aspects of coping which are subject to the individual's discretionary control. Because of the design of previous studies, the best predictors of successful coping were variables about which a person has no control. It does little good for a somewhat disappointed young newlywed to know that age, length of marriage, and degree of pretrauma happiness are positively correlated with coping success. Further, these data provide little bases for understanding the operative mechanisms in successful coping. Perhaps of more importance are the types of coping strategies used by particular women and the degree to which these strategies are successful. Subjects for the study were "successful" copers, in that all were

experienced and were not selected from the rolls of those receiving
therapy (Pearlman 1970; Isay 1968).

Purpose of the Study

The study, then, was designed to answer two questions: (a) What
coping strategies are used by navy wives as they go through transitions caused by their husband's tours of sea duty? and (b) Which of
these coping strategies is most effective in the successful handling
of transition? Based on the theory of the "coordinated management
of meaning" (Pearce 1976; Boynton 1977; Pearce, Cronen, and Conklin 1977), transitions were defined as the disruption of a person's
repertoire of episodes. Episodes are patterned sequences of social
action which have subject-punctuated boundaries and an internal order
(Harre and Secord 1973). As Mead (1934) and Sullivan (1953) argued,
a person's concept of self is identified with those recurring patterns
of interpersonal relationships which he is able to achieve with others.
To have a "significant other" suddenly unavailable for sociation constitutes a stress-producing disruption, and Isay's description of
"The Submariners' Wives Syndrome" indicates that the anticipation
of such a separation or the return is itself stressful.

This analysis suggests an initial, a priori taxonomy of three
coping strategies. Internalization occurs when a person simply
accepts the disruption in his repertoire of episodes and attempts to
live with it, using intrapersonal coping strategies. Substitution
occurs when a person reproduces the original structure of his repertoire by recruiting and training new people to enact episodes which
have the same meaning as the ones affected by the transitions.
Replacement occurs when a person learns and adds to his repertoire
a set of episodes which have a different meaning than any which
existed before the transition. In terms of the social dimension of a
person's life-space, internalization constitutes a net loss; substitution results in a change in the specific episodes in the repertoire but
no change in its structure; and replacement involves the addition of
a structural element to the repertoire.

The Sample

Thirty wives of naval officers stationed at the New London Naval
Base in Groton, Connecticut, were the subjects in this study. The
subjects were selected from a roster of officers' families on the
basis of four criteria. First, all subjects had experienced at least
two deployments (periods of sea duty) by their husbands. Second,

all subjects' husbands were attached to fleet ballistic missile (FBM) submarines, which maintain a regular duty cycle. Each FBM submarine has two crews, one of which is on shore duty while the other is at sea for a period of three and one-half months. Third, subjects were systematically selected to stratify husbands' ranks. Since the social prestige among wives is largely based on husbands' ranks, we ultimately included the wives of eight commanders, six lieutenant commanders, eight lieutenants, and eight lieutenants (jg). Finally, subjects were selected such that 15 were in the husband-home and 15 in the husband-away phase of the cycle. These wives were in various phases of their husbands' duty cycles at time of data collection.

Collection of Data

Each of the 30 wives was given a self-administered questionnaire designed to measure coping strategies and personal adjustment. The questionnaire solicited information considered to be descriptive of a subject's repertoire of episodes. The questionnaire consisted of a list of activities characteristically engaged in with significant others. In addition, for both the "husband-home" and "husband-away" conditions, subjects listed and ranked, in order of importance, as many as five persons whom they would miss the most if those persons were not available. Subjects then described on color-coded cards (indicating whether they occurred when their husband was home or away) as many as three episodes ("characteristic activities") which they enacted with each significant other in each condition. (The maximum number of cards was 30, with no more than 15 of each color.)

Subjects then performed an unforced card sort in which they piled and labeled those cards which (regardless of color) described episodes which had similar meanings for them. These piles were then combined, again on the basis of the subjects' perception of their similarity, until no more than four stacks were obtained.

The card sort provided information about the subject's repertoire of episodes and coping strategies. By stacking cards and merging stacks, the dimensional structure of their interpersonal life-space was obtained through a procedure viewed as similar in purpose but alternative in method to Forgas' (1976). An inspection of the colors in each stack provided a measurement of the three coping strategies described above. Internalization was defined as occurring if a stack had only "husband-home" (green) cards. This pattern indicated that a distinguishable part of the subject's concept of self was simply terminated by her husband's departure. The disruption in the repertoire of episodes was handled internally. The strategy of substitution was defined as producing a stack of mixed colors. Using this strategy, a woman would participate in similar episodes (although perhaps with different people) regardless of her husband's presence. Replacement was defined as producing a stack with only "husband-away" (blue) cards. A woman using this strategy would develop as part of her interpersonal repertoire episodes which were enacted only when her husband was at sea.

Subjects were also asked to describe their marital happiness, perception of self as a "good navy wife," happiness as a navy wife, and happiness with their husbands. Each of these variables was measured on a 1-item scale on which judgmental anchors were established by having subjects first place "the happiest person you know" and "the most unhappy person you know" on the continuum between "perfectly happy" and "awfully unhappy." Each item was scored by counting the number of spaces between the one identified as representing themselves and the one identified as representing the most unhappy person they knew. Since the scale had seven spaces, potential scores ranged from 1 (if they described themselves as six spaces more unhappy than the unhappiest person they knew) to 13 (six spaces more happy than the unhappiest person they knew). Obtained scores for perception of own marital happiness ranged from 6 (as unhappy as any known) to 12 (very much happier than the unhappiest known) with a mean of 10.44. Obtained scores for perception of self as a good navy wife ranged from 8 to 13, with a mean of 10.00. The subjects described their happiness as a navy wife as ranging from 7 to 13, with a mean of 9.86, and their happiness with their husbands from 1 to 13, with a mean of 10.03.

Finally, subjects were asked if their responses "adequately described the way you deal with the adjustments to your husband being away on patrol and to his return home." Twenty-seven of the 30 subjects wrote in the approximately 9" by 9" space provided. A content analysis of these responses was performed by a panel of three judges. The judges were adults, unconnected with the study, who were trained for approximately three hours to use a 9-category system. The authors divided the written material into 149 units, each of which represented a single, complete thought. Each of these was independently categorized by two of the raters. In 120 instances (81 percent), the independent judgments agreed. Where there was disagreement, the judges conferred. This produced agreement in 24 of the remaining cases. Where the two judges could not quickly reach agreement (N = 5) the third judge made an independent decision which produced a majority view. The category system is described in Table 10.1.

TABLE 10.1

Frequency of Occurrence in Content Categories

Category of Statement	Frequency of Occurrence (N = 149)	Number of Subjects (N = 27)
Positive Adjustment		
Independence – Statements which express positive emotion associated with separation	12	8
Dependency – Statements which express reliance on another person or other persons	12	10
Inhibition – Statements which express the cessation or avoidance of some behavior(s)	11	8
Diversion – Statements which express involvement in absorbing or substitutive activities	18	11
Negative adjustment – Statements which express negative emotion associated with separation	19	11
Distribution of Blame – Statements which imply that self, someone, or something is to blame for negative emotions	4	4
Denial of Adjustment – Statements which express a denial of any change in self or life style	9	7
Assertiveness – Statements which express mental preparation of stance for attack of the problem	15	7
Unrelated – Statements which express thoughts unrelated to the other categories	49	19

Source: Compiled by the author.

Findings

One objective of this study was to determine how a group of
"practiced copers" handled a regularly scheduled transition. This
question was answered by analysis of the subjects' card sorts and
by content analysis of their responses to the open-ended item on the
questionnaire.

Using the definitions of internalization, substitution, and replacement given earlier, each subject had one coping strategy for each
stack of cards. A total of 116 instances of coping were obtained (two
subjects' original card sorts used only three stacks; one subject's
original sort used only two). Substitution was used far more than
the other coping strategies ($N = 86$), with internalization ($N = 20$)
being used twice as often as replacement ($N = 10$). However, this
scheme proved unsatisfactory because it ignored the relative number
of blue and green cards in each stack, and it produced multiple scores
for each individual. These deficiencies were handled by deriving one
score, S, based on the summation model:

$$S = p_1 w_1 + p_2 w_2 + p_3 w_3 + p_4 w_4$$

where p_1 is the proportion of husband-home (green) cards to the total
number of cards in the ith stack, and w_1 is a weighting of the importance of the ith stack compared to the others. The weighting was
empirically derived, post hoc for each subject, as the product of the
proportion of the total number of cards used by the subject which
were in the ith stack and of the adjusted mean rank of the persons in
the significant-other list of the questionnaire who were identified as
episodic enactants in the ith stack. The adjustment to the mean rank
consisted of subtracting the score from 6 so that persons who were
ranked as most important (for example, as 1) would contribute a
greater weighting than those ranked as least important (for example,
as 5).

The value of S represents a description of the subject's coping
strategies across the repertoire of episodes, with each differentiated
area weighted by the relative importance of each stack of cards.
The strategy of internalization (in which the proportion of husband-
home cards in a stack was high) produced high values, substitution
produced moderate values, and replacement produced low values.
The obtained range of S scores was relatively small (1.06 to 2.62)
due to the preponderance of substitution as the coping strategy most
frequently used by these subjects.

The results of the content analysis of subjects' descriptions of
their coping strategies indicated that replacement was underrepresented in the card-sort procedure. Of the 27 subjects who responded

to this item, 13 described private, nonsocial activities performed only or primarily when their husband was at sea which included reading, sewing, crafts, and work. Because only those episodes associated with persons were sampled, those private coping strategies did not appear on the cards.

Seven subjects made statements, categorized as "assertive," which offered advice about how recurrent transitions can be best handled. Several wives emphasized the necessity for mental preparation: "If you don't plan for the inevitable, it's going to come up very suddenly and catch you unprepared," and "You have to accept the fact that patrol is coming—it's going to tear up a well-ordered family life." Another subject described the adjustment to her husband's return: "You must also learn to relinquish some of the absolute and total independence you sustained while alone."

To determine if there were systematic relationships between various coping strategies and the success with which the person negotiated the transition, the S values were correlated with marital happiness, perception of self as a "good navy wife," happiness as a navy wife, and happiness with husband, but none of these correlations were statistically significant.

A hypothesis grounded in these data suggests a curvilinear relationship between S values and various indexes of satisfaction. It may be assumed that these subjects were not only practiced, but were also successful copers. All had experienced at least two cycles of sea duty and were still married, able to function, and had not insisted their husbands leave the navy. Further, only 11 expressed negative reactions to the separation transition. Results indicated these wives used substitution predominantly (although this finding may have been exaggerated by the procedure used). Substitution produces midrange values of S; replacement and internalization extreme scores. From this, we infer the hypothesis of a curvilinear relationship between S and indices of successful coping, such that the highest values of success are obtained with midrange scores of S. Unfortunately, an inspection of scatterplots indicated that the obtained values of S in this study were too restricted to make a post hoc test of this hypothesis.

DISCUSSION AND CONCLUSIONS

Earlier in this chapter three stressful conditions were described as emerging due to the prolonged separations experienced by submariners' wives: instability, aloneness, and role ambiguity. The theory and research presented in this chapter focused on the first, instability, which was defined as a consequent of recurrent transitions.

The methodological protocol developed for the study, in general, worked well. The card-sort technique proved to be a useful, relatively unobtrusive way of eliciting subjects' perceptions of their interpersonal communication networks and the episodes of which they are constructed. Future research may benefit from a structured, unforced Q-sort approach to test the theoretical implications derived from this study and those of earlier studies (McCubbin et al. 1975; McCubbin, Hunter, and Dahl 1975; McCubbin, Dahl, Lester, Benson and Robertson 1976; Bey and Lange 1974; Pearlman 1970; Isay 1968) which focused on the effects of extended separations.

The content analysis of subjects' descriptions of their coping strategies indicated that replacement was underrepresented in the card-sort procedure. Such information would not have been obtained had the research relied solely on questionnaire-item responses, thus corroborating Mischel's (1977) defense of subjects as "the best experts on themselves" and "eminently qualified to participate in descriptions and prediction—not to mention decision—about themselves" (1977: 249). Future studies might benefit from the use of self-reports and interviews as a means of eliciting information not usually obtained through the use of questionnaires. Thus, the pitfall of assuming that persons are unaware, when in fact they are "simply being asked the wrong questions" may be avoided (1977: 249).

The most significant limitation of this study was the synchronous nature of the data. Subsequent research will observe transitioning subjects longitudinally, noting stages or phases in their use of coping strategies and describing the interaction between communication ability, the use of support services, and the use of coping strategies. When coupled with measures of how they "construe" (Kelly 1955) their family, their personal roles, and the transitions, this procedure may be able to test and extend the curvilinear hypothesis suggested by these data of the effects of particular coping strategies.

The second stressful condition associated with separation is aloneness, a state usually culturally defined as negative. Winnecott (1958), described aloneness as a "capacity" which develops or does not develop as a result of early childhood experiences. Moustakas (1961) distinguished loneliness from alienation, the latter appearing to be more debilitating since it is characterized by powerlessness, meaninglessness, normlessness, isolation and/or self-estrangement (Seeman 1959), rather than the mere absence of others.

It is imperative that families of military personnel be made aware that such feelings are actually quite natural, especially since we are raised from childhood in a society which provides little, if any, preparatory training for the experience of being alone. However, there is evidence that aloneness need not be a negative trauma if a person perceives it as an opportunity, and is prepared to function well in it (Moustakas 1961). One can then perhaps deal with it as a chosen situation rather than one that is imposed.

The third stressful condition examined by this study was role ambiguity, derived from Cottrell's contention that adjustment to roles depends upon the clarity with which they are defined (1942: 618-25). Today's military wife is exposed to messages which contradict earlier traditional female roles. Many women are thus placed in a role-conflict position without the benefit of societal rules as guides, since those which do exist apply to persons who live traditional married lives rather than the "married but single" role of the military wife. The consequences of poor role definition were described by Jackson as stressful conditions which necessitate a systematic method of specifying the structure of a norm system. From this perspective, the accuracy with which one perceives his or her role(s) depends ultimately upon the "degree to which a situation and a social system provide opportunities for learning about the roles" (1966: 45).

Such opportunities do not at present exist for military families. Recreational and social organizations are a partial answer for some, but until the military provides programs which inform rather than distract attention from the stresses of being alone, the problems will continue to exist. Instability, aloneness, and role ambiguity are three symptoms of a problem which is, if not curable, at least controllable.

11 Midlife Crisis Among Submariners' Wives

Alice Ivey Snyder

Recent anthropological field research among the submarine community of the United States Navy on Oahu, Hawaii, has focused on the effects of separations upon submariners' wives. In the course of evaluating coping behavior, it was discovered that wives of senior, career-oriented submariners universally experienced a midlife crisis, which most frequently occurred between the ages of 30 and 37, earlier than the age the limited literature indicates for the civilian sector. In addition, it resolved prior to the husband's facing retirement and career change, the point at which he is undergoing a midlife transition. Although midlife crises in the submariner population share many similarities to those described in the literature for other samples, there are distinct characteristics as well. This chapter describes the typical passage through midlife crisis for submariners' wives.

Sometime during the middle years of life, after adolescence and before senescence, one makes the transition from regarding her/ himself as young to seeing her/himself as mature or middle-aged. According to Jung, in this shift in life stage from young maturity to middle age we see "a significant change in the human psyche is in preparation" (1933: 104). Erikson noted that all life stage shifts are defined by marked change; he termed a life-stage shift a "crisis" which he uses "in a developmental sense to connote not a threat of catastrophe, but a turning point" (1968: 96). Applying Erikson's definition, a midlife crisis requires some measure of upheaval in one's life with the end result being either positive or negative change.

The content of this midlife crisis, or transition, is generally recognized. Introspection and stocktaking (Neugarten 1970) and deillusionment, which is the weeding out of invalid or no longer applicable illusions (Levinson 1977), are involved, as well as a growing realization of a time squeeze (Gould 1972) between generations or a sense of having been trapped. One may experience a change in time perspective from chronological to situational time. There is

a general discomfort and dissatisfaction, and the source of this dissatisfaction is often unknown. During this period, one may be forced
to face her/his own mortality (frequently triggered by the death of a
parent or terminal illness of a friend). One is in turmoil, has a
sense of aimlessness or purposelessness, and seeks, more than just
survival, to be less fragmented. Thus, one also seeks integration
of self through reformulation. The midlife crisis provides the opportunity to establish personhood through "I-encounter."

How the crisis is acted upon depends on one's life style, the
alternatives available to the individual when the crisis occurs, and
how severe it may be. A midlife transition and many of its causes
are unique to the individual undergoing it.

There is disagreement on how marked the transition is and just
when it occurs. Gould (1972) argued for a universal, all stops out,
period of instability; Levinson (1977) pointed out that a period of
transition may be mild or severe, but one who defers the transition
pays a price. Neugarten (1970) believed that a crisis is not evitable
but may be precipitated by a significant event occurring off-time in
the scheme of one's life. The range in age for the crisis is usually
said to be from 35 to 45.

Most of the work which has been done on the midlife crisis has
been for white, middle-class, urban, and predominantly U.S. male
populations (Wachowiak 1977). Levinson did a study (1977) based on
40 males from New Haven, ranging from 35 to 45 in age. Gould
(1972) discussed midlife crises from two studies, the first of which
was a sample of Los Angeles-based psychiatric outpatients between
the ages of 16 and 60 (sample size, sex, and social class distribution
were not noted), and the second, a sample of 524 acquaintances of
eight medical students and "several" hospital volunteers, again in
the Los Angeles area. This second group was white, middle-class,
with about half being women disproportionately represented in the
45+ age group, and, therefore, beyond the midlife transition period.
Neugarten (1970) presented data on over 2,000 men and women between the ages of 40 and 90, all of whom were white, from middle-
and lower-middle classes, and from metropolitan areas in the
Midwest. Neugarten's work dealt with a population almost totally
beyond the midlife crisis.

The transition to middle age specific to women is even less substantially represented in the literature. Although Lowenthal et al.
(1975) described life transitions for both men and women, the segment
closest to female midlife transitioning was their middle-aged sample
of 27 women with a mean age of 48. Other investigators have de-
emphasized the significance of the empty-nest syndrome in causing
crises for women, since the climacterium and the emptying of one's
nest occur past the midlife crisis range. Sheehy (1976) extracted

data from the twentieth reunion booklet of the Radcliffe class of 1954 and found that 89 (of 127 on whom she had sufficient information) became wives and mothers soon after graduation. Two-thirds of the 89 had gone back to school or to work by the age of 40, thereby implying a midlife crisis, or, in Sheehy's terminology, a "passage," which had been acted upon.

The conclusion which can be drawn from a review of the literature is that there is much left to be done in the study of midlife crises. The absence of midlife material is partially attributable to the fact that the nature of middle age changes from culture to culture and place to place; it certainly changes over time. As the length of one's life is continually extended, the middle years are extended, making middle age and transition to it difficult to define and explore.

THE STUDY

The present chapter reports on anthropological field research conducted during 1976-77 among the submarine-associated community located on Oahu, Hawaii. The average seagoing submariner is in his early to mid-twenties. If he is married, he and his wife are within two years of the same age. Submarine crew size can be from 75 to 140, depending on the particular type of submarine. (Fleet Ballistic Missile submarines operate primarily from an overseas base with the crews on an approximate three months home and three months gone cycle. When husbands are away, there is letter and telephone contact between spouses for the first month and then no communication whatsoever from husband to wife for the second and third month. Fast Attack submarines operate, in contrast, on an irregular schedule with five to seven month deployments every eighteen months to two and half years and frequent at-sea periods in between. Fast Attack subs put into various ports and there are opportunities for interchange of letters as well as telephone communication.) Ten percent of the crew are officers and 10 percent are chiefs.

An enlisted submariner can expect a 20 or 30 year service pattern, consisting of four to five years of sea duty alternating with two years ashore, with certain exceptions. He retires as a chief petty officer at the age of 37-40 on 20 years or at 47-50 on 30 years service. A career submarine officer typically spends up to 80 percent of his time in seagoing assignments. Only officers may be awarded command, and command of a submarine is achieved after 13 to 15 years of service by only 20 to 25 percent of those men who originally began officers' submarine training. Being the commanding officer is regarded as the culmination of one's naval career. Post command, the officer does not return to sea; if he retires "on 20," he is 41-44 years of age. The average career length for an officer is now 22 to 25 years and is affected by economic trends and the desire to attain the rank of captain. Both the enlisted man and the officer face transfer to new assignments every two to three years, either to a different submarine or to/from shore billets. A transfer can be within the same area or may require moving some distance to a different submarine base—12,000 mile transfers are not unheard of.

THE FINDINGS

During the study two periods of noncoping behavior on the part of the wife became evident. The first period was typified by the young wife who was new to the life style and did not possess the necessary skills to manage frequent and often lengthy separations from her spouse. The second period was about ten years later when the wife was in her early thirties and had coped for many years. The first period, it is believed, is attributable to inexperience in the life style, or incomplete socialization, and the second period is attributable to midlife crisis.

These women undergoing midlife crisis gave evidence of all the characteristics of such a critical period but with the variations reflective of each unique life history. The life style of the community also had its effect. Common threads observed were increased responsibilities because of the husband's career position, the end of active childbearing, increased leisure time, and ambivalence toward the husband's success. All crisis periods observed appeared to have been resolved, however, prior to the husband's retirement.

The women under study began to evidence some disruption in their coping styles at the onset of the crisis period, often when another separation was impending. A wife who had managed through ten or twelve years of family separations, many moves, bearing children while the husband was gone, Christmases and birthdays missed, anniversaries celebrated alone, and deaths of parents, would find herself depressed and feeling incapable of facing one more at-sea period.

These women were very knowledgeable of their coping skills and had indeed managed very well for years. They were also aware of the emotional cycles associated with the separations. They were married to successful career-oriented navy men who were reaching or had reached the pinnacles of their careers in submarines. Nonetheless, senior chiefs' wives, executive officers' wives, and commanding officers' wives variously expressed dissatisfaction, evidenced depression, acted out, or embarked on new careers or other ventures. They were no longer meeting the traditional stereotype which is associated with these womens' roles within the military context.

The traditional role assigned to such women has been that of "Super Mother" to younger wives, the source of information for problem resolution and, frequently, their husband's representative when he is at sea. The commanding officer's wife (the CO's wife), the executive officer's wife (the XO's wife), and the chief of the boat's wife (the COB's wife, usually the wife of the ranking noncommissioned officer) are thought to be significant sources of relevant information and, indeed, are utilized by the navy to relay information to crewmen's wives and are expected to deal with the various difficulties the wives experience when husbands are at sea.

EXAMPLES OF MIDLIFE CRISES IN WIVES

Unfortunately, these increased responsibilities for the wife when her husband is promoted to such a position are sometimes the straws that break the proverbial camel's back. To illustrate what can happen, an extreme case is cited below.

A thirty-four-year-old woman who had been married 13 years to a thirty-four-year-old submarine officer reported that her husband was considering leaving the navy after 14 years of service and just prior to his taking command of a submarine. He was experiencing some personality conflicts on the submarine of which he was executive officer, there were many at-sea periods, they had two small children, and the wife was worried and simply not managing. After 13 years she could no longer cope; he was not able to understand why.

Let us take a closer look. What happened was that the woman was able to handle her own stress concerning her husband and the separations and those of her family quite well. She also had energy left over to give to other military-associated activities, such as volunteer work with Navy Relief, and to chair various fund-raising activities. But, the wife simply could not manage her own problems and the problems of all the other wives who were supposed to contact her for assistance. She was the XO's wife and was known to be competent, sympathetic, and able to handle the traditional role expectations. Wives came to her in droves with all types of difficulties.

It was too much. She worried about her husband's personality conflicts; she exhausted herself trying to help others, and there was nothing left for herself.

In discussing the crisis she was facing, the woman recognized that the distress she was experiencing was not due to frequent separations or inadequate coping, but instead was due to the implications of the life style itself at her particular time in life. She felt her distress was directly related to the growing process. In effect, she saw that she was experiencing a <u>midlife crisis</u>. But she was frustrated by her attempt to grow and individuate without her husband consistently there. She needed the supportive relationship as she made the transition; the lack of face-to-face communication angered her.

The whole issue came to a head when the woman found that she was depressed—very depressed. She lost between 30 and 40 pounds, lost interest in the projects over which she had before exhibited a great deal of enthusiasm, experienced sleeping problems, and she recognized a radical change in herself. Fortunately, she acted upon this knowledge and sought the assistance of a psychiatrist.

She told her husband of her decision to seek mental help when he returned from sea. He responded that he wanted very much to help her, although it would involve giving up his entire career and his ambitions for command at sea, only a year away. However, he would be willing to do this for her sake. But he was at a loss as to how he could help her—his time and energies were consumed by his job.

The woman decided not to make such a demand, and with the assistance of the psychiatrist over a period of two years, was able to work through her crisis. She termed the working through "painfully difficult," but it resulted in a more stable outlook accompanied by a radical reorganization of priorities and profound self-redefinition. As the wife saw the crisis, it was precipitated by her becoming XO's wife, and, in her words, in that role, "I'm symbolic to other people; I'm supposed to be strong and field problems for other wives." But being XO's wife "capped it off" for her and led to a severe wrenching of the entire family. Other factors which contributed to the severity of the crisis included delayed grief work and a sense of not having met the expectations of demanding parents. The husband went on to take command of a submarine.

Within the submariner community, women in their thirties have usually completed their families and most utilize effective forms of contraception or their husbands have been sterilized. Additionally, there are no sanctions against placing young children into readily available military child-care or preschool programs. The result is that the senior submariner's wife has increased leisure time, much of which is spent while her husband is out to sea; there is time to reflect and reconsider one's role in life.

Let us examine other examples. The thirty-two-year-old wife of a chief petty officer had been married for 14 years and had three school-aged children. During one at-sea period she became quite depressed and cried almost continually for five weeks; no one really seemed to need her much. She began to improve as the date of her husband's return from sea drew closer and, after he had left for sea again, she had worked through her stocktaking to the point where she applied for, and obtained, a part-time inventorying job. She also made several careful furniture purchases. These were momentous decisions for a woman who before had consistently depended upon her husband's opinion and regarded herself only as wife and mother.

Another woman, thirty-four, with a brilliant college performance and intriguing job history prior to bearing children, rigorously outlined her choices for action and rated them in priority: law school was top on the list. She took time to investigate the implications of each item on the list and how it would coordinate with her husband's upcoming command tour. Where the impending transfer would take them was unknown at the time of the interview, but she knew which possibilities could be pursued in each area without detracting from her supportive role as CO's wife. When details of the transfer are known, she intends to act. A mild crisis confrontation; a mild crisis resolution.

The submariner's wife can harbor feelings of mild dissatisfaction, or more strongly, resentment because of the great amounts of time her husband spends at sea or, when in port, at work on the submarine. For the senior submariner's wife, this is also a form of status envy. The husband achieves success which the wife shares, but hers is reflected success, an ascribed status. The wife works for her husband's achievements by her support, either active or passive, but only reflects her husband's achieved status.

In illustration, the thirty-six-year-old wife of a commanding officer said, only half in jest, "Don't call me Sue Anne, just call me Mrs. CO." The terms of reference for wives of senior submariners, such as CO's wife, XO's wife, and COB's wife, underline the reflective status these women maintain. In all fairness, however, it must be noted that this reflective situation is certainly not unique to submariners' wives, but is the common pattern in the U.S. civilian sector as well.

If one combines this ascribed status with a sense of having given up one's own career or limiting it because of frequent transfers of the husband, or if the woman has unwillingly chosen to have no career beyond that of housewife, and mother, and navy wife, then the choice she has made can begin to chafe, especially if the husband's success means less time for the family.

One especially biting commentary was made by a thirty-five-year-old XO's wife:

As for me, his career and mine were incongruous from the start, so I never amounted to anything. After all,

how can you expect to land a decent job with two months
notice on orders and no control over your destination?
I might even resent my husband for having cheated his
family for all those years, except that I haven't the
heart. . . . I have had to sacrifice my life to his, and
. . . I resent the menial "wifesy" chores we're given
to do. I feel that I have great potential, but I am not
able to direct it toward any constant goal since our life
is always "up in the air."

The time and effort involved in continuing to do a good job as a
senior submariner is extensive. The woman sees her husband spend-
ing more time, and working more intensively, at his job and returning
home spent emotionally and physically. One thirty-four-year-old
commanding officer's wife said, "I think he's more married to that
big grey whale than to me!" Although this increase in work time
may result in feelings of jealousy in a woman, it can also cast doubt
upon herself as a woman and upon her adequacy in meeting her
spouse's needs. It is one more factor which must be dealt with in
redefinition of self and finding the "I" in "We" (Harris 1975).

If one compares the midlife transitioning of submariners' wives
to those described in the literature, we find that, first of all, the
crisis occurs earlier. Secondly, it is associated with increased
responsibilities which are tied to the husband's position, the end of
active childbearing, and more leisure time, and that ambivalence
towards the husband's success is also a contributing factor. The
crisis can be the extreme form Gould (1972) postulated but can also
be a much less severe reaction. Forms of both have been presented
as illustrations.

Levinson (1977) asserted that deferral of a crisis will result in
a more difficult passage when the crisis is finally faced. In this
particular sample, the only cases of lengthy deferral prior to facing
of the midlife crisis were women whose husbands were particularly
outstanding successes in the navy and were not 20-year career men,
but 30-year career officers. One mid-forties wife of a senior officer,
when questioned, got tears in her eyes and said, "I always regarded
myself as very strong, not emotional, but when my daughter, the
youngest child, went away to college, I just stopped living for a
while." Her midlife crisis, by the process of deferral, came
approximately ten years later than other submariners' wives, and
she associated it with the empty-nest syndrome, but it did not appear
particularly difficult for her to deal with.

Another wife of a 30-year career man apparently deferred the
crisis because of a large family, with the last child being born while
she was in her mid-thirties. When she felt able to leave the family,

and her husband had shore duty and could support her by assuming
increased responsibilities for the family, she returned to college
for advanced degree work. When interviewed she was seeking part-
time positions which would mesh with her other roles, but anticipated
difficulties. However, the deferral of her crisis did not appear to
intensify her reaction.

Although the supportive evidence is not extensive, for this group
of women, extended deferral did not imply a more difficult passage.
Deferral of the midlife crisis and its consequent working through
occurred in women whose husbands had always intended a 30-year
career in the navy. Therefore, the women could wait for their own
midlife crises to occur later in life.

A significant event occurring "off-time" (Neugarten 1970) contributed to the crisis reaction of one thirty-four-year-old wife,
married almost 16 years. Her husband, who had been in the navy
for 18 years, had not been advanced to chief petty officer. He had
taken the requisite exams for eight years straight, had letters of
recommendation, but never had placed highly enough to be selected.
It was a severe strain on the entire family. A second, unexpected
event, the violent death of a parent, served to intensify emotions,
and the woman worked and reworked her life repeatedly. Although
she did not act out, her sense of confusion was very evident. Finally,
the husband was promoted, she did her grief work, and resolution
was rapid.

The most distinctive feature of midlife transitioning among submariner's wives is that the woman faces <u>and</u> resolves her crisis
<u>prior</u> to her husband's retirement. At 20-year retirement he is
between 37 and 44 years of age and certainly capable of making an
entirely new career before retiring a second time. Even if the man
stays in the military for 30 years, he is still distinctly in his midlife
period when he leaves the service. McNeil states it succinctly:
"Retirement is a misnomer . . . it is rather a change of career at
middle age. . . ." (1976: 257). Midlife career change of military
retirement is often disruptive and surrounded by problems. The
husband's retirement, occurring at the approximate time usually
posited for his midlife crisis is, in all likelihood, the major reason
for disruption. Berkey (1972), Berkey and Stoebner (1968), Greenberg (1973), McNeil and Giffen (1965, 1967), and McNeil (1976),
among others, discuss the implications of military retirement on
men, their wives, and children.

Wives of most military men are very aware of the problems
and upheaval which may be associated with their husband's retirement. Submariners' wives seem to perceive that they must confront
their own midlife crisis before the retirement period and be stabilized
in order to minimize the difficulties connoted by retirement from the

military, career change, and frequent attendant loss in status for the male. There is no altruistic motive implied by the woman facing and resolving her midlife crisis prior to her husband's retirement. Perhaps it is even selfish. The family simply cannot support the upheaval of her crisis and his retirement at the same time. If the wife desires to act upon her stocktaking, she had better do it while the husband is stable; indeed, his stability may fan the fires of her dissatisfaction.

Conversations in groups of submariners' wives give ready evidence that the wife fully expects upheaval when her husband retires and that she must support him through what is a preordained and complex midlife crisis for him. While the retirement may be relatively smooth for any given family, the wife is prepared for far worse. The body of folklore associated with the life style includes myriad stories of how difficult it is for the man to make the transition to civilian life, although actual fact may not bear this out in specific situations.

A second, special case must be argued for the man who is the commanding officer of a submarine. Command at sea is the sought after goal of a career naval officer and is a one-time, peak experience with great status and heavy responsibilities which include total accountability for a highly sophisticated vessel and its crew.

The CO is the epitome of Levinson's BOOM, or Becoming One's Own Man, where his goals are "to become a senior member . . . , to speak more strongly with one's own voice, and to have a greater measure of authority. This is a fateful time in a man's life. Attaining seniority and approaching the top rung of his ladder are signs to him that he is becoming more fully a man (not just a person, but a male adult). However, his progress not only brings new rewards, it also carries the burden of greater responsibilities and pressures" (Levinson 1977: 105).

The submarining folklore is replete with stories of the emotional letdown following the command at-sea tour. One bitter joke refers to postcommand officers being sent to the Pentagon to be janitors. The wife of the submariner CO is cognizant of the implications of postcommand doldrums and of retirement from the navy, and she is pressured toward crisis resolution prior to this period.

In association with scheduling the woman's midlife transition to precede the husband's pending retirement or postcommand tour is a necessary space creating maneuver in roles. Greenburg (1973: 488-89) noted that the woman most subject to emotional problems at the time of her husband's retirement is the one who, among other things, places great stock in her role as a military wife. Thus, those women who seek additional education, start careers, begin new ventures and, concomitantly, begin dropping those activities within the military which they had supported before are beginning the separation of themselves from the military and resolving their midlife crises simultaneously.

As in the case of the wife of the commanding officer, the wife may pull away from many military activities in order not to be riding high when the husband is "gearing down." This maneuver would explain the crisis-resolution activities of the thirty-five-year-old CO's wife who had been extremely active in many military social affairs but suddenly had nothing to do with any of the wives' club's functions. It also explains the postcrisis thirty-seven-year-old wife of a submarine officer who had his command at sea and was preparing to retire. She had canceled all her navy-associated activities and had begun a full-time commitment as a professional painter.

False starts at resolution of the midlife crisis sometimes occur. One thirty-five-year-old woman had a baby when her other child was over ten years old. She subsequently purchased a small business and has found that resolution to be more satisfying. It is also preparation for her husband's retirement, for they plan to expand the business when he is free to join her.

These are examples of anticipatory socialization, "the process of learning the norms of a role before being in a social situation where it is appropriate to actually behave in the role" (Burr 1972: 408). In terms of traditional role expectations, these wives are behaving inappropriately, but they are nonetheless transitioning into new roles they expect to maintain after their husbands retire.

It is obvious that crises are dealt with and managed well in this population, probably in part because of the requisite coping skills needed to deal with the stresses of the life style. Few women were encountered who had severe problems in meeting the midlife crisis and passing through it successfully.

The common case is typified by the following. One thirty-five-year-old woman had been depressed and tenuously suggested to her husband, a CO, that perhaps she should seek counseling. He was upset by her suggestion and the matter was dropped. Later, however, she learned of a six-week series of counseling lectures and enrolled. These lectures, sponsored by a local private college and funded by a federal grant, dealt with providing alternative resolutions to conflicts women encounter. Self-realization was encouraged. During the six weeks the women were to take stock of themselves and list pie-in-the-sky aspirations as well as realistic goals. As a result of participation, this woman evaluated her priorities and decided that she was unwilling to divorce herself entirely from her role as a senior officer's wife and that she was unwilling to spend a great deal of time away from her children. Her solution was to take a part-time, minimally paying secretarial position for a local charity, which she finds rewarding.

It is significant to note that this counseling program was conceived by, and is directed by, a woman whose husband only recently retired from the navy after 20 years and command of a submarine. Its founder was assisted by another senior submariner's wife with training as a counselor. Word-of-mouth passed the positive aspects of this program, and increasing numbers of submariners' wives have been in attendance at the sessions.

Most women, however, do not require even this type of assistance. They are able to deal with their self-definition issues entirely by themselves. Others turn to Parent Effectiveness Training, or Adlerian-based family counseling (both programs are offered on base or in military housing areas). Still other submariners' wives seek professional help from civilian psychiatrists, psychologists, psychiatric social workers, and other counselors (no military mental health care was available in the community studied). Unfortunately, the numbers utilizing professional caregiving resources were unobtainable. Not surprisingly, a number of wives reported going to the library and checking out a book; talking with friends; or talking with their husbands when they are home from sea. Extreme acting out is rare. Alcoholism at this juncture is infrequent but does occur. There are but few examples of extramarital liaisons for one would be hard put to keep such affairs quiet and hidden. Some women return to church and achieve a "born again" type of faith, but not often. Parameters of appropriate behavior are clearly prescribed in the submariner community to conform to white, urban, middle-class standards.

CONCLUSIONS

Midlife crises affect virtually all submariners' wives between the ages of 30 and 37 but in varying magnitude. The only exceptions appear to be wives of 30-year career men who experience a midlife crisis somewhat later but not of increased intensity. All midlife crises for these wives occur prior to the husbands' military retirement. These crises seem to occur in order for them to be worked through before the impending crisis of retirement of the husbands. Thus, space is created between the women and the military context. The resolution of a midlife crisis is a form of anticipatory socialization.

The crisis itself is typified by the features commonly attributed to the midlife transition. It is also associated with some ambivalence on the part of the woman toward her husband's success and status, the increased leisure time available as she completes her family size, and the increased responsibilities associated with the traditional roles the wife is supposed to assume in the life-style context.

On the basis of the field research conducted in the submarine-associated community on Oahu, Hawaii, it was found that what originally looked to be a noncoping sequence on the part of the wife in dealing with at-sea separations of the husband was not that at all. It was, instead, a midlife period of crisis requiring redefinition of self which was not directly caused by separations.

PART IV

CHANGING FAMILY ROLES

"In a rapidly changing military system, the role of the military wife becomes dysfunctional if practiced in a traditional manner."

Ellwyn R. Stoddard

12 Changing Spouse Roles: An Analytical Commentary

Ellwyn R. Stoddard

Using a sociological perspective, this chapter examines the changing female spouse of military officers roles.* More a position paper than an intricate collection of specific research data, it is designed to focus on the husband-wife stresses and officer-wife role pressures associated with structural and functional changes within the military establishment.

A survey of literature by Lang (1972) and an excellent update by Kourvetaris and Dobratz (1976) reveal mostly prescriptive accounts of military family life such as those of Janowitz (1960: chapters 9, 10) and Little (1971: 257-70). An earlier description of families operating within these prescriptive limits is Lindquist's (1952) analysis of an air force unit. Various "guide book" supplements are those by Shea (1954), Murphy and Parker (1966), and Kinzer and Leach (1968).

One recent research report (Stoddard and Cabanillas 1976) departs significantly from the former trend of considering deviancy from prescribed spouse roles as a form of personal pathology. It traces the mechanisms developed by military officers' wives to avoid the rigidly prescribed roles expected of them by military tradition, in an effort to live in the milieu of today's changing military system.

This chapter presents a brief historical view of military policies supportive of the family institution, an examination of military and civilian "wife models" and their appropriateness within the current military system, and a discussion of some of the stresses felt by military spouses in these rapidly changing roles.

---

*Although the inclusive term "military officer" is used throughout the chapter, most of the scientific data upon which this commentary is based refer to army officers or air force personnel, and less to navy families.

MILITARY POLICY AND FAMILY UNITY

Until the World War II era, military policy did not allow for nor encourage family propinquity or family satisfactions as supportive of military efficiency. No budgetary items could be used for wives and children to accompany their officer husbands from post to post, and few officers' wives did so (Goldman 1976: 119-23). No facilities existed for mass billeting of families, transportation of household goods, family living allotments, or per diem allocations for temporary duty away from a permanent aid station. Up to that time the recruiting of enlisted men had not been focused on the stable family man. In addition, the family relationships between officers and their wives were institutionally jeopardized by restrictions of celibacy during military academy training and by setting the priority of professional military obligations over familial concerns.

In the army branch, an inbred officer corps, consisting of a regional and social elite class, operated as an inherited occupational category. This traditional military endogamy was perpetuated as graduating military cadets tended to select marriage partners from among the daughters of families already part of the military community (Janowitz 1960). Thus, both the neophyte officer and his bride had been socialized into a military life style compatible with the prescribed expectations of the military establishment. The officer's rigorous and disciplined isolation from close civilian contacts in the military academy[*] was reinforced by prospective brides who had been raised in military families and were aware of the established supportive role of the wife in the career of her officer husband. The subsequent experiences in assignments, mobility, transfer patterns, and residence among the wives of more senior officers provided an informal school wherein the wives of junior officers learned the critical lessons of supportive military etiquette.

Commensurate with the technological revolution experienced by the military during World War II came a further reliance on business management models for officer training. The West Point curriculum

---

[*]See Dornbush 1955. In the less regimented ROTC milieu, Picou and Nyberg (1975) still see the military reference group even in a civilian milieu. Both of these authors concentrate on military socialization as the source of military cohesion and homogeneity whereas the psychological studies of Lovell (Janowitz 1964: 119-57) attribute military socialization to a self-selection process of specific personality types being drawn to a military career. The latter argument is far more persuasive during long periods of peacetime than during the eras of mass mobilization in World War II.

of basic engineering courses was altered to include leadership and personnel management skills. These courses, infused with worker satisfaction procedures from the fields of industrial psychology and sociology, were considered a necessary part of the new officer-management product, and vast policy changes were instituted to normalize the family life of military personnel. Allotments, compensations, and services for military dependents were soon available for the large number of family men entering the service during the mass mobilization of World War II. Studies of the U.S. soldier (Stouffer et al. 1949) reveal the strong priority for personnel with family responsibilities. This priority was reflected in the "points system" in which assignments and time spent in active war zones were based upon the man's family responsibilities. This preoccupation with military families and dependents turned into an economic and organizational subsidy for normalizing family life for military personnel. Due to the shortage of on-base dwellings, housing officers maintained lists of housing available in the immediate surrounding area. The rapid influx of "civilian-oriented" wives created a social and functional cleavage between the traditional military spouses and the uncommitted officers' wives. The close-knit brotherhood of "ring rappers"* preserved what they could of the "old ways" against the numerical superiority of ROTC and OCS junior grade officers.

Unlike the professional soldier in the military academy who underwent intensive socialization, the ROTC officer was a "civilian student." Quite likely he did not major in engineering or business management; thus, his curricular training differed from the older military officers who controlled the system. In addition, these men were generally from lower-class origins. It may be that the attraction of ROTC may have been more economic than career-motivated. Viewing a limited officer tour as a preferable alternative to being drafted as an enlisted man does little to promote total commitment to the military profession. Although the ROTC-trained officer may be just as valuable in meeting the primary mission objectives of the military establishment, he is partially a civilian with civilian friends, social contacts, and possibly a civilian career as his long-range goal. His wife comes from the civilian society and is involved in his occupation only to the extent that other college students' wives are involved in the training of their husbands. As evidenced by current married status, family life has a high priority for the ROTC student, and his

*Also known as "ring knockers"—West Point officers whose distinctive rings are a symbol of elitism among army general officers and whose near monopoly of high military office is called by the "outgroup" the W.P.P.A. (West Point Protective Association).

military training is coordinated with his family-centered life style. His wife and children are aware of his lack of total commitment to a military career "when the war is over" and, thus, do not feel pressure to participate fully in the military life to the exclusion of civilian reference groups.

The OCS officers also departed significantly from the officer model of pre-World War II days. More than likely he was an NCO with lower-class origins; he did not have the "elitist" orientations inspired by military academy training and selection procedures. The OCS officer came from all regions of the country, and his family had already established a "military life style" hardly in keeping with that of the senior officer's family. The OCS officer might even have been in the service longer, but as an enlisted man. A social barrier prevented total acceptance of the wives of OCS officers in the more exclusive cliques of senior officers' spouses.

The avalanche of nontraditional military officers had an impact on some of the traditional officers' wives, causing them to escape the restrictive life assigned to them and become involved more with civilian groups—advanced educational training, hobby groups off post, local PTA or service organizations, leisure clubs, off-post church or fraternal orders. In other words, they abandoned the total supportive role of the traditional military wife. A further examination of wife role models will provide some insight into the incongruity introduced into the military system by the adoption of civilian-oriented wife roles.

MILITARY WIFE ROLE MODELS

Two major military prescriptions for wives are evident—the matricentral and the complementary—and these roles vary with branch of service. The matricentral type is a variation of the wife of the civilian salesman who is absent for extended periods of time. This role corresponds to wives of navy officers and those in other branches of the military service who are assigned tours to locations at which dependents are not authorized (that is, diplomatically sensitive bases, research sites such as Antarctic regions). The second type of wife role is one in which husband and wife are residing together and working as complementary partners.

The matricentral home has a wife-manager who is in full charge of familial responsibilities during the long absences of her military husband. Although he may dictate overall policies and general goals for the family commensurate with his earning power and career plans, most routine details and decisions are left to the wife. The infrequent visits of her military husband are a major disruption in her

decision-making monopoly, but one which she can plan for. Much
like the routine of the traveling salesman's spouse whose husband
leaves "on the road" for the week, her normal routines begin at his
departure and cease at his arrival. During the week, children invite
their friends over, the house becomes littered, and a relaxed attitude
prevails. However, on his expected arrival day (usually Friday after-
noon), the house patterns abruptly change. Children may not litter
the house which is now spotless; it may not be used for nonessential
activities; and the wife prepared herself for a "honeymoon weekend."
The cycle begins again with the husband's departure. Early in the
marriage, the departure of a husband for extended periods may lead
to days of grief, crying, and self-pity. But after a few years, the
excitement of personal freedom enjoyed by a wife left with total power
to make her own decisions and engage in those activities which suit
her, is carefully guarded against a returning husband who might
suggest that he "come home to stay permanently" and take over the
management and discipline of the family. Even an unannounced
arrival of an absent husband is frequently upsetting to the normal
family routine and is merely tolerated, as compared to the romantic
and emotional shift which occurs when the wife is given advance notice
of husband's return.

The complementary wife role represents the wife as an integral
unit of the husband's occupation and a necessary component of his
work-related routine. This role is clearly articulated in a case study
of the ambassador's wife (Hochschild 1969) who, in her quasi-legal
capacity, must correctly convey the official sentiments of her husband's government through the informal milieu of ceremonial and
entertaining occasions. Moreover, the socialization for this role
performance comes with time spent as the wife of a junior embassy
employee. In this subservient role she is informally trained by the
senior wife, the wife of the ambassador, in the subtleties of diplomatic
life and the reciprocal social opportunities afforded her. In like manner, the officer's wife is placed at the status level of her husband's
rank. Under the unspoken rules of protocol, she does not flagrantly
disregard the prerogatives of wives of senior officers, lest her husband's career be damaged.

The wife of a military officer is differentiated from most civilian
occupation wives in many ways. First, the separation between work
and place of residence so characteristic of most urban occupations
has been minimized (Janowitz 1960). Moreover, the unique work
contract requiring an unlimited call on the officer's time without
overtime compensation is without a civilian equivalent. Although
many occupations require frequent movement, none are so predictably
mobile as the three- to four-year military tour of duty. As a result
of this geographic mobility, the male's identity is enhanced through

upgrading or promotion, while the female's (without the complementary aspect of her relationship to her husband) is shredded since she
is unable to transfer her credentials of status and attainment as
effectively (Seidenberg 1973). This pattern further alienates her
from civilian involvement and "community roots" for her and family
members. Formal publications such as guide books and pamphlets
for officers' wives prescribe specific duties, obligations, as well as
her contribution to her husband's chances of becoming a general officer (Froehlke 1972).

Although guide books such as Murphy and Parker (1966) or Kinzer
and Leach (1968) are distributed to aid the army wife to adapt to her
prescribed role in the military system, these become ultimately a
model of acceptability, the deviancy from which is seen to be a personal weakness in the character of the wife herself. This blinds the
scientific observer from considering an outmoded structure as the
source of maladaptive spouse patterns in the military, rather than
the convenient approach of blaming the wife for her recalcitrant nature
and personality.

CIVILIAN WIFE ROLE MODELS

The housewife role (Lopata 1971) features a total isolation of
the wife from her husband's work. This isolation is not determined
by the employer or the circumstances surrounding the occupation
itself but rather, reflects a lack of personal interest or husband-wife
agreement of nonintervention. The female entering marriage finds
that she has received little training for becoming a housewife, other
than that received from her own mother. Her activities and involvement patterns before marriage now change abruptly as her new
"clients"—husband and children—become the focus of her daily routine.
Housewives refer to the husband's occupation as "his work," and
they do not concern themselves with him or his work from the time
he leaves until he returns. Sex roles are rigidly categorized in this
relationship with the responsibility of provider resting squarely upon
the husband, while the housewife assumes the domestic tasks and
carries out the child-rearing functions with little or no assistance.
Officers' wives who enter the military service with the housewife
model as their "game plan" are soon identified as apathetic. Rather
than their family responsibilities being seen as a high priority in
their lives, their actions are often interpreted as overt rejection of
their military-connected duty.

The companion role, the ideal auxiliary of a corporate or bureaucratic executive, is one which fluctuates between total isolation and
total involvement depending upon the employer demands. This fluc-

tuation is not modified or controlled by domestic agreements between the spouses but is regulated by the functional necessities of the husband's occupational needs. Whyte's (1951, 1952) research with wives of corporate executives found only one company in four attempting to make the wife an "organic member of the corporate family"; the remaining companies sold her on the corporate view of affective support for her husband, without interference with his corporate duties. They do not want the wife and the company to become adversaries, tugging on the husband-employee in an attempt to make him conform to each of their expectations (in which case he usually compromises, and loses the respect and support of both). If she is invited to become a member of the company, it is with the implicit understanding that together—wife and company—they can use the attributes with which they are endowed to encourage the husband to concentrate his efforts on being a success in business. The wife, in return, receives financial rewards, security, and increased social standing for the family. The aggressive wife who insists that her husband advance faster than his ability warrants, who discusses company business to outsiders, or tries to run the company is isolated, or the husband is discouraged from continuing with the company (Seidenberg 1973). To become a Mrs. Success (Wyse 1970) takes a purposeful, realistic approach to support her husband's work with a minimum of recognition. In an era of growing discontent of women playing seemingly "love object" roles as the males take the bows for brains, originality, initiative, and persistence, the companion wife receives a negative image from those wives who wish to pursue their own successful careers.

While the companion role of the military officer's wife might be mistaken for the complementary role, the latter involves a great deal more responsibility and personal initiative. A wife playing the companion role may "stay out of the way," but the complementary wife would "stay out of the way" only when appropriate. The companion wife might find the obligatory military activities, such as the wives' club and formal dinners, annoying and perform her duties mechanically—not so for the complementary wife (Kinzer and Leach 1968).

ROLE DISCREPANCIES IN THE
MILITARY WIFE ROLE

In a rapidly changing military system, the role of the military wife becomes dysfunctional if practiced in the traditional manner. Yet, if too much change in the expectations of military wives' behavior is initiated, it develops a generational cleavage between the

older "hard core" wives of general officers and the younger wives of
aspiring junior and field grade officers.

Role conflict, an overload of role obligations from multiple social
roles (that is, wife, mother, neighbor, citizen, church member,
Brownie Scout leader) occurs in all families and with all wives. However, those playing the traditional military wife roles seem to be
able to adapt less effectively than those playing civilian wife roles
in which less responsibility and initiative are required. One army
wife's diary gives an account of a party held for the general and his
staff while her son was very ill. Her very punctual guests were just
about to arrive when her officer husband (who had dressed in the
guest bathroom upstairs while she was finishing up the cooking and
cleanup chores in the kitchen) descended the stairs:

> . . . where he left a ring on the tub and my best bath mat
> as sodden as a dishrag. . . . He brought out bottles and
> glasses, demanding, "Where's the ice? You never have
> enough ice. Hand me the olives. What did you do with
> the oranges?" While I was stirring the Hollandaise that
> persisted in curdling like buttermilk. . . . Leaving the
> lamb to roast and the salad to crisp in the icebox, I rushed
> upstairs to take Tex's (the son) temperature again, wet
> myself briefly in a shower and tug on my best lace
> dress. . . . As I gave a final check to the dining room,
> the front doorbell rang announcing the arrival of the
> guests. . . . I took a quick slug of bourbon and tried
> to appear like a charming hostess who had no children
> and a chef in the kitchen (Lopata 1971: 6).

A great deal of role strain is contained in the expectations of an
officer's wife. Her wifely duties demand time and energy which are
drained off as a result of demands made by the military on the "wife
of a senior officer" such as that reported in Okinawa. An officer
had been subjected to harrassment and embarrassment by members
of the local Communist party. His wife, as befitting the wife of the
civil administrator, felt some commitment to strengthen and support
her husband in his dealings with the local citizenry.

> A capable Nisei civilian employee . . . called to ask
> if I would make a speech to several hundred Okinawan
> women. . . . The next day I was scheduled to have lunch
> at the village of Itoman and the day after that attend a
> groundbreaking ceremony at a school. I made the speech
> in the theatre . . . (to the women) but I didn't go to the
> school. To Johnny (her husband) I said "My joints ache

from sitting for hours cross-legged on the floor and I
ate two packages of Tums and still have indigestion.
No woman can keep up the schedule mapped out for
me. . . . The Army can get someone else for the public
relations job."
    Johnny said, "They expect you to do it."
    "Well," I retorted, "they can just go on expecting."

But she saw that many local people were helping to maintain good
army-citizen relations on Okinawa and yet she, the wife of the administrator, was doing nothing.

. . . I decided I'd just have to develop indigestion and
arthritis. The next time (they) . . . called to ask if I
would attend an official function, I said yes. I said yes,
too, to becoming a board member of the gift shop, to
visiting old people's homes, TB hospitals, and pottery
and lacquer factories to promote native industry; I said
yes to giving out diplomas to Okinawan graduates of the
Brides School who were marrying GIs and to attending
endless official parties. I didn't do it for Johnny's career.
I did it because it was my responsibility and because I
wanted to (Johnson 1967: 85).

Much role alienation occurs among officers' wives wherein they
no longer feel compelled to fulfill the prescribed obligations for
military wives, a sentiment often shared and supported by their
officer husbands. The general officer's wife cited earlier on Okinawa
had followed the traditional wife role throughout her husband's successful career; but, when sweeping changes occurred within the army
converting to business management procedures, she became alienated
and rebelled. Her personal account follows.

The change . . . affected even the women who, like the
wives of business executives, were supposed to be a "help"
to their husbands' climb to promotion. No longer could
they devote themselves to their own interests. They had
to assume civic responsibilities—the Women's Club, the
Red Cross, the PTA, the Dramatics Club, the Gold Group,
the Church Guild. They had to know how to ask for a
treasurer's report and to give a speech.
    They all did, too. ALL BUT ME.
    The first year I had an excuse because I was having
a baby . . . and when she was a year old, the commanding
general's wife indicated that I should accept my share of

civic responsibilities. Johnny was G.I. . . . and I was
a senior officer's wife. Since accepting civic responsibilities would only make more work for me, I saw no
reason to volunteer . . . I liked to ride horseback, play
golf, or loll around the house reading mystery stories.

A classmate's wife exclaimed, "Oh, but you have to
belong to the Women's Club and the PTA!"

"Nuts," Johnny said. "You can do what you want"
(Johnson 1967: 69-70).

Role ambivalence, the inability to assign priorities to the different aspects of role responsibilities, is not a common problem among
military wives. They are more apt to get caught in role conflict, a
situation demanding the time and energies of the person in two or
more role responsibilities. As one wife in the air force related:

I want to be a part of the civilian community but don't
really want to throw myself whole hog into fund raising
for good causes, building or holding together an idealistic
organization, working on political campaigns, correcting
social ills and injustices, putting on plays, seeking knowledge, or anything else. These things are important in my
value system but they require a great deal more time and
energy than I have to give and more community identification than I am able to muster, and they end up conflicting
with other values about family responsibility . . . (Seidenberg 1973: 19).

The woman had little ambivalence since she had decided that family
responsibilities were of greater importance than those dealing with
voluntary service, community programs, going to college, and other
worthwhile activities. However, the priority of family roles did set
up a conflict situation with the military expectations of an officer's
wife.

THE MILITARY WIFE IN A CHANGING ARMY:
IMPLICATIONS AND COMMENTARY

The military has prescribed the roles they wish their officers'
wives to play. These are articulated quite clearly in formal guide
books, in informal socialization techniques, and in many other ways.
However, if recent research results showing the marked changes in
officers' wives attitudes and behavior (Stoddard and Cabanillas 1976)
are representative of military wives generally, they are no longer

satisfied with these role prescriptions arbitrarily assigned to them. They reject those traditional patterns which today provide so little personal satisfaction and reward. Rather, at the expense of unquestioned loyalty to women's auxiliaries and officers' wives clubs, they increasingly choose the new emergent model of a woman who participates fully in the larger society. While there is no evidence that wives are fully supportive of the role of women officers working in concert with their husbands and competing directly for advancement and assignments, officers' wives do support a married woman's right to choose and work toward her own destiny.

The military is now left with a choice—to recognize a new kind of military wife who is uniquely independent and who no longer lives in the shadow of her husband's occupational success or to confront the problem with rules and administrative bulletins which might further alienate the husband and widen an already visible breach between military husbands and wives. Either way, the military can no longer depend upon tradition and established routine to solve the problem.

With the growing technological sophistication of military hardware,* most scholars see a functional convergence of military and civilian worlds supplanting the prewar military isolation from the larger society (Biderman and Sharp 1968; Moskos 1973; Segal et al. 1974; Segal 1975). Sarkasian and Taylor (1975) openly advocate the civilian education of military officers. Similarly, Segal et al. (1974) advocate service policies leading to further integration of the soldier into the larger society to deal with some of the problems of military life. It is recognized that were the military system to advocate policies leading to further integration of the soldier into the larger society as they suggest, it would lead to dysfunctions elsewhere. The military intelligence agent comes closest to being a "civilian" in his dress and daily contacts, and yet endures family stresses (Stoddard 1972: 578-81). As soldiers come to mimic civilian institutions more and more, the threats of military unionization and its destruction of traditional military command functions looms large. Thus, the amelioration of one military problem may cause serious side effects elsewhere within the military establishment.

It would appear that the only alternative to a patchwork ad hoc system of policy changes is to authorize an overall research project

---

*A rapidly changing and sophisticated military technology alters significantly the social organization of the military service as demonstrated by Bailey (1974). When civilian specialists are required to assist in maintenance and operation of this hardware, there is a partial resocialization among the military and civilian workers as each becomes aware of the world of the other.

dealing with organizational stresses and changes which would be anticipated by functionally modernizing the military organization to more effectively meet its new mission, developed for it in recent decades. Otherwise, an increasingly unworkable system of pre-scribed bureaucratic procedures will be circumvented by an increas-ingly effective informal system of pragmatic operational techniques.

If these trends continue, the military wife will demand more and more freedom from the traditional service wife role previously ascribed to her and will wish to have the various military and civilian wife models available to her, without negative sanctions attached to any of them.

13 Separation and Female Centeredness in the Military Family

Janice G. Rienerth

The U.S. military establishment of today contains a higher proportion of married personnel than ever before in its history. The presence of the service family is, further, a relatively new phenomenon arising from the need, since World War II, for a large, standing armed force as an aspect of national policy. The military family can be seen as either an asset or a liability to the individual's traditional performance of military duty and, in itself, is a unique type of family, different in structure and attitude from that found in the civilian community in general. The service family is faced by the ever present, often actualized, threat of separation of family members from one another and is subjected to chronic mobility requiring repeated family adjustments to new environments. These conditions can produce stress that is disruptive both to interpersonal family relations and to the performance of military duty.

The purpose of this chapter is to examine the effects of separations of the husband-father on the structure and organization of the military family. While military families are obviously not the only examples of families affected by male absenteeism (other examples include some black families, corporate families, commuter families, and families where the father is institutionalized), it is felt that military families provide an opportunity to examine the phenomenon of male absenteeism in a subcultural environment.

Each family's adjustment to the stressful situation of an absent parent, whether due to desertion, institutionalization, occupational commitments, or wartime mobilizations, is unique. In one sense the family is a battleground for conflicts between the demands of the

This chapter is an adaption of Rienerth, J., "The Impact of Male Absenteeism on the Structure and Organization of the Military Family," a Ph.D. dissertation prepared for Southern Illinois University, 1976.

community and those of the individual family members. In some cases society may prepare the family and its members for the stress of separation by providing roles and norms of appropriate behavior even before the separation becomes a reality. This suggests that some degree of chronic stress may be functional in preparing the family for crisis by predefining roles or developing institutionalized modes of adjustment. Yet as a general trend, in families where male absenteeism occurs, regardless of its length or reason, this predefinition has not occurred, and it becomes necessary for the remaining marriage partner, the wife, to assume aspects of the husband's role in order to retain a functional family unit. In some cases this adaptation may be necessary only for the duration of the husband's absence, while in other instances restructuring of family roles may become permanent. Thus, although the role of the male is important in understanding family structure, in families experiencing separation, it is the role of the wife which requires the most readjustment. While these families may have become "female-centered," they are not truly matriarchal, since the restructuring of family roles occurred out of necessity rather than by choice. In families experiencing separation, the marriage partners have altered their images of ideal husband/wife behavior and have adapted to the situation of father absence.

In this century many societal changes have occurred which have both caused father absence and legitimized and supported female-centeredness as a mode of adaptation. One of these has been the increased mobility of U.S. families in search of, among other reasons, educational and employment opportunities. Since the father is still viewed as the primary family supporter, this mobility is often for his benefit. In some cases, the father may leave the family behind until he finishes his education or secures employment. In other instances, the father and the family may both move to a new area at the insistence of an employer. In any case, the wife is expected to maintain the family unit until the father returns and to repress any ambitions which may negatively affect her husband's career. Situations of this type foster the development of what can be called the two-person single-career family. A general societal example of this situation is the corporate family, while a subcultural example is the military family, the focus of this research. In both cases father absence, whether externally or internally caused, has resulted in the development of a female-centered family.

THE TWO-PERSON SINGLE CAREER FAMILY

Traditionally, a woman's status and social class follow that of her husband—regardless of what other roles she may play. Horner

(1970) found that many women have chosen, perhaps unconsciously, not to develop either their potential or individuality but rather, to live through and for others. A woman who achieves her own success may lose her self-esteem and her sense of femininity, a standard internalized quite early in the socialization process. When studying this sex-role ideology, Lipman-Blumen (1972) found it necessary to examine modes of achievement; one of which was that of vicarious achievement. Papanek (1973) pointed out that vicarious achievement is most typical of members of the middle class, since the corporate institutions that foster it and the educational institutions that make it possible function primarily at that status level. Formal and informal institutional demands are placed upon both members of a marital unit, but only the man is employed by the institution. Women in such marital units, the best-known example being the corporate wife, are husband-oriented, have dependence on their husbands' jobs, and exist in a special combination of roles that constitutes the two-person single career. This study of the two-person single career further found that the above pattern played an especially significant role where an explicit ideology of educational equality between the sexes conflicted with an implicit inequality of access to occupations. The two-person single career pattern partially alleviates this conflict by providing a social control mechanism that serves to shift the occupational aspirations of educated women into noncompetitive channels, while preserving the rewards of occupational success.

Papanek's (1973) study revealed that ambivalence is a characteristic of the two-person single-career pattern. This ambivalence is particularly destructive to a woman's self-esteem, since women participate in activities that they may personally reject but are nonetheless expected to perform. Such a career pattern not only occurs among couples involved with corporate businesses but also in large, complex institutions that require the employment of highly educated men, such as colleges, large private foundations, and the United States government—particularly the armed forces. The greatest pressures on a wife to adopt the two-person single-career pattern occurs in situations where the employing institution operates within a social enclave as on an army post, or in a college, or company town.

The typical pattern of adaptation to the two-person, one-career family pattern is illustrated by the experience of the corporate wife. Precedent dictates that the wife follow the husband in his need for achievement. When the corporate husband and his wife adhere to their traditional roles, the conventional behavioral expectations arising from these roles often require excessive accommodations from the woman. It is these demands for excessive accommodations, and not personal immaturity nor unresolved childhood conflicts, that often account for grave problems within these families (Seidenberg 1975). The entire corporate life style encourages the wife to be cooperative, to get along, and to live solely through and by her husband; any personal aspirations or ambitions are to be promptly extinguished. The executive's hope is that the new breed of wife would eternally submerge her identity into that of her husband and the corporation. Two people for one salary—paycheck addressed to the husband—for his and her lifetimes (Seidenberg 1975).

One aspect of corporate life is the necessity of moving to a new location, often at the company's discretion. For the corporate wife, the burdens, deprivations, and penalties of moving are hers alone. The stressful effects of U.S. geographic mobility have been underestimated; moving often places inordinate demands on the individual to adapt and raises continued challenges to identity. In moving, the only seasoned relationship the wife takes with her is that of the nuclear family. Most central is the relationship with her husband, who is the reason she moved in the first place—to cleave unto him. If, after this move, in which she stripped herself of old and true relationships, trouble arises with her husband, the wife is more alone than ever (Seidenberg 1975). Commentators on the corporate wife agree that her principal disease is loneliness. Yet this may not be an endemic but an epidemic illness, contagious in every segment of society. For the corporate wife there are few compensatory mechanisms. She is very vulnerable and therefore feels the effects of isolation and estrangement more intensely.

The "military wife" could be substituted in the above discussion of the corporate wife with the same results. Lopata (1965) found that the air force officer's wife is also an example of a husband—oriented wife. The social enclave of a military base involves continued affiliation with the military organization, and the philosophy of the military fosters the two—person single career. The absence of an extended kin structure and the dependence on military neighbors and voluntary associations increases the social isolation of the base and further involves the wife within the military institution (Janowitz 1960). In addition to her family role, the military wife has definite, though limited, obligations to participate in voluntary associations within the military's system of self-help. Such participation of the military wife in the two—person single—career pattern is a major factor in her reluctance or inability to develop an independent career.

Military wives, subjected as they are to their husbands' many moves and long absences, share a destiny similar to their civilian counterparts. Yet, in many ways they are better off than their corporate sisters. While the financial and material rewards may not be as great in the military, a greater protective spirit appears to work in her behalf. The majority of "how-to" books say that the service wife "accepts" her military responsibilities and duties. Perhaps those who write about the "typical" military wife might be overlooking the fact that many officers are not career-minded, and both spouses may see the military, not as a way of life, but as an "interruption" in it.

Regardless of the differences, in both corporate and military families, father absence is an externally caused stressful event which requires some type of adjustment on the part of the wife and family. As discussed earlier, the most functional form of readjustment to this situation is the formation of a more female-centered family. Support for this contention comes from the research cited below on adjustments to service-related separations.

A classic study of World War II families who experienced separations of the husband-father due to military service (Hill 1949) found that the degree of family adjustment could be measured by the effectiveness of the family's role organization, and in general, by whether the family continued to satisfy the needs of its members. Hill concluded that the family's adjustment to separation was a function of (a) the wife's perception of the separation, (b) the resources the family brought to the situation, and (c) the hardships of the separation. Families who experienced separation also engaged in a "closing of the ranks" type of behavior which fostered the development of a family type independent of the father (McCubbin, Dahl, and Hunter 1976).

Studies by MacIntosh (1968) and Belt and Sweney (1973) viewed separation as a developmental task which may be more difficult in early married life than it is later. Additionally, frequent prior military tours, resulting in absences of the husband-father, may help some wives with adjusting to later separations. Military wives also frequently identify with their husband's rank and status, and this may provide enough gratification to overcome the difficulties of separation (MacIntosh 1968). Pcarlman (1970) pointed out that each separation is a psychological crisis that may hinder a couple from learning to interact maturely.

In a study of the effects of prolonged separation in prisoner-of-war families, McCubbin, Hunter, and Dahl (1975) found that the social and psychological stresses of prolonged separation encouraged families to develop behaviors and styles of life which lessened the possibility of successful reunions. In part fostered by the Women's Liberation movement, the wives had moved toward total autonomy during their husbands' absence and had become increasingly independent. Family tasks were redistributed with the wife assuming greater responsibility for making decisions, disciplining the children, and handling the finances. The children also assumed responsibilities which had traditionally belonged to the father, such as "caring" for the mother.

Stresses and strains exist between families and the military as separate systems. The military seeks to make the family instrumental to its mission of developing and maintaining a highly effective combat-ready body of men, mobile enough to be deployed where needed. Wives and children of the military must be socialized to subordinate their personal desires and needs to the "good of the service," and to minimize claims on the time and presence of the husband-father (McCubbin, Dahl, and Hunter 1976). The type of family which develops in the military is an adaptation to the military social structure. Men who elect career military status must not only accept the risks of separation and mobility but also place their wives and children in a subordinate position.

THE MILITARY ENVIRONMENT

Military life is in many cases institutional life. Traditionally the military has existed as an isolated community sharply segregated from civilian society. Men and their families were located on frontier outposts where they developed a distinctive way of life. The traditional service community molded family life to the requirements of the profession. Bases were organized to provide the goods and services necessary for the maintenance of life.

Today, changes in the nature of warfare and in the organization of the armed forces have altered service life, and many of the changes which have occurred in our society have been reflected in the military. The traditional picture has been altered. First, the civilian pattern of separating work and residence is becoming the norm. One reason for this is that a sufficient amount of base housing is rarely available. The increasing number of married personnel has also contributed to this separation. Second, the increase in the number of people in the military has made the close primary type of group life impossible. This increase in personnel, which includes a large number of civilians, has increased the size of the military bases. These larger populations have contributed to the greater importance of secondary groups. Third, the backgrounds of military people today are more heterogeneous than in the past. There are few traditional service families with a long history of military careers. The present-day officers and enlisted men come from a much broader social base. Fourth, social stratification is becoming ambiguous, especially in off-duty hours. The stratification system which once tended to increase the sense of solidarity has given way to the intermingling of groups. Fifth, the increasing similarity of military and professional jobs has made it impossible for many servicepersonnel to see their profession as unique. This is primarily the result of the technological revolution. Finally, the ties of the military family to the base have weakened. A wife was once believed to have an important influence on her husband's career; today the secondary group nature of the base has weakened this influence.

Other factors such as the effects of war, extended separations, frequent residential changes, and the idea of "duty" have affected the service family. Time has produced changes in the organization and professional culture of the military. Although these changes may have weakened some of the distinctive characteristics of the military, it is still a unique style of life externally and internally (Coates and Pellegrin 1965). It is significant that the distinguishing features of the military—mobility and separations—are also becoming more apparent in civilian society. Thus, there is both a convergence and a divergence between service and civilian families.

It has been observed that the military social structure and the subsystems within which the family operates provide the sources for both the family's destruction and its growth. The sociocultural environment presents the service family with conflicting values and expectations which cannot be easily resolved. On the one hand, society places great emphasis on preserving the integrity of the family and its effective functioning in order to ensure its contribution to society. At the same time social recognition is given to the soldier's role in implementing national goals, and society sanctions extended separations of the husband-father during the performance of his military duties. Both of these values cannot be fully attained by the family without substantial adaptations and emotional, as well as financial costs, to the family system (Montalvo 1976).

ROLE SHIFT IN THE MILITARY FAMILY

Various writers have suggested that the military family has the following unique and distinguishable features: strong group identification, separation from the general society, a ranked system, uncertainties due to assignments, stressful family situations resulting from mobility and separation, conflicting military and family requirements, relegation of the family to a secondary position, and heightened family cathexes. The research reported in this chapter deals specifically with one of these features—separation. It examines not only the type, duration, and frequency of father absences but also the relationship of these absences to family structure. The goal of this study was to answer the question: How is the internal organization of the military family affected by separation?

Research relevant to this study comes from a variety of sources. A summary of the role research points out that the family is composed of a number of roles and statuses which are learned and, especially for women, involve contingency planning. In some cases marital roles may conflict, necessitating some form of reorganization in family structure. Family roles can be viewed as a male-instrumental, female-expressive dichotomy, yet this dichotomy may disappear in the two-person single-career group.

Stress research states that the family is exposed to external and internal pressures. In order to understand these pressures one must consider both the people involved and/or the community in which the stresses occurred. In the military family the exterior pressures include periodic residential moves, potential hazards of training, always being on call, threat of permanent loss in wartime, and the possibility of separation. The interior pressures include the adjustments to the presence of children and the general adjustments to married life. Separations are one example of a chronic stress for which the military has set up norms of appropriate behavior. Entering the armed forces independently or as a couple may be viewed as a stressful situation for it entails adjusting to an entirely new way of life.

Research conducted on the military family leads to the conclusion that separations are common in the military, and the degree of stress they produce is dependent on the adaptability, integration, and previous separation experience of the family. Separation has different effects on the internal role organization of the family depending on the type of separation, its frequency of occurrence, and the total number of months separated. The uncertain presence of the father places stress on the mother who must sometimes assume his role. This alteration of roles, or the "closing of ranks," may have functional and/or dysfunctional effects on the family. Adjustment to separation may be viewed as a developmental task with problems occurring before, during, or after the actual separation.

Military separations may occur regularly or sporadically and are due to a variety of circumstances, from training exercises to wartime mobilizations. Three types of separation will be examined in this research: general separations, extended or long-term separations, and combat separations. The major hypothesis posed by this research is that families which have been separated are more likely to be female-centered than those which have never been separated and, further, that the number and total length of each type of separation is also directly related to the degree of female-centeredness. Of the numerous factors which might influence the relationship between separation and female-centeredness, only married service time and children will be examined in this study.

Research has shown that married service time is related to separation and female-centeredness (Duvall 1945; Lindquist 1952;

Coates and Pellegrin 1965; MacIntosh 1968; Little 1971; McCubbin, Hunter, and Dahl 1975). As length of married service time increases, female-centeredness increases, regardless of the occurrence of separations. Children are related to female-centeredness due to the fact that role organization may be different in the family with children than in the husband-wife pair (Lynn and Sawrey 1959; Landis 1962). While the presence of children may have little influence on the occurrence of separations, they will affect the family reactions before, during, and after the separation and make these families more female-centered.

METHODOLOGY

Data were collected by a questionnaire covering five general areas: (a) introductory questions, (b) questions related to the military, (c) questions related to family roles and organization, (d) general questions regarding family characteristics, and (e) additional information on the role of the air force wife.

The sample for this study included 156 wives of United States Air Force officer personnel at two bases, a midwestern Military Airlift Command base and a northern midwestern Strategic Air Command base. Only wives of officers were included in the sample. Their husbands were felt to form a more homogeneous group, based on similar educational, socioeconomic, and preliminary training backgrounds, than would be true of enlisted personnel.

The variables specifically related to this research deal with the various dimensions of separation, service time, children, and female-centeredness as defined below.

The independent variables included: (a) separations (number of separations of all types and total number of months separated); (b) extended separations (six months or more, tabulated by number of extended separations and number of months separated); and (c) combat separations (hazardous duty assignments, tabulated by number of combat separations and total number of months separated).

The dependent variable was female-centeredness, for example, the degree to which the mother takes on the "instrumental" family tasks while not discarding her "expressive" tasks, and was measured by a scale of 11 items statistically derived from the 36-item family life section of the questionnaire. The items which made up the final scale were as follows:

1. sets up family budget
2. decides how much to spend on necessities
3. decides how much to spend on luxuries

   4. decides how much to spend on recreation
   5. decides personal items wife will buy
   6. handles money for household
   7. handles money for charge accounts
   8. handles money for checking and savings accounts
   9. does the yard and garden work
 10. makes household repairs
 11. takes care of car

The test variables included (a) married service time: [length of married service time, military wife time (married time before the arrival of children); military mother time (married time after the arrival of children); rank of husband, career intent of husband (yes, no, undecided) and status of husband (reserve versus regular)], and (b) children: [absence or presence of children; number of children; age of the oldest child; and sex of the oldest child.]

DEMOGRAPHIC FINDINGS

The majority of the husbands in this sample (57.1 percent) held the rank of captain. Over 60 percent (62.8) planned on making the air force a career, 12.8 percent had negative career plans, and 24.4 percent were undecided. The officers were almost evenly distributed between those holding regular (56.2 percent) and those holding reserve status (46.8 percent). More officers were from urban (59.6 percent) than from rural (34.6 percent) backgrounds, and over 90 percent were not from military families. With respect to religion, 13.5 percent were Catholic, 72.4 percent Protestant, 3.2 percent Jewish, and 10.9 percent reported other affiliations. Fewer than 20 percent (18.6) of the families had no children, 24.4 percent had one child, 33.4 percent had two children, 14.7 percent had three, and 8.9 percent had four or more. Results showed that almost 40 percent (39.1) of the men were college graduates at the time their first child was born.

As for the wives, more than half married after their husbands were already in the service. At the time of the first child, 34.0 percent of the women had some college education, and 28.2 percent were college graduates. Almost 70 percent (67.9) of the wives were Protestant, 18.6 percent were Catholic, and 10.9 percent had Jewish or other religious affiliations. More of the wives were from urban (62.8 percent) than from rural (34.6 percent) backgrounds, and 90 percent were from nonmilitary families.

RESULTS

The major hypothesis of this research states that separation of the husband-father is directly related to female-centeredness in the military family. Separation was first treated as a general variable, in the initial analysis, and then broken down by type. In each case the cumulative number and cumulative length of separation experience were examined. Once the independent effects of separation were analyzed, control variables were introduced to determine whether various family and/or military experiences had any significant mediating effect upon the relationship between separation and female-centeredness. Statistical significance was determined by means of the x^2 test at $p \leq .05$.

Analysis of the effects of separation upon female-centeredness suggest that the major hypothesis is correct. Those wives who have experienced separations are more likely to be female-centered than those wives who have not been separated ($x^2 = 12.48$, df = 1, $p \leq .05$). Further, a significant relationship was obtained between female-centeredness and number of separations ($x^2 = 13.81$, df = 5, $p \leq .02$) and female-centeredness and length of separations ($x^2 = 13.40$, df = 4, $p \leq .01$). It appears that as the number of separations and the total amount of time separated increases, the likelihood of a woman reporting a high level of female-centeredness also increases.

The results further suggest that women who have never experienced separations of the husband-father are the ones with the lowest female-centeredness scores. There is, however, little difference between the female-centeredness scores of women who have experienced a single separation and those who have experienced more than one separation. The same pattern seems to hold for total duration of separation experience. Those women who had not been separated from their husbands were the lowest on the female-centeredness scale, but once separated, the cumulative length of separation made little difference toward increasing the reported level of female-centeredness. Hence, it appears that the critical feature of separation as an influence upon female-centeredness is simply the fact of separation, or more specifically, the first separation, rather than the intrinsic dimensions of number or duration of separation.

When the data for those wives who had experienced separations of the husband-father was cross-tabulated by type of first separation, the results were also statistically significant ($x^2 = 16.30$, df = 4, $p \leq .002$). The patterns resulting from this analysis indicated that while any type of separation leads to female-centeredness, the experience of an extended combat separation, as the first separation, seems to be the most stressful, or at least the most likely to move the family toward female-centeredness.

The analysis utilizing the control variables of married service time and children revealed that certain of the dimensions of each of these variables affected the relationship between separation and female-centeredness. Since the earlier analysis found that separation per se, rather than the number, length, or type, was the significant factor, in the subsequent analysis the variable of separation was treated dichotomously and subsumed under the concept—experience of separation.

Controlling for the dimensions of the variable—children—only presence of children, number of children, and sex of the oldest child were found to be significant. For presence of children the analysis indicates that neither the presence nor absence of children significantly modified the effects of separation upon female-centeredness. Those women without children who had experienced separation of the husband-father were as likely to report high female-centeredness scores ($x^2 = 6.17$, df = 1, $p \leq .01$) as women with children ($x^2 = 3.81$, df = 1, $p \leq .05$). Comparisons among women, controlling for number of children, found that only those respondents without children were significantly influenced by separations of the husband-father ($x^2 = 6.17$, df = 1, $p \leq .01$). Thus, number of children does not seem to mediate the effect of separation upon female-centeredness. In all categories, separation experience seemed to result in increased female-centeredness, but the effect of separation upon childless women was greater than the effect upon those women with children. Additional analysis found that sex of the oldest child affected the relationship between separation experience and female-centeredness. Those women whose oldest child was male were more likely to be female-centered than those women whose oldest child was female ($x^2 = 3.94$, df = 1, $p \leq .05$).*

When the relationship between separation experience and female-centeredness was controlled for the dimensions of the variable—married service time—only length of married service time, rank, status, and career intent were found to be significant. Controlling for length of married service time, a significant relationship was obtained only for women married over 12 years ($x^2 = 5.24$, df = 1, $p \leq .02$). In addition, it was found that women whose husbands were of medium rank (captains or majors) tended to be more female-centered than those with husbands of lower or higher rank ($x^2 = 5.80$, df = 1, $p \leq .02$). Comparisons among women, controlling for status of husband, found that separation proved equally likely to increase female-centeredness for the wives of regular ($x^2 = 5.08$, df = 1, $p \leq .02$) or reserve officers ($x^2 = 6.80$, df = 1, $p \leq .01$). In addition,

---

*Some of the cells contained fewer than five cases.

it was found that the relationship between female-centeredness and separation was influenced by the career intent of the husband. If the husband planned a military career, the relationship was significant ($x^2 = 9.34$, df = 1, $p \leq .002$). If, however, the husband was uncertain or did not intend to remain in the military, the relationship was not significant.

DISCUSSION

This study of the family in a military environment initially posed the question: Is the internal organization of the military family affected by separation? Based on the findings, this question must be answered affirmatively, since female-centeredness was found to be significantly related to both number and length of separations. It was also found that the first separation had the greatest effect on the structure of the military family, especially if this separation was of the extended combat type. A second question posed was: What factors influence this relationship and what is their effect? This question is answered by the statistical results which demonstrate that presence of children, number of children, sex of the oldest child, married service time, rank of husband, status, and career intent of husband influence the relationship between separation and female-centeredness. These factors will be discussed below.

An explanation of the influence of presence of children and number of children is found in a discussion of role organization in the family. Research has indicated that family organization in the two-person family may be different from the organization of the family in which children are present. Both partners in the childless family may be task specialists, while neither is the social-emotional specialist. In the childless family, there is no need for the "traditional" wife-mother roles with respect to the care of children or other areas of family life, such as housework and cooking. The role of the father is also different in the childless family. There is no need for him to act as a role model or to take time away from his occupation to be with his children. The structure of the military itself reinforces this pattern by necessitating the reallocation of roles into a more female-centered family in order to retain a functional family unit during the father's absence. Thus, the childless woman can assume greater responsibility for all family tasks than can the woman with children. It should be noted that the wife who experiences loneliness during her husband's absence may view the presence of children either positively or negatively, for while children may prohibit some types or degrees of outside activity, they may also be a source of support and comfort.

Where children are present, separation is more likely to affect the family if the oldest child is a male. Father absence places greater demands on the oldest male child, giving him more responsibility, more opportunity to contribute to the family, and more opportunity to develop independence. A male oldest child, or first male child, is often viewed as a substitute father figure. When the husband-father is absent, the son is the "little man" in the family. However, problems may arise when father returns, and the son does not want to relinquish his position. Classical sex-role training also influences the degree of female-centeredness within the family since male children do not require "traditional" feminine models. Male sex-role training is more often occupation-directed, whereas female training involves contingency planning. Thus, the wife-mother is often less directly involved with the sex-role training of her sons, allowing her to sustain her female-centered role without reverting to a more "traditional" female pattern as would be necessary for daughters.

An explanation of the influence of married service time is based on the fact that as the length of married service time increases, a couple becomes more assimilated into the military culture. Those families or marriages which have found the military too stressful have either dissolved their marriages or left the military. In marriages of longer duration, children, if present, are usually beyond the infant stage and can assist the mother in family tasks. Thus, there is less necessity for the wife to revert to her "traditional" mother role. Families who have elected to remain in the military have learned to adjust to separations as a type of developmental task, best handled by a more female-centered family.

Recall that the relationship between separation and female-centeredness was significant only for the medium-rank category (captains and majors). In general, as military service time increases the serviceman's jobs often change and responsibility is increased. Lower ranking men and their families are less integrated into the military because of less service time, have usually experienced fewer separations, and are therefore less female-centered. Husbands of higher rank have more likely been transferred to administrative-type jobs which require less separation, decreasing female-centeredness in their families. However, men in the captain and major ranks are in the most mobile segment of their careers. They are the most deeply involved with their jobs, since they are being evaluated most critically by their superiors, and the most likely to experience separations. Thus, the wives of men in the middle ranks are the most likely to be affected by separation, and they tend to adjust by making their families more female-centered.

The effects of separation upon female-centeredness held, regardless of whether the husband was a regular or a reserve officer. Actually, the chance of separations is not very different for the two status categories. Thus, increasing female-centeredness in their families is more a function of other factors, rather than of the husband's status alone.

Positive career intent would seem to signify a greater degree of integration into the military as a way of life and could be expected to interact with female-centeredness and separation variables. Early integration of the husband necessitates integration of the wife and/or family, otherwise it would be unlikely that the couple or family would remain in the military after the period of original obligation. Those families who have experienced separation have learned to reallocate family roles to form a more functional family unit.

A final point—the subjective aspect of separation—should not be ignored. While statistical analyses may delineate the types and lengths of separation and their relationship to female-centeredness, they do not measure the degree of disruptiveness of the separation for the family. For example, not only are extended separations not necessarily the most disruptive type of separation, but the point in the family life cycle when the separation occurs may also influence its effect.

This is supported by comments from the respondents which revealed that for wives, the most disruptive separation lasted three months, while for mothers the most disruptive separation lasted 12 months. For 15.4 percent of the wives the most disruptive separation occurred in the United States, with the second greatest number of disruptive separations occurring in Southeast Asia or Korea. For mothers the reverse was true; 41.0 percent said that a Southeast Asian or Korean tour was the most disruptive, and 10.9 percent cited tours in the United States. The most disruptive separation as a wife was a nonhazardous assignment, while as a mother, the reverse was true with one-third of the men engaged in hazardous or combat duty during the most disruptive assignment. Thus, the subjective evaluations of the most disruptive separation varied greatly among the respondents. While this is not a statistically supported finding, it does show the variable influences of separation in the post-Vietnam period.

CONCLUDING COMMENT

In summary, a number of conclusions can be drawn from this study: (a) although separations are a normal part of military life, they have a disruptive effect on the family; (b) separations vary as to their length and type, but it is the first separation which has the greatest effect on the family, especially if it is an extended combat separation; (c) family separation is directly related to the degree of female-centeredness within the family; and (d) the relationship between experience of separation and female-centeredness is influenced by the presence of children, number of children, sex of the oldest child, married service time, rank of husband, status (regular/reserve), and career intent of husband.

14 Family Role Structure and Family Adjustment Following Prolonged Separation

Edna J. Hunter

Since 1972, the Center for Prisoner of War (POW) Studies in San Diego has been following longitudinally the process of adjustment to separation and reunion of the families of army, navy and Marine Corps POWs. This experience of family disruption, with its unprecedented length of husband-father absence, functionally necessitated a reshuffling of roles within each family, sometimes to the point of closing out the man's role completely during his long absence. It was through necessity that the wives had functioned independently as heads of households for up to eight or nine years, in some instances, developing behaviors during the husbands' absences which could have been expected to lessen the probability of successful reunions (Metres, McCubbin, and Hunter 1974). Over time the wives tended to modify their assessments of their marital satisfaction, indicating less satisfaction with the marriage immediately prior to the husbands' return than they retrospectively assessed them prior to casualty (McCubbin, Hunter, and Metres 1974). This reassessment often resulted in a new set of expectations with regard to their marriages by the time of homecoming. As reunion became imminent, it was not expected that one of the major concerns expressed by the wives during interviews with Center staff was the anticipated difficulty of their husbands' adjustment to the shifts in family roles which had occurred during the separation period (McCubbin, Hunter, and Dahl 1975).

Social role has been defined as the part played by an individual in a specific group situation where each person tends to occupy a functional position, and other members of the group tend to attach certain expectations to each member's behavior in the group. Within a family, marital conflicts arise whenever there is a failure to work out relationship rules or relatively stable roles that will be durable and equitable (Lederer and Jackson 1968), and conflict and tension arise whenever conflicting demands are imposed by the complex roles people assume as they interact with others.

Previous investigations have established that characteristics of the marriage partners, as well as family roles and structure, must be taken into account in trying to understand families' adjustment both to separation and reunion (Hill 1949; Webster, Hunter, and Palermo 1977). A recent study (Hunter and Phelan 1978) found that certain personality traits of these former prisoners of war are related both to the resistance stance they assumed during captivity and to the harsh treatment received at the hands of the captor. For example, when examined subsequent to release, the firm resister during captivity tended to test high on the personality traits of achievement, dominance, and endurance, and low on the trait of harm avoidance. The firm resisters were also more likely to be those men who received harsher treatment during captivity. Further, those who received harsher treatment scored higher on the personality traits, achievement, nurturance, and understanding, as measured by the Personality Research Form (Jackson 1967).

One would indeed expect the achievement-oriented, somewhat authoritarian, and extremely firmly resisting POW to relate to his family somewhat differently upon return from prolonged incarceration than the man who had demonstrated a more compliant resistance posture during captivity. The purpose of the study reported in this chapter is: (1) to examine family role structure, family adjustment, father-child relationships, and the personal adjustment of the POW after release; and (2) to relate the resistance posture assumed during captivity and the degree of harsh treatment received from his captor to various family variables.

METHODOLOGY

Since 1973, all navy and Marine Corps POWs returned from Southeast Asia have undergone extensive physical examinations annually at the Naval Aerospace Research Laboratory at Pensacola, Florida. At the time of the examinations, these men also completed self-report inventories, the Family Development Checklist (McCubbin et al. 1974-1975). Comparable self-reports were completed by their wives when personally interviewed by Center for Prisoner of War Studies' staff. From these reports, measures were obtained of the husbands' career adjustments, personal and family adjustments, and between-spouse agreements on the performance of a variety of family roles and tasks.

Analyses were carried out to explore these family and captivity factors (for example, family role structure, duration of captivity, harsh treatment, resistance posture) which might be related to personal and family adjustment subsequent to prolonged family separation.

Either the husbands' scores or the wives' scores could have been
selected as measures of personal, marital, father-child, or career
adjustment. For this study, however, the husbands' perceptions,
rather than the wives' perceptions, were used. It should be noted
that using the husbands' perceptions of adjustment can be expected
to result in somewhat different results than had wives' reports been
used. The wives' responses were discussed in an earlier study
reported by Webster, Hunter, and Palermo (1977). For example,
Webster and colleagues found that wives rated their marital satisfaction significantly lower than did their husbands. Moreover, with
respect to family roles, the earlier study also indicated the major
areas of disagreement between spouses centered around the performance of homemaker tasks and maintaining discipline of the children.
For husbands, but not for wives, discrepancy scores between spouses
on family role allocations were significantly related to marital adjustment (for example, larger discrepancies were associated with poorer
marital adjustment). For the wives, but not husbands, discrepancy
scores on disciplining children were significantly related to family
communication (for example, larger discrepancies were associated
with closed family communication). The differences between husbands' and wives' responses on who usually performed each family
role were also computed for the present study to obtain between-
spouse discrepancy scores for family role structure, that is, the
differences between husbands' and wives' perceptions as to which
spouse routinely performed specific family roles or tasks.

Research Instruments

    Five scales were constructed using items from the self-report
inventories to obtain measures of the POWs' personal adjustment,
perceived marital adjustment, father-child relationships, family
communication patterns (open versus closed), and their perceived
career adjustment. Items included in the Personal/Emotional Adjustment Scale, the Marital Adjustment Scale, the Father-Child Relationship Scale, and the Communication Scale were selected on the basis
of two criteria: (a) good face validity, and (b) their ability to discriminate (p ≤ .001) between families with above-average and below-
average scores on each dimension of adjustment, based upon ratings
of the families by skilled interviewers following two- to four-hour
in-depth personal interviews. Items for the Career Adjustment Scale
were selected solely on the basis of good face validity. Four-point
Likert-type items for the measure of Self-Esteem were selected on
the basis of face validity and were adapted from the Coopersmith
scales (1967).

Resistance posture during captivity was measured by the man's total score on the CPWS Resistance Stance Scale (Hunter et al. 1976), with higher scores indicating firmer resistance postures. The CPWS Resistance Stance Scale (RSS) provides an overall measure of resistance posture, as well as eight subscale measures of specific aspects of resistance.

The Harsh Treatment variable is a measure derived for each man using a composite of (a) the time spent in solitary confinement, (b) time in restraining devices, and (c) degree of mental and physical pressure by the captor as reported to the examining physician at homecoming (Metres et al. 1976).

A modified version of Hill's (1949) scales which were used in his classic World War II study of family adjustment to wartime separation and reunion were included to measure family Communication, the division of Family Roles, and the family's Agreement on Task Responsibilities.

The Sample

Fifty-two married former navy and Marine Corps POWs completed self-reports in 1974, one year after return. This particular subsample was comprised entirely of married men with intact families. These men had spent an average of 61.7 months in captivity. Mean age of the men at time of return was 35.4 years; they had completed 15.5 years of formal education; and had an average of 1.5 children per family. There were no significant differences between this sample and the total sample of married navy and Marine Corps POWs on basic demographic and captivity variables.

RESULTS

First we shall examine factors which were significantly correlated with the husbands' perceptions of their Personal/Emotional Adjustment, Marital Adjustment, Father-Child Relationships, and Career Adjustment. The question which we shall then attempt to answer is: How are these measures, as well as other factors (for example, Family Communication, Self-Esteem, Harsh Treatment by the captor), related to the particular resistance posture (firm versus compliant) assumed by the POW while in captivity?

Personal/Emotional Adjustment

The man's perception of his marital satisfaction and his level of self-esteem were both positively and significantly related to his

personal/emotional adjustment. His perception of his agreement
with his wife about who handles family finances, who advises and
teaches the children, and their agreement about his future career
plans, as well as their agreement on her having or not having a
career outside the home, were all factors which were significantly
related to the husband's perceived personal/emotional adjustment.
Family role structure—that is, who actually performs which role
regardless of feelings about who ought to perform the role—was also
highly related to husband's personal/emotional status. Where the
husband rated himself as better adjusted, the family tended to show
a more egalitarian role structure. Neither resistance posture nor
harsh treatment by captor was significantly related to the man's
personal/emotional adjustment, as he perceived it, one year subsequent to release (see Table 14.1).

Marital Adjustment

The variables which were highly correlated with the man's perceived marital adjustment one year following return included openness
of family communication, his level of self-esteem, and personal/
emotional adjustment, between-spouse agreement on his future career

TABLE 14.1

Variables Related to POW's Personal/
Emotional Adjustment One Year
Subsequent to Release

Variable	r	df^*	p
Marital adjustment	.40	48	.01
Self-esteem	.52	48	.001
Agreement on handling family finances	.54	47	.001
Agreement on advising and teaching children	.47	35	.001
Agreement on husband's future career plans	.48	46	.001
Agreement on wife having own career	.48	40	.01
Family role structure	.42	47	.01

*$N = 52$, but df varied because of missing data.
Source: Compiled by the author.

plans and on the various family tasks, roles, or philosophies, such as demonstration of affection and religious matters. The extremely high correlation (.71) between family communication and the man's perception of his marital adjustment reflects the importance of open communication on better marital adjustment. Also, it would appear that agreement or disagreement between spouses on "who does what" within the family is more important in explaining perceived marital adjustment than who actually performs each family role, as evidenced by the significant correlations between marital adjustment and spousal agreement on roles and the lack of significant relationships between marital adjustment and actual role structure within the family. In other words, it was not whether the family structure was traditional, egalitarian, or role reversed, but whether the marital partners agreed on the role relationships that determined the level of perceived marital happiness. There was no apparent relationship between marital adjustment and the resistance posture assumed by the man during captivity. (See Table 14.2.)

Father-Child Relationships

Factors highly correlated with the POW's perception of his relationship with his children one year following reunion, included the wife playing an important part in the family decision-making

TABLE 14.2

Variables Related to POW's Marital
Adjustment One Year Subsequent to Release

Variable	r	df*	p
Family communication	.71	48	.001
Self-esteem (husband)	.62	48	.001
Agreement on husband's future career plans	.65	46	.001
Agreement on demonstration of affection	.68	47	.001
Agreement on religious matters	.56	45	.001
Personal/emotional adjustment (husband)	.40	48	.01

*N = 52, but df varied due to missing data.
Source: Compiled by the author.

TABLE 14.3

Variables Related to POW's Relationship
with Children One Year Subsequent to Release

Variable	r	df*	p
Wife involved in decision-making	.48	37	.01
Agreement on demonstration on affection	.42	37	.01
Agreement on recreational matters	.44	37	.01
Between-spouse differences on who disciplined children	.48	37	.01

*N = 52, but df varied due to missing data.
Source: Compiled by the author.

process and agreement between spouses on demonstration of affection and recreational matters. Better father-child relationships were perceived by father where the family tended toward the more traditional structure—that is, the husband-father performed the stereotypic male roles, and the mother performed the more typically female-type tasks. When discrepancy scores were computed between husbands' and wives' responses on the self-reports, the largest discrepancies found for any specific family role were for the role of family disciplinarian. Further analyses showed that harsh treatment by captor was highly related to discrepant spousal perceptions as to which parent performed the role of disciplining the children. In other words, the harsher the treatment the man experienced at the hands of his captor during captivity, the more disagreement existed between the parents in the postreunion period about whose role it was to discipline the children (see Table 14.3).

POW's Career Adjustment

The variables which correlated highest with the former POW's perceived career adjustment one year subsequent to return were the marital partners' overall agreement on the performance of various family tasks, their agreement on demonstration of affection, matters of recreation, and the man's future career plans. Good father-child relations and high self-esteem for both the husband and the wife were

TABLE 14.4

Variables Related to POW's Perceived Career
Adjustment One Year Subsequent to Release

Variable	r	df*	p
Overall agreement on family tasks	.62	48	.001
Agreement on demonstration of affection	.60	48	.001
Agreement on recreational matters	.56	48	.001
Agreement on POW's future career plans	.53	48	.001
Good father–child relations	.60	37	.001
Self-esteem (husband)	.53	48	.001
Self-esteem (wife)	.60	48	.001

*N = 52; df varied due to missing data.
Source: Compiled by the author.

also associated with better career adjustment of the husband. Thus, it would appear that where both marital partners have high regard for themselves, and if they agree on "who does what," the man is also likely to perceive that he is doing well in his career one year after release from captivity. Also, if he believed he was doing well on the job, he also appeared to be relating well to his children. Resistance stance in captivity was not significantly related to perceived career adjustment, nor was harsh treatment in captivity related to later perceived career adjustment (see Table 14.4). Results indicated the firm resister tended to be the more authoritarian father, and his family reflected the more traditional sex roles for family members. Greater harsh treatment was related to a firmer resistance posture, and larger spousal differences in responses as to who performed specific family roles were found in those families where the husband had received harsher treatment by the captor during the separation period.

CONCLUSIONS

If between-spouse discrepancies with regard to the performance of family roles and tasks do indeed reflect the degree of family reintegration following prolonged family separation, then one may conclude that the extremely firm resisters were not reintegrating into the family as quickly as those who assumed more moderate resistance postures in captivity. However, we would not be able to conclude from the findings, based upon data collected one year subsequent to return, that there is any significant relationship between resistance behavior and the harshness of treatment received while in captivity and the man's subsequent career adjustment. Nor can we say that those two captivity variables (resistance posture and harsh treatment) are related to the man's level of personal/emotional adjustment at that particular point in time (one year postreunion).

Although this report has not focused on the wife's perception of her personal/emotional adjustment and perceived marital adjustment, perhaps it should be noted that measures derived from her responses on similar self-reports also indicated the absence of any definitive relationship between her husband's resistance behavior or the captor's harsh treatment of him and her perceptions of personal and marital adjustment (Webster, Hunter, and Palermo 1977). It would seem that the effects of those captivity variables are seen only in the areas of parent-child adjustment, where they are associated with higher levels of disagreement between parents regarding the discipline of the children.

Also, since we were dealing only with married POWs with still intact families following many years of family separation, we are unable to make any statements from these data about the subsequent personal and career adjustments of those former POWs who remained unmarried or of those who had experienced dissolution of marriage since return. It could very well be that captivity factors would take on added importance where the returning man was faced with the trauma of marital disruption, deprived of his father role, or was unsupported by satisfying close emotional relationships which could perhaps counteract problems with regard to his career, when and if they should arise. This is an issue yet to be examined in a future phase of the longitudinal study of former army, navy and Marine Corps POWs which is currently ongoing at the Center for Prisoner of War Studies.

15   Effects of Couple Communication Training on Traditional Sex-Role Stereotypes

Richard J. Brown, III

Concern about the present and future states of marriage in our society has led to a marked increase of interest in factors which may contribute to marital stability and growth. The major focus of marital adjustment today is interpersonal, rather than the adjustment to predesigned roles which was once the case (Bernard 1964). Roles are still important, but appear to be less significant than the interrelatedness of persons. An increasing emphasis upon interpersonal relatedness is required by an "open" structure in marriage (Rausch, Goodrich, and Campbell 1963). The following statement concerning the interrelatedness of marriage and family was written by a family therapist:

> . . . Going is the illusion that the rugged individual, or the tight nuclear family, or the aggressive corporation, or the powerful country, times n, could cut its swath forever, with solitary purpose and immunity. Our purposes are joint, juxtaposed, shared—all people, all creatures. Our having to face our relatedness to the physical systems of the planet may provide a model for confronting the complexity of the social environment, its massive interdependence (Napier 1972: 39).

If our traditional division of roles is no longer the predominant pattern among couples (Hurvitz 1960; Tharp 1963), then couples will need additional skills or "technologies" to deal effectively with the interpersonal marital model in which the primary goal is that of achieving personal happiness and interpersonal growth and fulfillment (Saxton 1968). Many couples lack these skills, especially in the area of communication. The importance of communication in developing an interpersonal marriage which can deal effectively with the new alternatives and expectations faced by couples was emphasized by O'Neill:

The real bridge that makes it possible for partners to
know and love one another in intimacy and to sustain a
relationship in depth and through time is the verbal one.
All marriage relationships must ultimately be distilled in
the crucible of words (O'Neill 1972: 108).

When something goes wrong in a social interaction system such
as marriage, the result is always disequilibrium, and this imbalance
must be dealt with if the system is to be preserved (Lennard and
Bernstein 1969). The importance of verbal communication in maintaining marital equilibrium was further developed by Bernard:

Interaction implies—indeed, consists of—communication.
Communication may be explicit or tacit. Explicit communication is usually verbal, although it may also use
other conventional symbols. . . . Explicit communication
is basic to any form of adjustment which seeks to persuade
or cajole or bargain (1964: 691).

These concerns point to a need for increased research in the
skills of dyadic communication, especially as they relate to role
expectation and interpersonal relatedness.

REVIEW OF THE LITERATURE ON
COMMUNICATION AND MARRIAGE

A number of research studies have been conducted relating communication to various aspects of marital adjustment and growth. One
such study found a positive relationship between the degree of affect
or feeling which is verbally communicated between married partners
and marital satisfaction (Levinger and Senn 1967). A second study,
focusing upon the relationship between communication and marital
adjustment, examined the hypothesis "that couples who make a good
or 'happy' marital adjustment are those whose communication skills
have been expanded to deal effectively with the problems inherent in
marriage" (Navran 1967: 174). He concluded that "communication
and marital adjustment are so commingled that any event having an
effect on one will have a similar effect on the other" (1967: 183).

Eastman (1958) found support for the hypothesis that marital
happiness is related positively to self-acceptance, as defined in
terms of congruent perception of self and ideal self. Luckey (1959)
evaluated the concepts of self and ideal self as relating to perceptions
of the spouse. In that study, two groups of couples comprised the
sample. One group was self-defined as satisfactorily married and

the other self-defined as unsatisfactorily married. Results indicated that satisfaction in marriage was related to the accuracy of the <u>wife's</u> perception of her husband's self-perception. Unexpectedly, marital satisfaction was not related to the accuracy of the <u>husband's</u> perception of the wife's self-perception. In an examination of the influence of several factors, one of which was communication styles, upon marital satisfaction during the first six years of marriage, Corrales (1974) concluded that the shaping of marital satisfaction is influenced equally by input from both husband and wife:

> Whereas some studies in the literature (for example, Luckey 1961) emphasized the wife's crucial input to marital satisfaction, these findings indicate that, at the interactional level, husband's input is equally crucial for marital satisfaction (1974: 237).

In an attempt to integrate role theory and self-theory, Mangus (1957) concluded that role theory and the self-theory of Carl Rogers are quite similar except for their emphasis. A close relationship exists between one's perception of self and one's perception of his or her marital role. There also appears to be a close relationship between how one views the mate and how one perceives the mate's marital role. Moreover, the accuracy of these perceptions seems to relate closely to the degree of satisfaction in the marriage. It has further been suggested that the accuracy of the perceptions is strongly influenced by the degree of communication skill practiced in the relationship (Mangus 1957).

PROGRAMS TO INCREASE MARITAL GROWTH AND ENRICHMENT

In recent years programs have been developed to assist marital growth and enrichment. David Mace, former Executive Director of the American Association of Marriage and Family Counselors, together with his wife, founded the Association of Couples for Marriage Enrichment (ACME). ACME is an international organization that offers growth-oriented experiences designed to support marital enrichment through contact with other couples who are also interested in marriage enrichment. The program is both a "support system" and a means of access to couple-oriented learning experiences (Mace and Mace 1974). A similar effort, the Conjugal Relationship Program (CRP), was designed by Bernard Guerney, Jr. (1964) to build upon the strengths already present in marital relationships. The major emphasis of the CRP program is to teach couples to reflect feelings.

Evaluations of the effectiveness of CRP which have been carried out using pretest-posttest designs indicated increased marital communication subsequent to participation in the program (Rappaport 1971; Collins 1971).

Still another communication program developed by Carl Clarke (1970), employs a six-session procedure designed to increase positive feedback between partners. Clarke (1970: 328) indicated that "Most couples experienced awareness of the other's feelings and a better understanding of the needs of the other" as outcomes of their participation in the sessions.

The Human Development Institute produced a programmed text designed to enhance couple communication which was evaluated by comparing it with both conjoint marital counseling and a nontreatment control group. Although marriage counseling appeared to be most effective in producing change, the communications program was evaluated as being more effective than no program or no treatment at all (Hickman and Baldwin 1971).

The above programs focused almost exclusively on communication in relationships, although many other programs have placed some emphasis upon communication skills. One such marriage enrichment program was reported by Hinkle and Moore (1971). The communication aspect was only one segment of the program, but the participants indicated it was the most helpful part. The communications emphasis was upon verbal and nonverbal communication, constructive expression of aggression, intimacy, and affection.

The Couple Communication Program

One of the most highly developed and widely used programs of marital communication is Couple Communication (CC), designed by Miller, Nunnally, and Wackman (1971). Originally entitled The Minnesota Couples Communication Program, CC was designed to intervene into intimate dyadic processes through the implementation of a full range of specific communication skills or behaviors. These skills are built into conceptual frameworks or perspectives which serve to give the couple a basic understanding of effective communication and the skills to recognize and correct dysfunctional communication. Since the emphasis in CC is upon learning specific communication skills, the program allows the partners to change their communication patterns in the directions they choose.

The Couple Communication (CC) program is a group of learning experiences involving five or six couples who meet together for four three-hour sessions over a four to six week period. Leadership is provided by instructors certified by Interpersonal Communications,

Inc. (the corporate name for the CC program). Couples are asked
to read <u>Alive and Aware</u> (Miller, Nunnally, and Wackman 1975), a
book prepared for use during the training program. Reading, lectures,
discussions, and exercises teach a variety of specific communication
skills. The entire format is structured and designed toward the
acquisition of these skills. All participatory aspects of the program
are voluntary. A common framework is provided by the handbook
and short lectures to help couples understand and choose effective
communication patterns.

Several evaluative studies have been conducted with the CC program. Campbell (1974) found the CC training to be significantly
effective in increasing self-disclosure between married partners
during their child-rearing years.

The CC training has also been found to be effective in increasing
verbal work skills among engaged couples between pretest and posttest measures prior to their marriage (Miller 1971). Work skills
are defined as the ability to express personal thoughts and feelings
and to move to a mutual understanding of those thoughts and feelings.
There is strong support for the hypothesis that open communication
styles have a positive influence on marital satisfaction (Corrales
1974).

The Growth Group Program

Although the CC program focuses upon specific communication
skills, other programs promoting marriage growth are more broadly
oriented. One such program is the Growth Group (GG) model sponsored by the Association of Couples for Marriage Enrichment. Marriage enrichment growth groups are unstructured groups of five or
six couples that meet about two hours weekly for six to eight weeks.
All participation is voluntary, and the couples are encouraged to
share from their own experiences rather than opinions or theoretical
formulations. Couples are also encouraged to talk as much as possible with each other about concerns related to their marriage, instead
of talking "to the group." Counseling type interpretations and probing
are not allowed, and the facilitator couple functions as any other
couple in the group except where necessary to maintain the guidelines
or schedule (Mace and Mace 1974).

Studies of Sex Stereotypes

During the past decade, the questions raised by the feminist
movement have led to a renewed interest in the study of sex stereo-

types. It could be theorized that women, as well as men, have been seen and treated stereotypically rather than as persons with individual traits and characteristics. A variety of studies have attempted to define sex-role stereotypes (Rosenkrantz et al. 1968; Spence, Helmreich, and Stapp 1974; Williams and Bennett 1975). Various methods were used, but the Williams and Bennett study was the only one to employ a previously standardized instrument, the Gough Adjective Check List (ACL, Gough and Heilbrun 1965). Using college students as subjects, the Williams and Bennett study established a hypothetical male stereotype and a hypothetical female stereotype. The effects of couple communication training upon a variety of factors within dyadic relationships have been examined by a number of investigators (Miller 1971; Nunnally 1971; Corrales 1974; Larsen 1974).

Couple communication training appears to result in a better balance in communication, and this improved balance seems to be the result of changed perceptions of each other by the couple in relation to sex-stereotype roles (Campbell 1974). Thus, the manner in which marriage partners view themselves and their spouses in relation to the ACL sex stereotype can be used as a measure of self and spouse perception in this specific area.

THE STUDY

Since communication has been shown to be related to marital adjustment and satisfaction in various ways, it was decided to study the communication variable in relation to changes in sex stereotype perceptions subsequent to Couple Communication training.

The hypotheses tested were threefold: (a) that both self and spouse perceptions of sex stereotypes will significantly decrease following the Couple Communication workshop; (b) that there will be some decrease in the self and spouse perceptions of sex stereotypes following participation in a Growth Group, but the change will not be as great as for the couple communication training; and (c) that the decrease in the control couples' perceptions of each other in terms of sex stereotypes will be less than that observed in the Couple Communication training group or the Growth Group.

Subjects

Experimental subjects were twenty married couples engaged in Couple Communication (CC) workshops. Control subjects composed two groups. The first control group was 20 married couples engaged in marriage enrichment Growth Groups (GG), and the second control group consisted of 20 married couples not engaged in any educational or marriage-oriented group experience (NG) during the six to eight week duration of their participation in the study. They did, however, have some interest in marriage enrichment since they were involved in ACME. The subjects were predominately white, middle-class adults from 25 to 55 years of age.

Task and Materials

Materials used were the <u>Gough Adjective Check List</u> (ACL) and an individual information form which requested basic personal and demographic information.

The ACL consists of 300 alphabetically arranged adjectives, has 24 scales, and may be used either as an individual instrument or as a group instrument. Completion of the instrument takes approximately ten to fifteen minutes and does not usually arouse anxiety or resistance. The instrument is useful in determining how a person perceives himself or another person.

The ACL also provides information regarding behavioral tendencies and is a useful instrument, not only for diagnostic and counseling purposes, but also for research purposes. In recent years the ACL has been used with increasing frequency in behavioral research, as it is able to yield a unique picture of an individual's self-image because it presents an extensive list of adjectives routinely used in daily life.

Procedure

At the first group meeting, each person was asked to complete two ACLs. On the first form they were asked to choose the adjectives which they considered to be self-descriptive, and on the second form to choose the adjectives which they considered to be descriptive of their spouse.

At the close of the last meeting of the Couples Communications training each person was again asked to complete two ACLs, one for self and one for spouse. Subjects were told that this research was being carried out in an attempt to study the effectiveness of the communication program. No reference was made to sex roles or sex stereotypes.

The same procedure was followed with couples in the Growth Group condition, with the exception that they were told that the research was being carried out in an attempt to study the effectiveness of growth groups in marriage enrichment.

The couples in the nongroup condition were not engaged in any type of growth or educational group for the six to eight week period between the pretest and posttest administrations. These couples were randomly selected from ACME members, and they completed the pre- and post-ACLs at regular ACME meetings.

Analysis of Data

Data consisted of prescores and postscores obtained on the 24 scales of the ACL and scores on the sex-stereotype scale designed by Williams and Bennett (1975). Age, sex, years married, whether or not previously married, number, age, and sex of children, and occupation were also available for each subject. The relationship between the various treatments and the sex-stereotype perceptions was analyzed using a 3 (Couple Communication training, Growth Group, and No Treatment) $\times$ 2 (self-perception, spouse perception) analysis of variance.

Negative and positive change scores on the ACL sex-stereotype scale (Williams and Bennett 1975) on each subject were derived by subtracting pretest scores from posttest scores so that a negative number indicated a less stereotypic score for the individual on that particular rating. In other words, a negative change score indicated a lower number of stereotypic adjectives marked on posttest than pretest.

Findings

When looking at the CC, GG, and NG groups without regard to sex, there was a significant difference between the three groups on self-perception, $F (2, 114) = 3.67$, $p < .05$. There were no significant differences between the means of the three groups on spouse perception.

When the means of all three groups were compared for self-perception and spouse perception, the greatest changes were found, in the direction of less stereotypic perceptions, among the CC group. Within that group, the more egalitarian change was on self-perception (see Table 15.1). With respect to changes in self-perception, females changed more than males (see Table 15.2).

Note also that in all groups, the female ratings of self and spouse changed more than the ratings of males (see Table 15.3). Moreover, the CC females changed more than the females in the other two groups (see Table 15.4). When means on self- and spouse scores for the CC, GG, and NG groups were compared using the $\underline{t}$ test, a significant

TABLE 15.1

Mean Differences by Group and Change
in Sex-Role Perception

		$\bar{X}$	s.d.
Couple communication group	Self	-1.17	3.44
	Spouse	-.45	2.43
Growth group	Self	.55	2.52
	Spouse	.50	4.16
Nongroup	Self	.07	2.71
	Spouse	.45	2.98

Source: Compiled by the author.

TABLE 15.2

Mean Differences by Sex of Rater and
Change in Sex-Role Perception

		$\bar{X}$	s.d.
Males	Self	.15	2.65
	Spouse	-.33	3.51
Females	Self	-.48	3.28
	Spouse	.25	3.44

Source: Compiled by the author.

TABLE 15.3

Mean Differences by Sex of
Rater and Sex-Role Perception

		$\overline{X}$	s.d.
Males	Self	.15	2.65
	Spouse	.25	3.44
Females	Self	-.48	3.28
	Spouse	-.33	3.51

Source: Compiled by the author.

TABLE 15.4

Mean Change in Sex-Role Perception as a
Function of Group and Sex of Rater

Group	Sex	Rating of Self		Rating of Spouse	
		$\overline{X}$	s.d.	$\overline{X}$	s.d.
CC	Male	-.70	2.61	.40	2.56
	Female	-1.65	4.14	-1.25	1.99
GG	Male	.95	2.56	.25	4.82
	Female	.15	2.47	.25	4.59
NG	Male	.20	2.64	.00	2.67
	Female	-.05	2.83	.90	3.24

Source: Compiled by the author.

difference was found only between the CC and GG self-scores (t = 2.44, p < .05).

DISCUSSION AND CONCLUSIONS

The conclusions of this study were compatible with the subjective data gathered from reports and observations of couples participating in CC training. The findings showed that Couple Communication training had some effect upon how couples saw themselves and each other in regard to sex stereotypes. The greatest change following CC training occurred in perception of self. There was no statistically significant change in spouse perceptions following CC training (p < .06). This study supports the use of CC training as a resource in enriching marital relationships if one accepts the position that the more egalitarian the self- and spouse perceptions of husband and wife, the more they will communicate with each other as persons, rather than as sex stereotypes.

It was hypothesized that the Growth Group couples would move in a more egalitarian direction, that is, less stereotypic, but would not experience as great a change in that direction as the CC couples. This was not supported by the data. In fact, the GG participants become more stereotypic than the NG participants (those with no training). One possible explanation could be the nature of the GG experience compared with CC. The Growth Group is a considerably less structured group in which couples are encouraged to become more aware of and open about issues which are most often relevant to marital growth. Through identifying with the concerns of other couples and experimenting with more open behavior in relation to each other, partners perhaps gain a more accurate assessment of self and spouse. Although these new perceptions may be more stereotypic, they may also be a more accurate picture of how the partners are actually relating to one another at that time. It should be noted that it is not the primary intent of GG to teach new communication behavior. On the other hand, CC is highly structured, and its major goal is to teach specific skills which will facilitate not only new and clearer perceptions of self and spouse, but also improve patterns of communication.

The major questions raised by the results center around the differences between groups. What actually transpires in Couple Communication groups that does not occur in Growth Groups? What are the salient differences between the two marriage enrichment experiences? Future studies of the effects of CC training upon changes in sex-stereotypic perceptions of husbands and wives should perhaps concentrate upon isolating or emphasizing the various components within CC to determine which were most responsible for the results found in this study. The greater change among females overall suggests the need for further research on sex differences in responsiveness to marriage enrichment experiences.

PART V

ADAPTATION TO CHANGE

". . . the provision of more services will not, in itself, solve the problem of failure to reach high-risk families . . . efforts might be better directed toward the provision of information systems which would increase the awareness of services, thus enabling those most vulnerable to take advantage of available service support systems."

Edwin W. Van Vranken and
Dorothy M. Benson

16

Family Awareness and Perceived Helpfulness of Community Supports

Edwin W. Van Vranken
Dorothy M. Benson

Increasingly, military organizational efforts are being directed toward service support systems which address the specific needs of the families of military members. There presently exists at most military installations a vast array of social, health, maintenance, and educational services available exclusively for the use of members of the military community and their immediate families. Experience has shown that failure to provide these family support services results in significant, often hidden, costs to organizational effectiveness. Retention rates, physical and social health, productivity, and general career satisfaction are often directly related to the service member's satisfaction with the support systems available to him and his family (see Chapter Two). The underlying issue is no longer whether the military organization has a responsibility to provide family support services, but rather, what should be the extent of these services, which methods of service delivery most adequately meet the needs of the military family, and how does the military family perceive existing services (Bennett et al. 1974).

One area of service delivery which is presently receiving increased attention is that of the adequacy of existing support systems which are designed to assist with the specialized needs of military families during those periods when the husband-father is away from home for an extended period such as prolonged training maneuvers, ship deployments, or unaccompanied overseas assignments.

Research conducted on the impact of prolonged separation on the family members of prisoners of war and of servicemen missing or killed-in-action suggests that the coping-with-separation repertoires of some families are more refined and extensive than the

The authors acknowledge the significant contributions of Dr. Hamilton McCubbin, University of Minnesota, and Mr. Gary Lester, Naval Health Research Center.

repertoires of other families during father absence but can, nonetheless, be minimized by the extension of a variety of family support services (McCubbin and Dahl 1974).

Military organizations, by their very nature, produce some degree of inconvenience for the serviceman and his family. Requirements for military readiness and the attendant need for training and preparedness exercises will continue to require the occasional separation of the military member from his or her family. The nature of the problem of military separation and the number of people affected by these separations is not expected to diminish in the near future. Assuming then that these occasional separations will continue to occur, it seems reasonable to address measures designed to prevent social and emotional dysfunctioning within families during these periods. First, it would seem reasonable to assume that the military effectiveness of servicemen separated from their families could be enhanced if they were assured that during their absences their families would have access to all necessary support systems. Secondly, the stress experienced by the family members who are left behind could be minimized, if not alleviated, by the availability of support services.

A conceptual model which interrelates an individual's awareness of social supports with increased adaptability and improved coping abilities in the face of stress has been advanced by Sidney Cobb (1976). He argues persuasively that social support, defined as information leading the individual or family to believe that they are cared for, esteemed, and members of a network of mutual obligation, is supportive and can protect people in crises from a wide variety of pathological states.

It seems reasonable to generalize from this evidence that the military wife and family unit would be better able to manage the stresses of separation if they were aware of one or more of the basic types of social supports available in their community. Using Cobbs' framework, these social supports would include: (1) information leading the wife and family to believe that they are cared for and loved; (2) information leading them to believe that they are esteemed and valued; and (3) information leading the wife and family to believe that they belong to a social network of communication and mutual obligation (Cobb 1976: 300).

Within the framework of this study of family coping and adaptation to the stresses of family separation, it is this third type of social supports that has been examined. The relevant information or belief that the wife is a member of a social network which includes communication and mutual obligation can be further clarified and broken down into two subelements. The first is an awareness of goods and services that are available on demand, including information about the accessibility of services that are occasionally needed, for example, specialized skills such as counseling services and technical information such as procedures for processing CHAMPUS claims. The second subelement is that of information that is common and shared with respect to the dangers of life and the procedures for mutual defense. For example, the knowledge that a competent dispensary staff is available for health care or that a wives' group or friendly neighbor is readily accessible for support if needed, is socially supportive.

Thus, it would appear that a military family's adaptability to the stresses of separation will be enhanced by a greater awareness of social supports available to them. How aware are families of available community supports? To what degree do they perceive the supports as being of potential value to them? Considering the variability in awareness and perceived value of specific supports across families, is it possible to isolate those characteristics of "families at risk" who appear to be less aware of community supports and who perceive available supports as being of little potential helpfulness?

In order to achieve greater understanding of the attitudes, awareness, and perceived helpfulness of community support programs, the study reported in this chapter examined the relationship of these variables to selected formal and informal support systems available in both the military and civilian communities.

For those readers unfamiliar with the military community, it should be noted that as in civilian communities, the military community has developed a variety of support systems designed to contribute both to individual and family stability. The vast array of health, welfare, recreation, and educational services underscores the military's recognition of the importance of the family. Janowitz noted that "the military community has been literally converted into an advanced form of a welfare and social service state" (1960: 175-76). As with civilian communities, however, the extent to which these services are developed frequently depends on the need and/or demand for services.

Also, as with their civilian counterparts, military communities provide a variety of structured, formal support services to military members and families. These service providers include the physicians, chaplains, lawyers, family service officers, and mental health professionals. These individuals are professionally trained and are usually members of the military community themselves. There also exists on most military installations a group of nonmilitary, formal support organizations whose primary function is to support the members of the military community. Organizations such as the Navy Relief Society, the American Red Cross, banks, and credit unions are examples of these formal, nonmilitary support systems.

Civilian communities provide similar formal support systems, either through professional practitioners such as physicians, lawyers, and so on or by way of more formalized organizations such as churches, legal aid societies, law enforcement agencies, family service programs, and welfare agencies.

Informal support systems also exist in both the civilian and military communities and include friends, relatives, neighbors, social and religious organizations, and wives' groups. The informal social network of families is believed to provide a major supportive influence in times of stress. This is especially true for the military community where it has long been recognized that mutual help is a time-honored tradition.

The primary focus of this research project was the identification of significant relationships between selected demographic, family, and adjustment variables and three indices of social support accessibility: (1) the wife's awareness of, or familiarity with, selected formal military support systems, informal military support systems, and civilian support services that might assist them with problem resolution; (2) the wife's estimation of how helpful these selected informal military, formal military, and civilian support programs might be in assisting with problems; and (3) the wife's reluctance to use professional help and services in times of stress.

METHOD

Subjects

Data for this study were obtained as one part of a larger more comprehensive investigation of family adjustment to separation. The 82 families included in the study were randomly selected from the complete roster of married naval personnel attached to attack and fighter squadrons scheduled for an eight-month tour aboard a carrier to be deployed to the Western Pacific. The families were drawn from two types of military communities: (1) an "open" military community in which families were an integral part of both an urban civilian and a military subculture and who were not dependent primarily upon the military community for their social and physical support; and (2) a "closed" military community in which families were physically located in a limited, somewhat rural area and were primarily dependent upon the military community for their social and physical support.

The sample of families were nearly equally distributed between the two communities with a slight majority (54.9 percent) of the families being based in the closed or rural community. A slight

majority (53.7 percent) of the husbands of the respondents were of
enlisted rank, and the remaining 46.4 percent were of officer rank.
Wives in the sample averaged 29 years of age with 13.5 years of
formal education at the time of the first contact with the research
team. The majority of the families (78 percent) had one or more
children, with an average of two children per family. The length of
marriage averaged 7.5 years. Twenty-eight percent had never experienced an unaccompanied tour and 17 percent had experienced
one previous separation. Most of the families (55 percent), however,
had experienced two or more previous separations.

Instruments

Data were collected from wives during the two- to three-month
period preceding the ship's scheduled deployment. Structured family
interviews and self-report questionnaires comprised the protocol.
Of particular interest to this portion of the study were three scales
which were developed to measure the dependent variables of awareness, helpfulness, and reluctance as related to community support
services. The "Awareness of Services" scale measures an individual's familiarity with how various formal and informal resources
available within the military or civilian community can assist with
various problems. The "Assessment of Helpfulness" scale provides
an estimation of how helpful each of the services available in the
military and civilian community might be for an individual in assisting with various problem situations. Finally, the "Reluctance" scale
measures an individual's reluctance to avail herself of professional
help and services. It should be noted that this latter measure was
used as both a dependent and an independent variable in analyzing
the data.

Procedure

In order to determine what, if any, relationship existed between
awareness, perceived helpfulness, and reluctance to use community
supports, three sets of demographic variables were examined:
I. Wife's Background Characteristics: (1) Location (open vs. closed
community), (2) rank of husband (officer vs. enlisted), (3) husband's
career intention, (4) wife's level of education, (5) length of time as
a military dependent; II. Family Characteristics: (6) number of
children, (7) family developmental stage, (8) length of marriage;
III. Wife's Adjustment Factors: (9) wife's feelings about life in the
military, (10) anticipation of hardships as result of husband's depar-

ture, (11) number of preparations for separation, (12) wife's reluctance to utilize services were the need to arise.

Analysis

Distribution tables by frequency and percentage have been utilized to denote levels of awareness of support services and assessments of helpfulness of services. In order to establish the degree of relationship between the independent demographic variables and the dependent variables of indexes of social support accessibility (awareness, helpfulness, and reluctance), Pearson product-moment correlations were calculated. This procedure permitted the identification and elimination of those variables having little or no relationship to the dependent variables.

RESULTS

Awareness of Services

Results showed that 40 percent of the sample wives reported having "no knowledge" of how the selected informal military resources could assist them. Over half (57 percent) of the wives reported "no knowledge" of how the selected formal military services could assist them, and almost 70 percent claimed "no knowledge" of how the selected civilian resources could assist them. At the other end of the awareness continuum, none of the sample reported having "extensive knowledge" of how either civilian resources or formal military services could help them. Only 12 percent of the wives reported "extensive knowledge" of how informal military resources, such as friends, neighbors, wives' clubs, and so on could be of assistance or a resource for help (see Table 16.1).

Significant, positive first-order correlations were found between awareness of help available from informal military services and the demographic variables of husband's rank (officer), husband's career intention, wife's education, her feelings about the military, and the preparations made for separation. Significant negative correlations existed between awareness and the husbands rank (enlisted), the wife's anticipation of hardship during the separation, and her reluctance to use service supports (see Table 16.2).

Awareness of help available from formal military services was positively correlated with those wives whose husbands were career-motivated, had been in the military longer, had more children at home, had achieved a more mature stage of family development, and

TABLE 16.1

Awareness of Family Supports

Awareness of Resources	Informal Military f(percent)	Formal Military f(percent)	Civilian f(percent)
No knowledge	33	47	57
	(40.2)	(57.3)	(69.5)
Some knowledge	39	35	25
	(47.6)	(42.7)	(30.5)
Extensive knowledge	10	0	0
	(12.2)	(0)	(0)
	82	82	82
	(100)	(100)	(100)

Source: Compiled by the author.

had been married longer. This group also had more positive feelings about life in the military and had made more preparations for the separation. Only one variable, reluctance to avail oneself of services, was negatively correlated with awareness of help available from formal military services (see Table 16.2).

Awareness of how civilian resources might help was also found to be positively correlated with the length of the marriage, preparations made for separation, and wife's feelings about life in the military. As might be expected, it was found that a negative correlation existed between a wife's awareness of how civilian resources might help and the reluctance to use helping services.

Assessment of Helpfulness

An analysis of the scale which provided an estimation of how helpful each of the selected military and civilian resources might be provided several noteworthy results (see Table 16.3).

The majority of the sample perceived all available supports as helpful. Approximately 85 percent of the sample wives felt that both informal military and formal military supports were "helpful," while almost 99 percent viewed civilian supports and either "helpful" and "very helpful."

TABLE 16.2

Significant First-Order Correlations between Demographic Variables and Service Awareness

Demographic Variables	Awareness of Services		
	Informal Military	Formal Military	Civilian
Wife's Background			
Open (vs. closed) community	NS	NS	NS
Officer (vs. enlisted) husband	.73**	NS	NS
Career intention	.29*	.23*	NS
Education	.35**	NS	NS
Time with military	NS	.28*	NS
Family Characteristics			
No. of children at home	NS	.25*	NS
Family developmental stage	NS	.25*	NS
Length of marriage	NS	.25*	.21*
Wife's Adjustment Factors			
Feelings about military	.39**	.49**	.31**
Anticipating hardships of separation	-.39**	NS	NS
Preparations for separation	.47**	.36**	.42**
Reluctance to use	-.39**	-.32**	-.33**

* = p < .05.
** = p < .01.
Sources: Compiled by the author.

216

TABLE 16.3

Perceived Value (Helpfulness) of
Family Supports

Assessment	Informal Military f(percent)	Formal Military f(percent)	Civilian f(percent)
Very helpful	4 (5.0)	13 (15.9)	8 (9.8)
Helpful	65 (81.3)	58 (70.7)	73 (89.0)
Not helpful	11 (13.7)	11 (13.4)	1 (1.2)
	80 (100)	82 (100)	82 (100)

Source: Compiled by the author.

The significant first-order correlations between estimation of helpfulness of informal military services and the demographic variables were: The estimation of helpfulness was positively correlated with the husband's rank (officer), the wife's higher level of education, and her positive feelings about life in the military (see Table 16.4).

Only one significant correlation was found between "estimated helpfulness of formal military services" and the various demographic variable; that is, the wife's feelings about life in the military was significantly correlated with helpfulness. Estimated helpfulness of civilian resources was found to be significantly correlated with those wives who were better educated and whose husbands were of officer rank.

Reluctance to Use Services

The final dependent variable to be examined was that of reluctance to use services. This measure of a wife's reluctance to avail herself of professional help or services was found to be negatively correlated with the wive's level of education and her preparations for separation. It was also negatively correlated with the wife's feelings about the military and the husband's officer rank. A significant positive correlation was found between reluctance to avail oneself of services and the anticipated hardship of separation (see Table 16.5).

TABLE 16.4

Significant First-Order Correlations between Demographic Variables and Perceived Helpfulness

Demographic Variables	Perceived Helpfulness		
	Informal Military	Formal Military	Civilian
Wife's Background			
Open (vs. closed) community	NS	NS	.23*
Officer (vs. enlisted) husband	.39**	NS	NS
Career intention	NS	NS	NS
Education	.34**	NS	.28**
Time with military	NS	NS	NS
Family Characteristics			
No. of children at home	NS	NS	NS
Family developmental stage	NS	NS	NS
Length of marriage	NS	NS	NS
Wife's Adjustment Factors			
Feelings about military	.32**	.28**	NS
Anticipated hardships of separation	NS	NS	NS
Preparations for separation	NS	NS	NS
Reluctance to use	-.36**	NS	NS

* = $p < .05$.
** = $p < .01$.
Source: Compiled by the author.

TABLE 16.5

Significant First-Order Correlations between
Demographic Variables and Reluctance to Use

Demographic Variables	Reluctance to Utilize Resources (N = 82)
Wife's Background	
Open community	NS
Closed community	NS
Officer husband	-.26*
Enlisted husband	.26*
Career intention	NS
Education	-.34**
Time with military	NS
Family Characteristics	
No. of children at home	NS
Family Developmental stage	NS
Length of marriage	NS
Wife's Adjustment Factors	
Feelings about military	-.29**
Anticipated hardships of separation	.34**
Preparations for separation	-.35**

* = p < .05.
** = p < .01
Source: Compiled by the author.

DISCUSSION

The focus of this study was to discover relationships which exist
between selected demographic, family, and adjustment factors and
the awareness, estimated helpfulness, and reluctance of military
wives to use available support systems. Specifically identified were
those systems which may be labeled as informal military supports,
formal military supports, and civilian supports. Using Cobb's (1976)
conceptual framework, it would seem reasonable to assume that if
a wife and family possess information which leads them to believe
that they belong to a social network, either military or civilian,
which makes available to them goods and services on demand and
information regarding procedures for mutual obligation and support,
they will be better able to manage the stresses of separation. To

examine the issue of available information and the perceived availability of services and supports, we tapped a sample of military families who were about to undergo a routine military separation to determine their awareness of available resources, their estimation of helpfulness, and their reluctance to use these service resources.

Findings suggest that although a majority of these wives had some knowledge of the type of help available from informal military resources, their knowledge of formal military services or civilian services was extremely limited. A significant number of families had no knowledge of the types of help available to them from either formal military services or from civilian resources. This finding suggests that important information regarding what services are available to assist in dealing with personal and family problems is lacking in a vast majority of military families. This is especially important if we consider "extensive knowledge" of available resources as being a desirable level of awareness for families facing the stress of separation.

Results also indicated that awareness of informal military resources was higher where the woman was the wife of an officer who was career-oriented, was better educated, and had positive feelings about life in the military. Typically, then, it would appear then that it is the career officer's wife, who is typically traditionally involved in numerous informal military activities, who may show high awareness of informal military resources.

Awareness of help available from formal military support programs tended to be associated with length of time in the military system and career orientation, regardless of rank. It is conceivable that length of time in the military and the attendant exposure to the military's formal services contributes to our findings of increased awareness for this group.

Analysis of the data regarding estimated helpfulness of available supports suggests that the majority of these wives perceived the supports as being either "helpful" or "very helpful." Caution must be exercised in the interpretation of these findings, however, given the extremely low level of knowledge regarding available resources. While further exploration of this phenomenon is indicated, it is possible that the positive responses were based on "expected value" rather than on a knowledge of what was actually available.

Perceived helpfulness of informal military services was found to be significantly associated with those characteristics most often found in the wife of the career officer. Again, it is possible that the officer's wife's involvement in informal military activities influences her perceived helpfulness of these resources.

Reluctance to avail oneself of available services was associated with those wives with less education, wives who had more negative feelings about life in the military, wives of enlisted personnel, and those wives who made fewer preparations for the separation.

If one were to generalize from the data obtained in this study, it would appear there exists a serious deficit among military wives in the awareness and knowledge of resource availability. This deficit in awareness could have considerable impact on families' abilities to manage the stresses of separation because they do not know where to turn for support. Again, using Cobb's framework, a family's lack of awareness could impact on its belief that it is cared for, appreciated, and valued—all factors related to coping and, according to Cobb, a source of protection from a variety of pathological states.

The data, although preliminary, also lend themselves to the development of hypotheses that those wives whose husbands were not yet career-oriented, who had been in the military a shorter period of time, and who were less committed to the military life style could benefit from an intensive educational effort directed toward improving awareness of available supports, thereby improving coping repertoires. This is especially important for first-term enlisted wives.

There is little question that the vulnerability of military families during separation could be partially offset by the availability of support systems. There exists, however, a growing body of information (Allen 1972; Bevilacqua 1967; Spellman 1965) which supports the findings that a definite relationship exists between awareness of resources, perceived social cost of service utilization (reluctance), and such factors as rank, education, age, and length of service. Therefore, the provision of more services will not, in itself, solve the problem of failure to reach high-risk families. It would appear that efforts might be better directed toward the provision of information systems which would increase the awareness of services, thus enabling those most vulnerable to take advantage of available service support systems.

17 Drinking and the Military Wife: A Study of Married Women in Overseas Base Communities

Gerald R. Garrett, • Betty Parker, • Suzan Day,
Jacquelyn J. Van Meter, • Wayne Cosby

Substantial attention by both military and civilian researchers has been given to the drinking behavior and misbehavior of men in all branches of the armed forces.* In contrast, comparatively little is known about the drinking behavior of their spouses. Reports (Subcommittee on Drug Abuse in the Military Services 1972) from hospital and mental health sources, psychiatric and counseling personnel, social actions officers, as well as occasional "human interest" articles by journalists (Druyor 1973; Lester 1975) provide some evidence which suggests that the rate of drinking pathologies among service wives is rapidly increasing. Yet, to date there is little available information on either the incidence of drinking pathologies or the characteristics of drinking behavior of women married to men in the military services.

The paucity of published research on the drinking of military wives is somewhat surprising, because there has for some years been an increasing amount of attention in research to the drinking, alcohol problems, and education and prevention programs of women in civilian populations (Garrett 1970, 1973; Gomberg 1974; Sandmaier 1975; Bahr and Garrett 1976). Furthermore, there is at present a heightened concern in all branches of the military services over alcohol abuse (Comptroller General 1976). This is evidenced by widespread publicity campaigns on the warning signs of incipient alcoholism, alcohol education and treatment programs, and an impressive array of newspaper and periodical articles on the social and personal problems associated with alcohol addiction, all of which

*For example, see Moore 1942; Harrison 1944; Monsour 1948; Subcommittee on Alcoholism and Narcotics 1970, 1971; Subcommittee on Drug Abuse in the Military Services 1972, 1973; Carman 1968; Pendergast, Preble, and Tennant 1973; Tennant 1974; and Goodwin, David, and Robins 1975.

have been directed specifically to a military audience.* Nevertheless, despite a current emphasis on prevention and treatment of alcohol problems in the armed forces, service wives seem to have largely escaped the attention of research investigators.

Although inattention to drinking by service wives no doubt reflects a longstanding research bias in favor of the military man, the problem of studying drinking and deviant drinking among these women is not altogether a simple one. For one thing, previous studies on civilian populations clearly show that women with drinking problems are generally more likely than men to remain "hidden drinkers," especially when their role is confined to that of housewife (Garrett 1970, 1973; Gomberg 1974; Bahr and Garrett 1976). For the heavy, or problem-drinking service wife, however, this pattern may be even more common than in the civilian population. Lester (1975), for example, cites the case of a military wife whose drinking was hidden during the early stages of her alcoholism because it was necessary to protect her husband's career in the navy. Yet, even after hidden drinking is discovered by the spouse, it is not uncommon to ignore the problem until it reaches a crisis level.†

But, if alcoholic military wives as a respondent population are difficult to locate for research purposes, so, too, are there potential obstacles in gathering information on the drinking practices and characteristics of nonalcoholic wives in the military. As one wife of an air force captain explains: "My husband's career, and my personal reputation as well, are the most important things in my life, and I'm not about to volunteer information to the air force about our lives that could damage our goals, particularly his career. In civilian life, it would be different; I'd have nothing to lose." Nevertheless, while even nonalcoholic service wives are often reluctant to provide information about something so personal as their drinking practices, they offer important clues about the attributes of a military life style and subculture which may be linked to alcohol abuse in a military setting, as well as useful information for promoting prevention programs.

---

*An especially good example of this type of journalism can be found in a newspaper series by Hoyer et al. 1976.

†Lester (1975) also cites the case of Eleanor, which is an excellent example of the effects of an alcoholic wife on the career of a navy man. It exemplifies a "typical" progression of alcoholic symptoms, deterioration of family relationships, and how the burden of an alcoholic spouse necessarily influences the job performance and career ambitions.

This chapter examines the drinking patterns and practices of married women dependents living in five overseas housing areas as an attempt to overcome the lack of available data and incomplete knowledge on the alcohol consumption patterns of military wives. Attention is given to: (1) assessing the extent of drinking and deviant drinking; (2) the characteristics of families living in overseas military housing; (3) respondents' perceptions of the role of drinking in military life; and (4) factors which are seen as promoting heavy and problem drinking. The research setting is a particularly interesting one, for there is some evidence suggesting that military life in overseas bases tends to increase alcohol consumption and presumably promotes a higher risk of alcohol abuse (Subcommittee on Alcoholism and Narcotics 1971).

METHODS

Data for this study were collected over a three-month period from five samples (n = 261) of dependent wives living in army and air force base-housing communities in Europe. Though conducted with the approval of the base commanders, field workers who contacted sample respondents emphasized that the study was neither sponsored nor funded by military organizations.

Research Setting

The housing communities selected as the research sites were located in two adjoining major military installations in West Germany. The surrounding area constitutes one of Germany's largest manufacturing and cultural centers, and it is the location also of major financial and banking interests. With a metropolitan population well in excess of one million, the area is also important for its agricultural products, and particularly renown for its wine.

Both the U.S. Army and Air Force have maintained large installations in the area since shortly after the close of World War II. These have come to be more important as administrative posts rather than as sites for the operation of field troops. The region's military population is one of the largest concentrations of U.S. Forces personnel in Europe, and the military community itself has well-developed facilities for U.S. families, including four large shopping and recreational centers within a 25-mile radius and several large family housing complexes.

Data Collection and Sampling

Five housing communities, two of which were occupied by air force families, were selected because housing authorities considered these to be "average" or "typical" communities of U.S. military families, and because at the time of data gathering, each housing community had a high rate of occupancy. The sampling frame was defined as all married women whose spouses were in active military duty and who resided in U.S. military housing.* Eligible respondents were identified through an initial prelisting of the sampling frame, and an interval or systematic sample design (f = 1/5) was used to distribute self-administering questionnaires. Special follow-up procedures were used to minimize the no-response rate (29 percent), and precautions were taken to protect anonymity by using return mail for completed questionnaires.

Each housing community contained a number of apartment buildings, which ranged in size from two-family units up to as many as 24 in a single complex. Units within a given cluster were designated as "officer" or "enlisted," and with the exception of senior ranking officers, quarters or apartments are assigned by the order of application.

The data-gathering instrument, which was pretested using non-sample respondents of military wives, included a battery of items on drinking, family and military life, and leisure activities. Qualitative data were collected through several open-ended items, including an item that solicited candid appraisal of military life and its influence on drinking practices. In the end, this item generated a great deal of important information, especially perceptual data, that the questionnaire itself did not tap directly. In addition, several unstructured interviews with nonsample respondents were conducted in an effort to construct a picture of alcohol and military life in greater depth than possible in the questionnaire instruments.

Measures of Drinking

Two measures were used in gathering information on the extent of drinking: a self-rating and a quantity-frequency (Q-F) index. Al-

---

*Military wives living in civilian housing within the German community could not be included in the sampling frame because of logistic difficulties in locating respondents. However, the proportion of U.S. families living on the German economy by comparison to those in military housing is relatively small.

though both are based on self-report information, the outcomes differ somewhat.

Self-rating Measure

Respondents were asked, "In thinking about your drinking, which of the following categories best describes your drinking in the past 12 months? Quite a lot, moderate, light, or none at all?" An affirmative reply led to several additional questions about their drinking patterns, including their drinking habits since their spouses' overseas tours began. Respondents who indicated that they did not drink were directed to an item on whether they had in the past been a drinker. These ratings of drinking status are, of course, self-perceptions, and, as such, are not subject to external validation. Thus, while distortions in their perceptions may be present, these data must be accepted at face validity.

Quantity-Frequency Measure

The Q-F index was based on items about quantity, frequency, and the type of beverage normally consumed on drinking occasions. Typically, the amount of drinking was reported in glasses, shots, bottles, quarts, liters, and half-liters; these quantities were then converted into ounces of beverage, and translated into "ounce equivalents; 1 oz. of spirits = 10 oz. equivalents). This procedure is similar to those in which the beverage is counted into ounces of absolute alcohol. The resulting index of quantity was then combined with information on the respondent's frequency of drinking (for example, daily, three to four times weekly, once a week). Hence, the resulting Q-F score provided a measure of the quantity of alcohol (in ounce equivalents) drunk over a standard period of time. Using previous findings on drinking and consumption patterns of women (Garrett and Bahr 1973, 1974; Bahr and Garrett 1976) as general guidelines, the following categories were devised based on ounce equivalents: (1) a "heavy" drinker had a score of at least 400 oz. equivalents per week; (2) a "moderate" drinker, 140-399 oz. equivalents; and (3) a "light" drinker, 139 oz. equivalents or less.* Although more refined quantitative measures of drinking were possible, the Q-F index was adequate for the purpose of this research.

---

*Further details on the construction of the Q-F index can be located in Bahr and Garrett 1971, 1976; Garrett and Bahr 1973, 1974.

FINDINGS

Analyses show a number of noteworthy findings for selected social and military-related characteristics for the 261 sample respondents. On the age factor, nearly three of every four women fell within a range of 25 to 35; the mean age is slightly over 30 years. One in every five had received at least an undergraduate college degree; one-third had completed some college work. Approximately one-fourth of the sample was employed at the time the study was made; one-third were active in some type of volunteer work outside the home. As expected, most women (81 percent) had at least one child. On religious preference, nearly six of every ten listed a Protestant denomination. Approximately 60 percent of the sample reported their spouse's military status as "enlisted," which was almost evenly divided between the E-1/E-5 (private/sergeant) and E-6/E-7 (staff sergeant/sergeant first class) categories; slightly fewer than 5 percent were reported as warrant officers (W-1 to W-4). Among those reported as officers, approximately one-half held ranks of 0-1 to 0-3 (second lieutenant/captain) and the remainder were classified as 0-4 to 0-6 (major/colonel).

Social Activities

For married women who accompany their spouses on an overseas tour of duty, opportunities for leisure and social activities are placed at a premium, particularly at bases situated in remote locations. Often confronted with a language barrier that restricts interaction with local residents, separated from relatives, friends, and acquaintances, the military wife faces a choice of confining her life to her family or of reconstructing a new social world in an overseas military life style. Respondents in this study generally agreed that their sense of self-satisfaction and contentment not only rested on family activities and responsibilities, but also on their available opportunities to engage in social activities outside the home.

Overall, the military wives chose a wide variety of leisure and recreational activities. As expected, considerably less than half (38 percent) reported attending church on a regular basis. Shopping on the German economy was the widely chosen weekly activity. However, sedentary activities (watching television, reading, hobbies, visiting) were the most frequent activities of these women.

Despite the variety of activities, the most common complaints among these women were boredom, a shortage of interesting leisure activities, or the lack of opportunity to seek outside activities. Sample complaints were:

I think there should be more activities for wives of the E-5
and below. We are needing more places to go and with some
time free (of) baby-sitting.

There isn't nearly enough for wives to do as most of our
husbands are always somewhere else on TDY. Most women
that I know sit and drink from sheer boredom!

There is nothing to do . . . (but) I have enjoyed isolating
myself here these past two years.

I think it is said that most military wives are so withdrawn
and keep to themselves. We just recently moved here and
it is very lonely . . . There are so many people . . . who
are reluctant to make friends.

With low income and small children I feel more tied down
here than when in the States.

Most military wives sit home with kids . . . all day.
There's nothing else interesting to do. . . . I sit home
all day—depressed.

For those of us who don't work and who have a family (and
that's most of us) there is not much exciting I can do,
especially with a limited income.

In summary, while military wives as a group indicate participation in a wide variety of leisure and recreation activities, the most
frequently chosen activities are those that are typically personal or
individual activities or those that do not involve recreation outside
the home: reading, television viewing, entertaining visitors. Furthermore, a separate analysis of data on the social life of the military
wife, such as entertaining, celebrations, parties, and so forth, show
that the vast majority (close to 90 percent) are military-related
functions, typically, promotion section/battery, squadron/battalion,
or "hail/farewell" parties. Here, however, there were major differences by rank of spouse. For example, among women married to
officers the median number of military-related social gatherings is
8.0 yearly; for wives whose spouse was enlisted the median is approximately one per year. This outcome, of course, is an expected one,
which in turn perhaps accounts for an undercurrent of dissatisfaction
with military life styles among wives of enlisted men:

I feel being a military wife is a lot harder than other
types—moving . . . not having family, the loneliness of
being overseas . . .

Most of the activities aren't for young mothers . . . who
can't afford sitters or have transportation. In the company
my husband's in, the women don't even know each other
and don't want to.

There is too much emphasis on being social in the military.
Bull!

We do not fit into the military community. Most military
people we know (and their wives) tend to pick their friends
by rank which tends to stifle real friendships.

If your husband is an officer, it can be swell. But if not,
boredom. . . . Most bases have lots of activities, but I
have no way to participate.

Extent of Drinking

In examining the characteristics of drinking among military
wives, we find that nearly nine out of ten are self-reported drinkers.
Thus, compared to results provided by Cahalan, Cisin, and Crossley
(1969) on the drinking patterns of U.S. women, military wives are
far less likely than married civilian women to be abstainers (10 percent vs. 38 percent). The two measures of extent of drinking, however, reveal interesting results. Approximately 5 percent of the
sample were self-classified as heavy drinkers, comparable to results
reported by Cahalan, Cisin, and Crossley; for married civilian women
the figure is 6 percent. However, a better comparison can be found
in the Q-F results, since the national study used a quantified measure
(the Q-F-V or quantity-frequency-variability) of classifying drinking
groups. The Q-F index used in this study shows that nearly one in
ten women could be classified as exhibiting heavy drinking patterns.
Similarly, the number of drinkers classified by the Q-F index as
"moderate" more than doubles (44 percent) over the self-reported
"moderates" (17 percent), as shown in Table 17.1. Quite apart from
the fact that military wives appear to be somewhat heavier drinkers
than married civilian women, the finding is especially interesting,
first, because it shows a distortion in self-perception of drinking in
relation to objective indicators of consumption patterns. This is

TABLE 17.1

Characteristics of Drinking Patterns for
Military Wives (N = 248)

Characteristic	Percent[*]
Percent self-reported drinkers	87
Self-rating of drinking	
Quite a lot	5
Moderate	17
Light	68

$$x^2 = 168.99, \ df = 2, \ p < .01$$

Quantity-Frequency (Q-F) Index	
Heavy	10
Moderate	44
Light	68

$$x^2 = 60.91, \ df = 2, \ p < .01$$

Consumption since overseas duty	
Far more often	17
Somewhat more often	19
About the same as stateside	56
Somewhat less often	5
Far less often	3

$$x^2 = 225.70, \ df = 4, \ p < .01$$

Most frequently consumed beverage	
Beer	14
Wine	67
Spirits	18
Other	1

$$x^2 = 249.72, \ df = 3, \ p < .01$$

(continued)

Table 17.1 (continued)

Characteristic	Percent*
Alcoholic beverages consumed during a "typical week"**	
Beer	25
Wine	74
Spirits	47
Liqueur	15
Social occasions where alcohol is used	
Always or almost always	45
About half	30
Occasionally or less often	25

$$x^2 = 16.12, \ df = 2, \ p < .01$$

Reasons for drinking, percent endorsement as important or very important**	
Relax	30
To be sociable	36
Taste	49
To forget troubles	18
Celebrate special occasions	69
Improve appetite	25
Polite thing to do	41
Cheers me up	10
Need alcohol for my nerves	16

*Percentages do not total 100.
**More than one response could be endorsed.
Source: Compiled by the authors.

perhaps not altogether unexpected in view of comments from respondents, such as: You have to watch what you say, especially at parties,
dinners, almost every place. I'm careful what I do; I watch my
drinking and behavior. I feel I must be on guard. Command/
supervisory paranoias!

However, at least one study has analyzed the relationship of
self-report and Q-F drinking statuses of both women and men. These
findings seem to indicate that women at all socioeconomic levels (in
civilian life) are far more likely than men to hold self-perceptions
of their drinking in line with classifications of objective measures,
such as a quantity-frequency index (Garrett and Bahr 1974). Preliminary results here, however, do not reveal this consistency.
Instead, the military life style presumably has an effect of clouding
or distorting the self-perceptions of drinking patterns, at least to a
greater degree than those of married women in civilian contexts.

Whatever distortions may intervene in the self-ratings of drinking, the vast majority of women in this study seemed quite aware of
an emphasis on drinking in military life in an overseas assignment.
In fact, regardless of their own drinking, most respondents com-
mented on the drinking by military wives:

> I think much drinking is done because of boredom and
> loneliness. Military wives (many of them) are like pris-
> oners in their quarters, especially overseas. Removed
> from family and friends, they find it hard to make new
> acquaintances.

> I have been living in the military for only three years
> now. I have seen more military wives and their hus-
> bands drink more than I have ever seen in my life.

> Too much emphasis is given to alcohol. More . . .
> should understand why they drink.

> It is sad that so many of the wives I see have to use
> booze like they do. Yes, there is a drinking problem
> in the military. They encourage it in many ways.

Drinking Patterns

Outcomes on beverage preference are expected, especially in
view of the fact that these overseas bases were located in an area
of Germany renowned for its wine. Their preference for wine, how-

ever, is somewhat higher than results from national studies, including the Cahalan, Cisin, and Crossley (1969) study. Approximately two out of three drinkers indicated that wine was the most frequently consumed beverage, and while many drinkers indicated that other beverages were also consumed in a "typical" week, wine (74 percent) is far above beer (25 percent) and spirits (47 percent) in usage.

Surely one of the factors that can be seen as promoting alcohol use among military wives as well as their spouses in an overseas assignment is its availability. Although spirits are rationed and controlled through military alcohol beverage outlets ("Class VI Stores"), the monthly ration for spirits is relatively generous since both spouses hold ration privileges. Together with willing friends who make purchases on behalf of others, large quantities of spirits are readily available at tax-free prices that run from 40 to 60 percent lower than those in most states. Neither beer nor wine are subject to rationing. In military clubs, such as the officer's or noncommissioned officer's (NCO) clubs, alcohol by the drink, like the cost per bottle, is a bargain by comparison to typical stateside costs.

Results showing changes in consumption patterns since their spouse's overseas assignment, therefore, are hardly surprising. For example, over one-third of the respondents rated their use of alcohol as more frequent than during stateside assignments, and about half of these indicated that they drank far more often since arriving overseas. The increase in frequency of drinking, of course, cannot be seen as a simple consequence of high availability or low cost. Instead, social factors intrinsic to the military life style itself are probably more important influences on drinking patterns. For one thing, the use of alcohol in military-sponsored social gatherings comes to be a prominent feature of life, regardless of one's personal drinking habits. Nearly half of the respondents in this study indicated that alcohol was consumed at nearly all military-sponsored social occasions attended in the past year, and one-third estimated that about half of the gatherings and private parties they attended included consumption of alcohol. At least one writer in reflecting on her socializing during her husband's career in the army, goes so far as to assert that heavy drinking is condoned by the military authorities:

> Our parties were usually command performance and sometimes prorated; which meant, that without any murmur of complaint, my husband and I (who drank four and one-third drinks during an evening) were paying for a lot of alcohol guzzled by others. This sanctioning of the heavy drinker by the top echelons, seems to me a flaw in army (and the other services) leadership (Druyor 1973: 9).

Reasons for Drinking

Although respondents were asked to comment on factors in the military setting that they perceived as influencing drinking patterns, they were also requested to indicate their personal reasons for drinking, regardless of how much they typically consumed. Not unlike results from past studies of women in civilian populations, the most frequently endorsed reasons were "to be sociable" (36 percent), "to celebrate special occasions" (69 percent), or because it was the "polite thing to do" (41 percent). But, not all respondents saw alcohol as part of convivial gatherings. Nearly one in five reported their drinking was in part an effort to "forget troubles"; approximately one in ten indicated that drinking was needed to "calm the nerves."

Comments from respondents, though seldom referring to personal motivations for drinking, add further depth and understanding to drinking by military wives:

> The wives sometimes drink because of pressures that are brought on by the military: TDY for the hubbies, PCS remotes, etc. There ought to be a program . . . specifically designed for problem drinkers who are military wives.

> Too many wives hid their drinking during the day and then don't drink at night to show they don't need AA.

> I think . . . most military wives are so withdrawn and keep to themselves.

> I can understand why more wives drink over here 'cause there really isn't much else to do unless you do have a hobby of some sort.

> So many wives in Europe sit and drink in their homes and clubs claiming they are so unhappy in the country and it has caused it.

An underlying theme of comments from many respondents, often unrelated to their personal drinking pattern, singles out the sense of isolation that the military wife experiences in an overseas environment. Removed from parents, in-laws, relatives, or close friends, there is an uprooting of ties and relationships that otherwise impose stability and security in her personal life. For women who do not work, opportunities to "get out of the household" come to be important in reestablishing new roots in what is an otherwise transient

society of neighbors and acquaintances. Yet, not always is the personal motivation to "reestablish" roots present. Respondents themselves seem to acknowledge a syndrome of indifference, which on
occasion is linked to drinking:

> Some wives just sit and drink. Their excuses for drinking
> are poor as there are many activities to do.

> Most bases have enough activities for one to do. You just
> have to get off one's lazy ass and go do it. Otherwise you
> can become very miserable.

> I understand how some women would get depressed enough
> to drink, especially if they're alone a lot and don't try to
> keep busy.

> Cultural shock, frequent absence of spouses, sexism, etc.
> provide excuses for drinking.

> The trouble with most military wives that consume large
> amounts of spirits, wine, etc. is that they are too lazy
> . . . to get out and look for a job or volunteer their time
> to some place.

> Much drinking is done because of boredom and loneliness.

The Heavy Drinker

Analysis of data on respondents classified as "heavy drinkers"
was restricted because of the small number of cases (N = 26). However, qualitative data gleaned from these respondents tentatively
indicated, first, a general dissatisfaction with military life. Succinctly described by one respondent: "I cannot live this way any
longer. Since we have come overseas, I feel the air force every-
where. At times I think they tell what, where, and when to eat!"
Similarly, boredom and chronic absences of their spouse on temporary
duty assignment were singled out in particular. ("I have nothing to
do. My husband is always on TDY. I can't drive. I am trapped.")
Other military wives face similar circumstances without taking
recourse to alcohol. Whether the factors that condition the choice
of solving these problems by alcohol are significantly influenced by
the military life style, whether these are attributes of one's personal
psychology, or, as is more likely the case, whether there is an interaction of both constellations of factors would seem an important line
of inquiry for future research.

SUMMARY AND CONCLUDING REMARKS

This study has examined drinking patterns and military-related characteristics of service wives in overseas base communities. Although a paucity of previously published research precludes comparison with earlier studies, the results on extent of drinking indicate that military wives are far more likely to be self-reported drinkers than their civilian counterparts and that their overall level of consumption of alcohol is higher than other groups of married women. Two measures of drinking—self-rating and a quantity-frequency items—were used in ascertaining drinking status. Classifications of drinking by the Q-F measure generally produced approximately twice as many respondents in the "heavy" and "moderate" categories than observed for self-ratings. Although inconsistent with an earlier report on womens' drinking patterns, this "underestimation" of drinking would seem to be a function of military base environment, which some respondents described as "feeling as if one is on display" and "being watched."

The data reported here also single out factors in the military life style that might explain why one in every three women reported an increase in the frequency of drinking since beginning their spouse's overseas duty assignment. The high availability of alcohol at a cost considerably below stateside prices and a relatively high frequency of informal as well as military-sponsored social gatherings where alcohol is served would seem generally to increase the probability of higher levels of consumption. But, for some respondents, increased consumption may also be due to their personal experiences within the military setting. The difficulties faced by some military wives in tolerating a spouse-absent situation, the inaccessibility of leisure activities and/or social relationships outside of her family, the consequences of boredom, as well as separation from immediate ties with parents, in-laws, relatives, or old acquaintances can be seen as "occupational risks" of the military wife which might promote changes in drinking patterns, including an increase in consumption.

Although the data reported here provide only tentative grounds on which to draw inferences about drinking problems of military wives, there is general evidence suggesting that service wives in an overseas setting may run a somewhat higher risk of drinking pathologies than their counterpart in civilian society. It seems clear that the drinking norms of the military, not unlike other occupational groups, are more permissive toward drinking, even heavy drinking. This is not to say that drinking misbehaviors are encouraged; rather, that norms seem to structure drinking patterns in such a way that they become as much a part of the military experience as the duty assignment. Earlier reports on alcoholism in the military clearly document that the risk of alcohol abuse by servicemen is generally higher than among the civilian population (Subcommittee on Alcoholism and Narcotics 1971). As Lester (1975) points out, some observers suggest that the rate of alcoholism in the military may be three times greater than in comparable civilian populations. But, if the risk is greater for the military man so, too, is it likely to be higher for his spouse. And, the difficulties in identifying the problem-drinking wife may be more complex. At least one alcoholism counselor at a base with 12,000 wives estimates that there are from 700 to 1,000 women with alcohol problems, yet fewer than ten had sought professional help (Lester 1975). Presumably, the first step toward the end of instituting effective alcohol prevention, as well as treatment programs, should be to develop an adequate body of knowledge about the military wife and her drinking patterns.

PART VI

EPILOGUE

Epilogue: Adapt or Opt Out

Edna J. Hunter

Until recently, military family research has been a much neglected area of concern among military planners, even though the research which has been carried out has usually pointed to definite relationships between family factors and the job satisfaction, performance, and retention of the service member. The all-volunteer service, the changing roles of men and women in society in general, and the integration of larger numbers of women into the military services are all factors which have increased the decision makers' interest in the impact of the family upon the military mission.

The Conference on Current Trends and Directions in Military Family Research held in San Diego in September 1977 grew out of the need to take a broader look at the field of military family research. The conference presented an opportunity for researchers, health services, and operations personnel to examine military family research more closely—to see what had been done in the past, what is being done at present, and what perhaps ought to be done in the future. During the two-and-one-half days of the conference, those in attendance heard a number of research reports and discussions of problems and issues concerning military families.

It would appear logical that the first step in finding the solution to any problem is defining the problem. Many of the presentations at the conference touched on the numerous changes taking place in family structure, function, attitudes, and values, such as the increasing alternative styles of marriage and the increasing number of single-parent families and dual-military career families. The special problems and requirements of children within the military system were also approached by participants in the meetings. For example, what happens during evacuation procedures to the children and families of those service persons who are not the "typical" family; for example, unmarried couples, single parents with children? Are these nontraditional families included in evacuation planning or deployment of the service member? Should they be?

Attendees discovered there are people in varying disciplines, including those from the civilian sector, who are interested in the military family. During the conference the need to balance care with research was discussed as well as the need to show that family research does have dollar payoff, and that family social support programs are actually cost-effective. It was pointed out that perhaps the military has something to contribute to the family "mission," as well as the other way around. The need to integrate the skills of the practitioner with the knowledge and skills of the researcher was also emphasized.

Conferees also heard how the structure of the military family is changing; about the value of "poor man's research;" about the increasing number of dual-military career families and single-parent families and how this creates additional problems for which research can find answers, such as the need for 24-hour day care if single-parent military personnel are to be able to perform their jobs effectively. Yet another question raised for consideration by attendees was: Is it possible that not all family forms can survive in the military organization? It was suggested by some participants that it was entirely possible that a single-parent family cannot survive in the military system. However, research could perhaps answer that question more definitively.

The special problems which have arisen in trying to integrate women in larger and larger numbers into a system with incongruent policies for women was also discussed during the conference sessions. It was suggested that special training may be necessary to undo the years of sex-role stereotyping ingrained in both men and women before maximum utilization of all servicepersonnel can be achieved. The need to look further into other subcultures, in addition to the male-female dichotomy, was emphasized during the meetings, for example, officer/enlisted, senior officer/junior officer, black/white, and others.

Answers were provided for many of the questions posed during the conference; however, most were tempered by statements about the need for further research efforts in order to reach more definitive conclusions. Unfortunately, the discussions provided more questions than answers. Which family support systems best meet families' needs? What new social or financial supports are perhaps required? When are interventions most effective? Does the need for social supports vary with time or life transitions? Are different supports needed at various points along the family's developmental life cycle? Which theories already developed in the field of family research can perhaps be applied to military family research?

Throughout the meetings the many unique problems faced by military families were reiterated, and yet our colleagues from academia pointed out that perhaps the military family is not really too much different from the civilian family in many ways. Although the military life style may certainly involve somewhat unique stresses, those stresses perhaps are not too different than those experienced by civilian families. In fact, in some respects the military family may even have an advantage over its civilian counterpart in its capacity to cope with family stresses.

One noteworthy observation coming out of the conference was that information about military families is widely scattered. If one wants to know about medical needs, one must go to the medical departments. If information concerning housing or commissaries is sought, then one has to go elsewhere. And when one wants to find out about unmet needs of families, sometimes the source of information is completely unknown. It was apparent that a better system for accessing reports written on military family research is needed. Family concerns often "drop through the cracks."

The conference demonstrated, however, that times are indeed changing. For many years it has been recognized that the military organization has a profound effect upon the military family. At the meetings, attendees learned that those in the top echelons of military operations, as well as those on down through the system, are beginning to realize that the family also impacts upon military effectiveness. For instance, the dual-career military family is creating increasing problems for military detailers. In very recent times, military planners are eager to know if the programs designed to support families are actually meeting families' needs. Payoffs of the research currently being carried out can perhaps eliminate some of the programs which prove to be cost-ineffective, and ones that are effective can then be substituted. From the medical departments conferees heard that certain family-practice clinics are now beginning to assess family functioning as a routine part of family care, indicating there is indeed increasing recognition that relationships exist among family crises, life events, and actual physical health—or at least the demand for health care services. Military family research was presented as a valuable and much needed tool and one with measureable payoffs, even though those payoffs are sometimes difficult to measure.

In the closing session of the conference, Dr. Benjamin Schlesinger of the University of Toronto philosophically stated:

> I am an optimist about the family; I believe it will survive. Let us look and do some research on what allows thousands of military families to manage. What makes these families tick? Percentage-wise, there are more military families who manage, despite tremendous pressures, despite the moving, and we can learn from those who are surviving and help those who are not. Let us never forget that families have tremendous strength; let us build on them. . . . If there's peace in the family, there's peace in the world.

REFERENCES

Aldous, Joan. 1969. "Wives' Employment Status and Lower-Class Men as Husband-Fathers: Support for the Moynihan Thesis." Journal of Marriage and the Family 31 (August): 469-76.

Allen H. 1972. "Schilling Manor: A Survey of a Military Community of Father Absent Families." Ph.D. dissertation, Catholic University of America.

Andrews, F. M., and S. B. Withey. 1974. "Developing Measures of Perceived Life Quality; Results from Several National Surveys." Social Indicators Research 1: 1-26.

Bahr, H. M., and G. R. Garrett. 1971. Disaffiliation Among Urban Women. New York: Bureau of Applied Social Research.

____. 1976. Women Alone. Lexington, Mass.: Lexington Books/ D. C. Heath.

Bailey, Glenn A. Jr. 1974. "Military Technology and Military Organizational Structure: A Case Study of Four Army Tactical Units." M.A. thesis, University of Texas.

Battalia, O. W., and J. J. Tarrant. 1973. The Corporate Eunuch. New York: Crowell.

Bauer, R., R. Stout, and R. Holz. 1977. "Measures of Military Attitudes." Army Research Institute Technical Paper, Arlington, Va.

Bell, D., and T. Houston. 1976. The Vietnam Era Deserter: Characteristics of Unconvicted Deserters Participating in the Presidential Clemency Program. Army Research Institute Technical Paper, Arlington, Virginia.

Belt, J., and A. Sweney. 1973. "The Air Force Wife: Her Knowledge of, and Attitudes toward, the Air Force." Paper presented at Military Testing Association Conference on Human Resources, October, San Antonio, Texas.

Bennett, W., H. Chandler, J. Duffy, J. Hickman, C. Johnson, M. Lally, G. Norbo, A. Omps, V. Popsin, R. Seeberg, and W. Wubbena. 1974. Army Families. Carlisle Barracks, Pa: U.S. Army War College.

Berkey, Carry R. 1972. "Military Retirement Syndrome: The Civilian Side." Military Medicine 137, no. 7: 278-81.

Berkey, Barry R., and James B. Stoebner. 1968. "The Retirement Syndrome: A Previously Unreported Variant." Military Medicine 133, no. 1: 5-8.

Bernard, J. 1964. "The Adjustment of Married Mates." In Handbook of Marriage and the Family, ed. H. T. Christiensen. Chicago: Rand McNally.

Bernard, Jessie. 1966. Marriage and Family Among Negroes. Englewood Cliffs, N.J.: Prentice-Hall.

Bevilacqua, J. 1967. "Civilianization and Health-Welfare Resource Participation on an Army Post." Ph.D. dissertation, Brandeis University.

Bey, Douglas R., and Jean Lange. 1974. "Waiting Wives: Women under Stress." American Journal of Psychiatry 131 (March): 283-86.

Biddle, Bruce J., and Edwin J. Thomas. 1966. Role Theory, Concepts, and Research. New York: Wiley.

Biderman, Albert D., and Laure M. Sharp. 1968. "The Convergence of Military and Civilian Occupational Structures." American Journal of Sociology 73 (January): 381-99.

Biller, H., and D. Meredith. 1975. Father Power. New York: Anchor Press/Doubleday.

Billingsley, Andrew. 1968. Black Families in White America. Englewood Cliffs, N.J.: Prentice-Hall.

Blaydon, Colin C., and Carol B. Stack. 1977. "Income Support Policies and the Family," Daedalus 106, no. 2 (Spring).

Blockberger, C. W. 1970. "Military Families: Differential Life Styles." Ph.D. dissertation, University of California.

Bowlby, J. 1960. "Separation Anxiety." International Journal of
    Psychoanalysis 41: 89-113.

Boynton, Kathleen R. 1977. "Episodic Deviation: A Precursor to
    Dynamic Homeostasis in Interpersonal Relationships." Unpub-
    lished paper, University of Massachusetts.

Bronfenbrenner, Urei. 1977. "Nobody Home: The Erosion of the
    American Family." Psychology Today 10, no. 12 (May): 41-47.

Burger, N. H. 1968. The Executive's Wife. London: Collier.

Burr, Wesley R. 1972. "Role Transitions: A Reformation of
    Theory." Journal of Marriage and the Family 34, no. 4: 407-16.

Busia, K. A. 1954. "The Shanti of the Gold Coast." In D. P.
    Forde, ed., African Worlds: Studies in the Cosmological Ideas
    and Social Values of African Peoples.

Butler, Robert N. 1975. "Psychiatry and Psychology of the Middle-
    Aged." In Comprehensive Textbook of Psychiatry/II, 2d edition
    2, no. 48, 2390-2404. Baltimore: Williams and Wilkins.

Cahalan, D., I. Cisin, and H. Crossley. 1969. American Drinking
    Practices. New Brunswick, N.J.: Rutgers Center of Alcohol
    Studies.

Campbell, A., P. Converse, and W. Rogers. 1975. Quality of
    American Life: Perception, Evaluation, and Satisfaction.
    Beverly Hills: Sage.

Campbell, E. E. 1974. "The Effects of Couple Communication
    Training on Married Couples in the Childrearing Years: A Field
    Experiment." Ph.D. dissertation, Arizona State University.

Carman, R. S. 1968. "Drinking Behavior as Related to Personality
    and Social Class Factors. Ph.D. dissertation, University of
    Colorado.

Chilman, N. C. 1966. Growing Up Poor. Washington, D.C.:
    U.S. Department of Health, Education and Welfare.

Clarke, C. 1970. "Group Procedure for Increasing Positive Feed-
    back between Married Partners." The Family Coordinator 19:
    324-28.

Coates, Charles, and Roland J. Pellegrin. 1965. Military Sociology: A Study of American Military Institutions and Military Life. College Park, Md.: Maryland Brooks Exchange.

Cobb, S. 1976. "Social Support as a Moderator of Life Stress." Psychosomatic Medicine 38, no. 5: 300-14.

Collins, J. D. 1971. "The Effects of the Conjugal Relationships Modification Method on Marital Communication and Adjustment." Ph.D. dissertation, Pennsylvania State University.

Comptroller General of the U.S. 1976. Report to the Congress by the Comptroller General: Alcohol Abuse Is More Prevalent in the Military than Drug Abuse. Washington, D.C.: U.S. Government Printing Office.

Coopersmith, S. 1967. The Antecedents of Self-Esteem. San Francisco: W. H. Freeman.

Corrales, R. 1974. The Influence of Family Cycle Categories, Marital Power, Spousal Agreement, and Communication Styles upon Marital Satisfaction in the First Six Years of Marriage." Ph.D. dissertation, University of Minnesota.

Cottrell, L. S., Jr. 1942. The Adjustment of the Individual to His Age and Sex Roles." American Sociological Review 7 (October): 618-25.

Cromwell, Ronald E., C. Edwin Vaughan, and Charles H. Mindel. 1975. "Ethnic Minority Family Research in an Urban Setting: A Process of Exchange." The American Sociologist 10, no. 3 (August): 141-50.

Culbert, S. A., and J. R. Renshaw. 1972. "Coping with the Stresses of Travel as an Opportunity for Improving the Quality of Work and Family Life." Family Process 11, no. 3: 321-37.

Cushman, Donald P., and Robert T. Craig. 1976. "Communication Systems: Interpersonal Implications." In Explorations in Interpersonal Communication, ed. Gerald R. Miller, pp. 37-58. Beverly Hills: Sage.

Daedalus. 1977. Special issue on "The Family." 106, no. 2.

Dahl, B., H. McCubbin, and G. Lester. 1976. "War-Induced
    Father-Absence: Comparing the Adjustment of Children in
    Reunited, Non-reunited, and Reconstituted Families." Inter-
    national Journal Sociology Families 6, no. 1: 99-118.

Darnauer, P. 1976. "The Adolescent Experience in Career Army
    Families." In Families in the Military System, eds. H. I.
    McCubbin, B. B. Dahl, and E. J. Hunter, pp. 43-66. Beverly
    Hills: Sage.

Davis, Allison, and John Dollard. 1940. Children of Bondage.
    New York: American Council on Education and Harper and Row.

Dickerson, W. J. 1964. "Child Psychiatry in the Naval Service."
    Military Medicine 129 (November): 1081-83.

Dobrofsky, L. R., and C. T. Batterson. 1977. "The Military Wife
    and Feminism." Signs: A Journal of Women in Culture and
    Society 2 (Spring): 675-84.

Dornbusch, Sanford. 1955. "The Military Academy as an Assimi-
    lating Institution." Social Forces 33 (May): 316-21.

Drake, St. Clair, and Horace R. Cayton. 1945. Black Metropolis.
    New York: Harper and Row.

Druyor, G. 1973. "Alcohol and the Military Wife." U.S. Magazine,
    December, 9, p. 42.

Dubois, W. E. B. 1909. The Negro American Family. Atlanta:
    Atlanta University Press.

Dupuy, H. J. 1965. Attitude toward Dependents' Housing and their
    Relationships with Career Intention, Report II. Washington,
    D.C.: U.S. Naval Personnel Research Activity.

Duvall, E. M. 1945. "Loneliness and the Serviceman's Wife."
    Journal of Marriage and the Family 7, no. 1: 77-81.

Eastman, D. 1958. "Self-Acceptance and Marital Happiness."
    Journal of Consulting Psychology 22, no. 1: 95-99.

Erikson, Erik H. 1966. "The Concept of Identity in Race Relations:
    Notes and Queries." Daedalus 95 (Winter): 145-71.

_____. 1968. Identity: Youth and Crisis. New York: Norton.

Etzioni, Amitai. 1977. "Science and the Future of the Family."
Science 196, no. 4389 (April):

Fagen, S. A., E. J. Janda, S. L. Baker, E. G. Fischer, and L. A.
Cove. 1968. "Impact of Father Absence in Military Families:
II. Factors Relating to Success of Coping with Crisis." Techni-
cal Report. Washington, D.C.: Walter Reed Medical Center.

Finlayson, E. 1976. "A Study of the Wife of the Army Officer:
Her Academic and Career Preparations, Her Current Employ-
ment and Volunteer Services." In Families in the Military
System, eds. H. McCubbin, B. Dahl, and E. Hunter. Beverly
Hills: Sage.

Forde, D. P. (ed.). 1954. African Worlds: Studies in the Cosmological Ideas and Social Values of African Peoples. New York:
Oxford University Press.

Forgas, J. P. 1976. "The Perception of Social Episodes." Journal
of Personality and Social Psychology 34, no. 2: 199-29.

Frazier, E. Franklin. 1932. The Negro Family in Chicago. Chicago: University of Chicago Press.

_____. 1939. The Negro Family in the United States. Chicago:
University of Chicago Press.

Fried, Barbara. 1967. The Middle Age Crisis. New York: Harper
and Row.

Froehlke, Robert F. 1972. "General Officer Promotion Criteria
Detailed." Commander's Digest, July 20: 1, 1.

Garrett, G. R. 1970. "Problem Drinking Among Women." New
York: Bureau of Applied Social Research.

_____. 1973. "Homeless Women." In Skid Row: An Introduction
to Disaffiliation, ed. H. M. Bahr. New York: Oxford University
Press.

Garrett, G. R., and H. M. Bahr. 1973. "Women on Skid Row."
Quarterly Journal of Studies on Alcohol 34 (December): 1228-43.

_____. 1974. "Comparison of Self-Rating and Quantity-Frequency Measures of Drinking." Quarterly Journal of Studies on Alcohol 34 (December): 1294-1306.

Gates, Thomas S. 1970. President's Commission on an All-Volunteer Armed Force. Washington, D.C.: U.S. Government Printing Office.

Giffin, Martin B., and John S. McNeil. 1967. "Effect of Military Retirement on Dependents." Archives of General Psychiatry 17 (December): 717-22.

Goldman, Nancy L. 1976. "Trends in Family Patterns of U.S. Military Personnel during the 20th Century." In The Social Psychology of Military Service, eds. Nancy L. Goldman and David R. Segal, pp. 119-33. Beverly Hills: Sage.

Goldschmidt, Walter. 1974. "Ethology, Ecology and Ethnological Realities." In Coping and Adaptation, eds. George E. Coelho, David Hamburg, and John E. Adams. New York: Basic Books.

Gomberg, E. 1974. "Women and Alcoholism." In New Psychotherapies for a Changing Society, eds. V. Franks and V. Burtle, pp. 169-88. New York: Brunner/Mazel.

Goode, W. 1956. After Divorce. New York: Free Press.

Goodwin, D., D. H. David, and L. Robins. 1975. "Drinking Amid Abundant Illicit Drugs: The Vietnam Case." Archives of General Psychiatry 32 (February): 230-33.

Gough, H. G., and A. B. Heilbrun. 1965. The Adjective Check List Manual. Palo Alto: Consulting Psychologists Press.

Gould, Roger L. 1972. "The Phases of Adult Life: A Study in Developmental Psychology." American Journal of Psychiatry 129, no. 5: 521-31.

Grace, G. L., H. A. Holoter, and M. I. Soderquist. 1976. Career Satisfaction as a Factor Influencing Retention. Technical Report No. 4. System Development Corporation TM-5031/004/00.

Grace, G. L., H. A. Holoter, R. J. Provenzano. J. Copes, and M. B. Steiner. 1976. Navy Career Counseling Research: Phase 3 Summary and Recommendations. Technical Report No. 8. System Development Corporation TM-5031/008/00.

Greenberg, Harvey R. 1973. "Psychiatric Symptomatology in Wives of Military Retirees." American Journal of Psychiatry 123, no. 4: 487-90.

Greenwood, G., and R. Soar. 1973. "Some Relationships between Teacher Morale and Teacher Behavior." Journal of Education Psychology 69: 105-8.

Grier, William H., and Price M. Cobbs. 1968. Black Rage. New York: Bantam.

Guerney, B. Jr. 1964. "Filial Therapy: Description and Rationale." Journal of Consulting Psychology 28, no. 4: 304-10.

Hall, R. C. W., and W. C. Simmons. 1973. "The POW Wife: A Psychiatric Appraisal." Archives of General Psychiatry 29 (November): 690-94.

Handel, Gerald (ed.). 1967. The Psychosocial Interior of the Family: A Sourcebook for the Study of Whole Families. Chicago: Aldine.

Hareven, Tamara K. 1977. "Family Time and Historical Time," Daedalus 106, no. 2 (Spring): 51-70.

Harre, Romano, and Paul F. Secord. 1973. "The Explanation of Social Behavior." Totowa, N.J.: Littlefield, Adams.

Harris, Janet. 1975. The Prime of Ms. America: The American Woman at Forty. New York: Putnam.

Harris, William. 1976. "Work and the Family in Black Atlanta, 1880." Journal of Social History 9, no. 3 (Spring): 319-30.

Harrison, F. 1944. "Alcohol Problems in the Navy." Quarterly Journal of Studies on Alcohol 5: 413-25.

Hartnagel, T. F. 1974. "Absent without Leave: A Study of the Military Offender." Journal of Political and Military Sociology 2 (Fall): 205-20.

Hayles, Robert. 1977. "Future and Black Values." Paper presented at the 10th Annual Convention of the Association of Black Psychologists, August 9-14, Los Angeles.

Hickman, M. E., and B. A. Baldwin. 1971. "Use of Programmed Instruction to Improve Communication in Marriage." The Family Coordinator 20: 121-26.

Hill, Reuben. 1949. Families under Stress: Adjustment to the Crises of War Separation and Reunion. New York: Harper.

Hill, Robert. 1972. The Strengths of Black Families. New York: Emerson Hall.

Hinkle, J. E., and M. A. Moore. 1971. "A Student Couples Program." The Family Coordinator 20: 153-58.

Hochschild, Arlie. 1969. "The Role of the Ambassador's Wife: An Exploratory Study." Journal of Marriage and the Family 31 (February): 73-87.

Hoffman, L. W., and F. I. Nye. 1974. Working Mothers. San Francisco: Jossey-Bass.

Holmstrom, Lynda L. 1972. The Two-Career Family. Cambridge, Mass.: Schenkman.

Holoter, H. A., G. W. Stehle, L. V. Conner, and G. L. Grace. 1974. Impact of Navy Career Counseling on Personnel Satisfaction and Reenlistment: Phase 2. Technical Report No. 3. System Development Corporation TM-5031/003/00.

Horner, Matina S. 1970. "Femininity and Successful Achievement: A Basic Inconsistency." In J. M. Bardwick, E. Douvan, M. Horner, and D. Gutman, eds., Feminine Personality and Conflict, Belmont, Calif.: Brooks-Cole.

Hoyer, B. et al. 1976. "About Your Drinking." Stars and Stripes.

Hunt, Bernice, and Morton Hunt. 1975. A Guide to the Pleasures and Opportunities of the New Middle Age. New York: Stein and Day.

Hunt, Janet G., and Larry L. Hunt. 1977. "Dilemmas and Contradictions of Status: The Case of the Dual-Career Family." Social Problems 29, no. 4: 403-16.

Hunter, E., and Phelan, J. 1978. "Personality of the Navy POW in Relation to Resistance Posture in Captivity and Harsh Treat-

ment by the Captor." Unpublished manuscript, Naval Health
Research Center.

Hunter E., J. Plag, J. Phelan, and E. Mowery. 1976. "Resistance
Posture and the Vietnam Prisoner of War." Journal of Political
and Military Sociology 4, no. 2: 295-308.

Hurvitz, N. 1960. "The Marital Roles Inventory and Measurement
of Marital Adjustment." Journal of Clinical Psychology 16
(October): 377-80.

Isay, Richard A. 1968. "The Submariners' Wives Syndrome."
Psychiatric Quarterly 42, no. 4: 647-52.

Jackson, D. 1967. Personality Research Form Manual. New York:
Research Psychologists' Press.

Jackson, Jay. 1966. "A Conceptual and Measurement Model for
Norms and Roles." The Pacific Sociological Review (Spring):
35-47.

Janowitz, M. 1960. The Professional Soldier: A Social and Political
Portrait. Glencoe, Ill.: The Free Press.

_____, (ed.). 1964. The New Military: Changing Patterns of Organi-
zation. New York: Russell Sage Foundation.

Jeffers, C. Living Poor. 1967. Ann Arbor: Ann Arbor Publishers.

Johnson, Charles. 1941. Growing Up in the Black Belt. Washington,
D.C.: The American Council on Education.

_____. 1934. Shadow of the Plantation. Chicago: University of
Chicago Press.

Johnson, P. V., and R. H. Marcrum. 1968. "Perceived Deficiencies in Individual Need Fulfillment of Career Army Officers."
Journal of Applied Psychology 52, no. 6: 457-61.

Johnson, Virginia W. 1967. Lady in Arms. Boston: Houghton-
Mifflin.

Joint Commission on Mental Health of Children. 1969. Digest of
Crisis in Child Mental Health: Challenge for the 1970's. New
York: Harper and Row.

Jung, Carl G. 1933. Modern Man in Search of a Soul. New York: Harcourt, Brace, and World.

Kadushin, A. 1970. "Single-Parent Adoptions: An Overview: Some Relevant Research." Social Science Review 44: 263-74.

Kahn, R. 1960. "Productivity and Job Satisfaction." Personnel Psychology 13: 275-87.

Katzell, R., R. Barrett, and T. Parker. 1961. "Job Satisfaction, Job Performance, and Situational Characteristics." Journal of Applied Psychology 45, no. 2: 65-72.

Kellian, Ray H. 1971. The Working Woman. American Management Association, p. 21.

Kelly, George. 1955. The Psychology of Personal Constructs. New York: Norton.

King, Edward L. 1971. "The Death of the Army, a Premortem." The Army Times, February 17, pp. 1-13.

Kinzer, Betty, and Marion Leach. 1968. What Every Army Wife Should Know. Harrisburg: Stackpole Books.

Knight, R. C., R. D. Neathammer, J. L. Pfeister, and R. M. Dinnat. 1974. "Attitudes and Preference of Occupants of Military Family Housing Communities." Executive Digest, Vol. I. (Technical Report D-22). Champaign, Illinois: Department of the Army Construction Engineering Research Laboratory.

Knitter, R. W., S. S. Stumpf, and S. E. Dow. 1969. "Navy Personnel Survey, NPS 68-1." (WSR 69-6). Washington, D.C.: Naval Personnel Research and Development Laboratory.

Kourvetaris, George A., and Betty A. Dobratz. 1976. "The Present State and Development of Sociology of the Military." Journal of Political and Military Sociology 4 (Spring): 67-105.

Kuhn, T. 1970. The Structure of Scientific Revolutions, 2d edition. Chicago: University of Chicago Press.

Ladner, Joyce A. (ed.). 1973. The Death of White Sociology. New York: Vintage Books.

Ladycom. 1973. "Tell Us about You." (A survey questionnaire for Navy wives.) October.

Ladycom Survey of Navy Wives. 1973. Unpublished survey results.

Lang, Kurt. 1972. Military Institutions and the Sociology of War: A Review of the Literature with Annotated Bibliography. Beverly Hills: Sage.

Lang, Kurt, and Gladys Engel Lang. 1964. "Collective Responses to the Threat of Disaster." In The Threat of Impending Disaster, eds. George Grosser, Henry Wichsler, and Milton Greenblatt. Cambridge, Mass.: MIT Press.

Larsen, G. R. 1974. "An Evaluation of the Minnesota Couples Communication Training Program's Influence on Marital Communication and Self and Mate Perceptions. Ph.D. dissertation, Arizona State University.

Lederer, W., and D. Jackson. 1968. The Mirages of Marriage. New York: Norton.

Leider, Richard. 1970. Why They Leave: Resignation From the United States Military Academy Class of 1966. Washington, D.C.: Department of the Army.

Lennard, Henry L., and Arnold Bernstein. 1969. Patterns in Human Interaction: An Introduction to Clinical Sociology. San Francisco: Jossey-Bass.

LeShan, Eda J. 1973. The Wonderful Crisis of Middle Age: Some Personal Reflections. New York: David McKay.

Lester, M. 1975. "The Alcoholic Wife." The Times Magazine, Army/Navy/Air Force Times, October 8, pp. 5-8.

Levinger, G., and D. J. Sen. 1967. "Disclosure of Feelings in Marriage." Merrill-Palmer Quarterly 13: 237.

Levinson, Daniel J. 1977. "The Mid-Life Transition: A Period in Adult Psychosocial Development. Psychiatry 40, no. 2: 99-112.

Libman, Joan, and Herbert Lawson. 1976. "The Future Revised: The Family, Troubled by Changing Mores, Still Likely to Thrive." The Wall Street Journal, March 18, p.

Liebow, Elliot. 1966. Tally's Corner. Boston: Little, Brown.

Lindquist, R. 1952. "Marriage and Family Life of Officers and
    Airmen in a Strategic Air Command Wing." Technical Report
    No. 5, Institute for Research in Social Science, University of
    North Carolina.

____. 1952. "The Family Life of Officers and Airmen in a Bomb
    Wing." Institute for Research in Social Sciences, University
    of North Carolina.

Lipman-Blumen, Jean. 1972. "How Ideology Shapes Women's Lives."
    Scientific American 226, no. 1: 34-42.

Little, Roger W. (ed.). 1971. Handbook of Military Institutions.
    Beverly Hills: Sage.

Lofland, Lyn H. 1973. A World of Strangers: Order and Action in
    Urban Public Space. New York: Basic Books.

Lopata, H. Z. 1965. "The Secondary Features of a Primary Rela-
    tionship." Human Organization 24, no. 2: 116-23.

____. 1971. Occupation: Housewife. London: Oxford University
    Press.

Lowenthal, Marjorie Fiske, Majda Thurnher, David Chiriboga, and
    Associates. 1975. Four Stages of Life: A Comparative Study
    of Women and Men Facing Transitions. San Francisco: Jossey-
    Bass.

Luckey, E. B. 1959. "An Investigation of the Concepts of the Self,
    Mate, Parents, and Ideal in Relation to Degree of Marital Satis-
    faction." Ph.D. dissertation, University of Minnesota.

____. 1961. "Perceptual Congruence of Self and Family Concepts
    as Related to Marital Interaction." Sociometry 24: 234-50.

Lund, Donald A. 1971. "Active Duty—Yes or No?" The Military
    Police Journal, February 20, pp. 15-17.

Lynn, D. 1974. The Father: His Role in Child Development.
    Monterey, Calif.: Brooks/Cole.

Lynn, D. B., and W. L. Sawrey. 1959. "The Effects of Father-Absence on Norwegian Boys and Girls." Journal of Abnormal and Social Psychology 59: 258-62.

MacIntosh, H. 1968. "Separation Problems in Military Wives." American Journal of Psychiatry 125, no. 2: 260-65.

Mace, David, and Vera Mace. 1974. We Can Have Better Marriages: If We Really Want Them. Nashville: Abingdon Press.

Mangus, A. R. 1957. "Integration of Theory Research and Family Counseling Practice." Marriage and the Family 19: 81-88.

Mannheim, K. 1936. Ideology and Utopia. New York: Harcourt, Brace and World.

Marmion, Harry A. 1971. The Case Against A Volunteer Army. Chicago: Quadrangle Books.

Martin, A. 1969. "Morale and Productivity: A Review of the Literature." Public Personnel Review 30, no. 1: 42-45.

Mbiti. J. 1970. African Religions and Philosophies. Garden City, New York: Anchor Books/Doubleday.

McCubbin, H., and B. Dahl. 1974. "Social and Mental Health Services to Families of Servicemen Missing in Action or Returned Prisoners of War." In Family Separation and Reunion, eds. H. McCubbin et al., pp. 191-97. San Diego: Naval Health Research Center.

McCubbin, H., B. Dahl, and E. Hunter. 1976. Families in the Military System. Beverly Hills: Sage.

McCubbin H., B. Dahl, E. Hunter, and P. Metres. 1974-1975. Family Development Checklist. San Diego, Calif.: National Health Research Center.

McCubbin, H., B. Dahl, G. R. Lester, D. Benson, and M. L. Robertson. 1976a. "Coping Repertoires of Families Adapting to Prolonged War-Induced Separations." Journal of Marriage and the Family (August): 461-71.

McCubbin, H., B. Dahl, G. Lester, and B. Ross. 1975. "The Returned Prisoner of War: Factors in Family Reintegration." Journal of Marriage and the Family 37 (August): 471-78.

McCubbin, H., E. Hunter, and B. Dahl. 1975. "Residual of War: Families of Prisoners of War and Servicemen Missing in Action." Journal of Social Issues 31, no. 4: 95-109.

McCubbin, H., E. Hunter, and P. Petres. 1974. "Adaptation of the Family to the PW/MIA Experience: An Overview." In Family Separation and Reunion: Families of Prisoners and Servicemen Missing in Action, eds. H. McCubbin, B. Dahl, P. Metres, E. Hunter, and J. Plag, pp. 21-47. Washington, D.C.: U.S. Government Printing Office.

McNeil, John S. 1976. "Individual and Family Problems Related to Retirement from the Military Service." In Families in the Military System, eds. H. McCubbin, B. Dahl, and E. Hunter, pp. 237-57. Beverly Hills: Sage.

McNeil, John S., and Martin B. Giffin. 1965. "The Social Impact of Military Retirement." Social Casework 46, no. 4: 203-07

_____. 1967. "Military Retirement: The Retirement Syndrome." American Journal of Psychiatry 123, no. 7: 848-54.

McQueen, Albert J. 1977. "The Adaptations of Urban Black Families: Trends, Problems and Issues." A Paper presented at the conference on Families in Contemporary America: Varieties of Form, Function and Experience, sponsored by the Department of Psychiatry and Behavioral Sciences, George Washington University, School of Medicine and the Center for Continuing Education in Mental Health, Psychiatric Institute Foundation, June 10-11, Washington, D.C.

Mead, George H. 1934. Mind, Self and Society. Chicago: University of Chicago Press.

Mechanic, David. 1974. "Social Structure and Personal Adaptation: Some Neglected Dimensions." In Coping and Adaptation, eds. George U. Coelho, David Hamburg, and John E. Adams, pp. 32-44. New York: Basic Books.

Merton, Robert K. 1959. "Introduction: Notes on Problem-Finding in Sociology." In Sociology Today, eds. Robert K. Merton et al. New York: Basic Books.

Metres, P., H. McCubbin, and E. Hunter. 1974. "Families of Returned Prisoners of War: Some Impressions on Their Initial

Reintegration." In H. McCubbin, B. Dahl, P. Metres, E. Hunter, and J. Plag, Family Separation and Reunion. Washington, D.C.: Government Printing Office, pp. 147-55.

Metres, P., J. Plag, K. Ross, and J. Phelan. 1976. "Psychological Dysfunction in Repatriated American Prisoners of War and Its Relationship to Captivity and Demographic Variables. Paper presented at the 5th Psychology in the Air Force Symposium, March, Colorado Springs, Co.

Miller, S. 1971. "The Effects of Communication Training in Small Groups upon Self-Disclosure and Openness in Engaged Couples' Systems of Interaction: A Field Experiment." Ph.D. dissertation, University of Minnesota.

Miller, S., E. Nunnally, and D. Wackman. 1971. The Minnesota Couple Communication Training Program: Instructor's Manual. Bloomington: Marital Resource Center, Inc.

_____. 1975. "Improving Communication in Relationships." Alive and Aware. Minneapolis: Interpersonal Communication Programs, Inc.

Mischel, Walter. 1977. "On the Future of Personality Measurement." American Psychologist 32 (April): 246-54.

Monsour, K. 1948. "Management of Chronic Alcoholics in the Army." Bulletin of U.S. Army Medicine 8: 882-87.

Montalvo, F. F. 1976. "Family Separation in the Army: A Study of the Problems Encountered and the Caretaking Resources Used by Career Army Families Undergoing Military Separation." In Families in the Military System, eds. H. I. McCubbin, B. B. Dahl, and E. J. Hunter. Beverly Hills: Sage.

Moore, M. 1942. "Alcoholism and Military Servide." Military Surgeon 91, no. 1: 29-39.

Moskos, Charles C. 1973. "The Emergent Military: Civil, Traditional or Plural?" Pacific Sociological Review 16 (April): 255-80.

_____. 1970. The American Enlisted Man. New York: Russell Sage Foundation.

Moustakas, Clark. 1961. Loneliness. Englewood Cliffs, N.J.: Prentice-Hall.

Moynihan, D. P. 1965. "Employment, Income, and the Order of the Negro Family." Daedalus 94, no. 3 (Fall): 745-70.

Muldrow, T. W. 1971. Navy Wives Perceptions of Conditions of Navy Life. Technical Report WSR 71-7. Navy Personnel Research and Development Laboratory, March (AD 722024).

Murphy, Mary K., and Carol Bowles Parker. 1966. Fitting in as a New Service Wife. Harrisburg: Stackpole Books.

Napier, Augustus. 1972. "The Primary Task." In The Book of Family Therapy, eds. A. Ferber, M. Mendelsohn, and A. Napier. New York: Science House.

Navran, Leslie. 1967. "Communication and Adjustment in Marriage." Family Process 6: 173-84.

Neugarten, Bernice L. 1970. "Adaptation and the Life Cycle." Journal of Geriatric Psychology 4, no. 1: 78-87.

Nichols, G. 1971. "Job Satisfaction and Nurses' Intention to Remain with or Leave an Organization." Nursing Research 20: 218-28.

Nobles, Wade W. 1974. "Africanity: Its Role in Black Families." The Black Scholar 5, no. 9 (June): 10-17.

_____. 1976. "A Formulative and Empirical Study of Black Families." A Final Report submitted to the Office of Child Development under Contract Number 90-C-255, December.

Nunnally, E. W. 1971. "Effects of Communication Training upon Interaction Awareness and Emphatic Accuracy of Engaged Couples: A Field Experiment." Ph.D. dissertation, University of Minnesota.

O'Beirne, Kathleen, P. 1976. "Waiting Wives." United States Naval Institute Proceedings 102 (September): 28-37.

Oborn, P. T. 1972. "Review of the Literature on Social Indicators." Denver: Social Welfare Research Institute, University of Denver.

O'Neill, Nena and George O'Neill. 1972. Open Marriage: A New Life Style for Couples. New York: Lippincott.

_____. 1974. Shifting Gears: Finding Security in a Changing World. New York: M. Evans.

Orthner, D. K., T. Brown, and D. Ferguson. 1976. "Single-Parent Fatherhood: An Emerging Family Life Style." *Family Coordinator* 25: 429-37.

Papanek, Hanna. 1973. "Men, Women, and Work Reflections on the Two-Person Career." *American Journal of Sociology* 78, no. 4: 852-72.

Pearce, W. Barnett. 1976. "The Coordinated Management of Meanings: A Rules-Based Theory of Interpersonal Communication." In *Explorations in Interpersonal Communication*, ed. Gerald R. Miller, pp. 17-36. Beverly Hills: Sage.

Pearce, W. Barnett, Vernon Cronen, and Forrest Conklin. 1977. "A Hierarchical Model of Interpersonal Communication." Paper presented to International Communication Association, Berlin.

Pearlman, C. A., Jr. 1970. "Separation Reactions of Married Women." *American Journal of Psychiatry* 126, no. 1: 946-50.

Pendergast, T., M. Preble, and F. Tennant. 1973. "Drug Use and Its Relation to Alcohol and Cigarette Consumption in the Military Community of West Germany." *International Journal of Addictions* 8: 741-54.

Picou, J. Steven, and Kenneth L. Myberg. 1975. "Socialization into the Military: A Study of University Cadets." Paper presented at American Sociological Association, August, San Francisco.

1977. "The American Family in Trouble." *Psychology Today* 10, no. 12 (May):

Rainwater, Lee. 1970. *Behind Ghetto Walls: Black Family Life in a Federal Slum*. Chicago: Aldine.

Rappaport, A. F. 1971. "The Effects of an Intensive Conjugal Relationship Modification Program." Ph.D. dissertation, Pennsylvania State University.

Rappaport, Thona, and Robert Rappaport. 1971. *Dual Career Families*. Baltimore: Penguin Books.

Rausch, H. L., W. Goodrich, and J. D. Campbell. 1963. "Adaptation to the First Years of Marriage." *Psychiatry* 26, no. 4: 368-80.

Reid, Ira, D. A. 1940. In a Minor Key: Negro Youth in Study and Fact. Washington, D.C.: American Council on Education.

Renshaw, J. R. 1975. "An Exploration of the Dynamics of the Overlapping Worlds of Work and Family." Family Process 14, no. 1: 143-65.

Rodman, Hyman. 1959. "On Understanding Lower Class Behavior." Social and Economic Studies 8 (December).

_____. 1963. "Lower Class Values Stretch." Social Forces 42 (December).

Rogers, Everett M., and F. Floyd Shoemaker. 1971. Communication of Innovations, 2d ed. New York: Free Press.

Rosen, H., and E. McCullum. 1962. "Correlates of Productivity." Personnel Psychology 15: 429-39.

Rosenkrantz, P., S. Vogel, H. Bee, I. Broverman, and D. M. Broverman. 1968. "Sex-Role Stereotypes and Self-Concepts in College Students." Journal of Consulting and Clinical Psychology 32, no. 3: 287-95.

Ryan, F. J., and J. J. Bevilacqua. 1964. "The Military Family: An Asset or a Liability." Military Medicine 129: 956-59.

Safilios-Rothschild, Constantina. 1972. Toward a Sociology of Women. Lexington: Xerox College Publishing.

Sandmaier, M. 1975. Alcohol Abuse and Women. Washington, D.C.: U.S. Government Printing Office.

Sarkasian, Sam C., and William J. Taylor, Jr. 1975. "The Case for Civilian Graduate Education for Professional Officers." Armed Forces and Society 1 (Winter): 251-62.

Saxton, L. 1968. The Individual, Marriage, and the Family. Belmont, Calif.: Wadsworth.

Scanzoni, John H. 1971. The Black Family in Modern Society. Boston: Allyn and Bacon.

Schank, R. C., and R. R. Abelson. 1977. Scripts, Plans, Goals, and Understanding. Hillsdale, N.J.: Erlbaum.

Schreiber, E., and R. Holz. 1973. "Determinants of Army Career Intentions among Enlisted Men and Non-Commissioned Officers." Unpublished manuscript, Army Research Institute, Arlington, Virginia.

Seeman, Melvin. 1959. "On the Meaning of Alienation." American Sociological Review 24: 783-91.

Segal, David R. 1975. "Convergence, Commitment, and Military Compensation." Paper presented at the American Sociological Association, August, San Francisco.

Segal, David R., John Blair, Frank Newport, and Susan Stephens. 1974. "Convergence, Isomorphism, and Interdependence at the Civil-Military Interface." Journal of Political and Military Sociology 2 (Fall): 160-62.

Seidenberg, R. 1973. Corporate Wives—Corporate Casualties? New York: American Management Association, Inc.

_____. 1975. Corporate Wives—Corporate Casualties? Garden City, New York: Anchor Books, Anchor Press/Doubleday.

Shea, Nancy. 1954. The Army Wife, 3rd edition. New York: Harper and Row.

Sheehy, Gail. 1976. Passages: Predictable Crises of Adult Life. New York: Dutton.

Slater, Philip. 1970. The Pursuit of Loneliness. Boston: Beacon Press.

Snyder, Alice Ivey. 1977. "Mid-Life Crises Among Submariners' Wives." Paper presented at the Conference on Military Family Research: Current Trends and Directions, sponsored by the Naval Health Research Center, Office of Naval Research, and Naval Postgraduate School, September 1-3, in San Diego.

Spellman, S. 1965. "Orientations Toward Problem-Solving Among Career Military Families: A Study of the Knowledge of Available Resources in a Military Community and Perception of the Social Cost of Using Them for the Resolution of Family Conflict." Ph.D. dissertation, Columbia University.

____. 1976. "Utilization of Problem-Solving Resources among
Military Families." In Families in the Military System, eds.
H. McCubbin, B. Dahl, and E. Hunter, pp. 174-206. Beverly
Hills: Sage.

Spence, J. T., R. Helmreich, and P. Stapp. 1974. "The Personal
Attributes Questionnaire: A Measure of Sex-Role Stereotypes
and Masculinity/Femininity." Catalog of Selected Documents
in Psychology 4: 43-44.

Stack, Carol B. 1974. All Our Kin: Strategies for Survival in a
Black Community. New York: Harper and Row.

Staff Writer. 1977. "Can They Be Happy, Though Wed?" Air Force
Times, November 14, p. 6.

Staples, Robert. 1971a. "Towards a Sociology of the Black Family:
A Theoretical and Methodological Assessment." Journal of
Marriage and the Family (February): 119-38.

____, (ed.). 1971b. The Black Family: Essays and Studies, Bel-
mont, Calif.: Wadsworth.

____. 1974. "The Black Family in Evolutionary Perspective."
The Black Scholar 5, no. 9 (June): 2-9.

Stoddard, Ellwyn R. 1972. "The Military Intelligence Agent:
Structural Strains in an Occupational Role." In Social Dimen-
sions of Work, ed. Clifton D. Bryant, pp. 570-82. Englewood
Cliffs, N.J.: Prentice-Hall.

Stoddard, Ellwyn R., and Claude E. Cabanillas. 1976. "The Army
Officer's Wife: Social Stresses in a Complementary Role." In
The Social Psychology of Military Service, eds. Nancy Goldman
and David Segal, pp. 151-71. Beverly Hills: Sage.

Stouffer, Samuel A., Edward A. Suchman, Leland C. DeVinney et
al. (eds.). 1949. The American Soldier, Vol. I, II, III.
Princeton: Princeton University Press.

Subcommittee on Alcoholism and Narcotics. 1970. Drug and Alcohol
Abuse in the Military. Washington, D.C.: U.S. Government
Printing Office.

____. 1971. Alcoholism Among Military Personnel. Washington,
D.C.: U.S. Government Printing Office.

Subcommittee on Drug Abuse in the Military Services. 1972. Drugs
    and U.S. Military Personnel–Germany. Washington, D.C.:
    U.S. Government Printing Office.

____. 1973. Review of Military Drug and Alcohol Programs.
    Washington, D.C.: U.S. Government Printing Office.

Sullivan, Harry Stack. 1953. The Interpersonal Theory of Psychia-
    try. New York: Norton.

System Development Corporation. 1972. "Analysis of MVA/VOLAR
    Actions Impact on Soldiers' Attitudes toward the Army and on
    Retention," Vol. 1 and Vol. 2. Unpublished manuscript, Santa
    Monica, Calif.

Tempels, P. 1959. "Ban to Philosophy," Presence Africaine.

Tennant, F. S. 1974. "Childhood Antecedents of Alcohol and Drug
    Abuse." Ph.D. dissertation, University of California, Los
    Angeles.

Tharp, Roland G. 1963. "Dimensions of Marriage Roles." Marriage
    and Family Living 25: 389-404.

Thomas, L. V. 1961. "Time, Myth and History in West Africa."
    Presence Africaine 11, no. 39: 50-92.

The Black Scholar. 1971. Issue on "The Black Woman," December,
    Vol. 3, No. 4.

The Black Scholar. 1974. Issue of "The Black Family," June,
    Vol. 5, No. 9.

The Journal of Afro-American Issues. 1976. "The Black Family:
    Black Child/Youth Development," Number I, Spring, Vol. 4,
    No. 2, and Number II, Summer/Fall, Vol. 4, Nos. 3 & 4.

The Western Journal of Black Studies, special issue on the Black
    Family, June 1977, Vol. 1, No. 2.

Toffler, Alvin. 1970. Future Shock. New York: Bantam.

U.S. Department of the Army. 1966. Family Housing: DA Survey
    of Married Male Military Personnel. (OPOSS Report 52-66-E).
    Washington, D.C.: Office of Personnel Operations, December.

____. 1969. Survey Estimate of Satisfying and Dissatisfying Aspects of Military Life as Indicated by Army Officers and Enlisted Men. Report Number 52-69-E. Washington, D.C.: Office of Personnel Operations, Personnel Management Development Office.

____. 1969. Survey Estimate of Officers' Wives' Satisfaction with Army Life as Expressed by Officers. (OPOPM Report No. 44-69-E). Washington, D.C.: Office of Personnel Operations.

____. 1971a. "The Modern Volunteer Army." Washington, D.C.: U.S. Government Printing Office.

____. 1971b. Survey Estimate of Dependent and Off-Duty Employment of Army Personnel. Report Number 53-71-E. Washington, D.C.: Office of Personnel Operations, Personnel Management Development Office.

____. 1974. Sample Survey of Military Personnel. Unpublished report. Washington, D.C.: Office of Personnel Operations, Personnel Management Development Office.

Vineberg, R., and E. Taylor. 1972. Summary and Review of Studies of the VOLAR Experiment, 1971. Human Resources Research Organization Technical Paper Number 72-18, Alexandria, Virginia.

Wachowiak, Dale. 1977. "Counseling Inside/Out." Personnel and Guidance Journal 55, no. 7: 387-78.

Waters, L., and D. Roach. 1973. "Job Attitudes as Predictors of Termination and Absenteeism: Consistency over Time and across Organizational Units." Journal of Applied Psychology 57: 341-42.

Webster, E., E. Hunter, and D. Palermo. 1977. "Changing Roles in Military Families Following Prolonged Separation." In Changing Families in a Changing Military System, ed. E. Hunter. Proceedings of Panel at 84th American Psychological Association, Chicago.

Weiss, R. 1975. Marital Separation. New York: Basic Books.

Whyte, William H. 1951. "The Wives of Management." Fortune, October.

Williams, John E., and Susan M. Bennett. 1975. "The Definition of Sex Stereotypes Via the Adjective Check List." Sex Roles 1: 327-37.

Willie, Charles V. (ed.). 1970. The Family Life of Black People. Columbus: Charles E. Merrill.

Willie, C. V., B. M. Kramer, and B. S. Brown. 1973. "Mental Health Action for Human Rights." In Racism and Mental Health, eds. C. V. Willie, B. M. Kramer, and B. S. Brown, pp. 581-87. Pittsburgh: University of Pittsburgh Press.

Willie, Charles V., and Janet Weinandy. 1963. "The Structure and Composition of 'Problem' and 'Stable' Families in a Low-Income Population." Marriage and Family Living 25 (November): 439-46.

Winnecott, D. W. 1958. "The Capacity To Be Alone." International Journal of Psychoanalysis 39: 416-20.

Wyse, Lois. 1970. Mrs. Success. New York: World.

INDEX

ABOUT THE CONTRIBUTORS

EDNA J. HUNTER, a clinical research psychologist, has been affiliated with the Naval Health Research Center since 1967. For the past six years she has been assigned to the Center for Prisoner of War Studies, where she has served as Head of Family Studies and Assistant Director for Administration. Recently she was appointed Associate Dean of the Graduate School of Human Behavior and Director of the Family Research Center, United States International University, San Diego. Dr. Hunter is presently a member of the Executive Council, Inter-University Seminar on the Armed Forces and Society. Dr. Hunter has coedited two books on the military family, several book chapters, and over 50 journal articles in the areas of family research and psychophysiology. Dr. Hunter received her undergraduate training at the University of California, Berkeley, M.S. from San Diego State University, and Ph.D. from United States International University.

D. STEPHEN NICE is a research psychologist at the Naval Health Research Center in San Diego, California. Current research efforts focus on the effects of prolonged family separation and family adjustment to remote assignments within the military organization. Dr. Nice has published in the areas of psychophysiology and family research. His articles have appeared in scientific journals such as Perceptual and Motor Skills and Psychophysics. He holds a B.A. from DePauw University, an M.A. from the College of William and Mary, and a Ph.D. from the University of Virginia.

KATHLEEN REARDON BOYNTON is a University of Massachusetts Fellow. As high school teacher, college instructor, and researcher, she has focused her interests on the study of interpersonal communication. Her current research includes the study of deviation from conversational rules, children's acquisition of conversational rules, humor usage in educational media, and the relationships among role ambiguity, marital type, and marital satisfaction in navy marriages. Ms. Boynton graduated Phi Beta Kappa with a B.A. from the University of Connecticut in 1971. She received an M.A. from the University of Massachusetts in 1973, where she is presently completing work toward her Ph.D. in communication studies.

RICHARD J. BROWN, III is a Marriage and Family Counselor in private practice and also a Chaplain in the United States Air Force Reserves. Chaplain Brown is presently a doctoral candidate in child development and family relations at the University of North Carolina at Greensboro, North Carolina. He also serves as a Student and Young Professional Representative on the Board of Directors of the National Council on Family Relations.

WAYNE COSBY works in educational services for the United States military educational programs in the overseas command. He holds degrees from the University of Maryland, European Division, and George Peabody College, England.

SUZAN DAY, currently at the University of Michigan, Ann Arbor, earned her undergraduate degree in sociology at the University of Maryland, European Division.

KATHRYN BROWN DECKER has worked as a social worker and researcher with military families in Norfolk, Virginia, and Monterey, California. Mrs. Decker holds a B.A. from the College of Idaho and an M.S.W. from Norfolk State College, Norfolk, Virginia. She has also studied at the National Catholic School of Social Service at Catholic University of America in Washington, D.C. Mrs. Decker, the wife of a United States Naval officer, currently resides in the British Crown Colony of Hong Kong.

GERALD R. GARRETT is Associate Professor of Sociology at the University of Massachusetts, Boston, and is currently Visiting Associate Professor of Criminal Justice at Washington State University. He also has held positions at Columbia University, Wisconsin, and the University of Maryland, European Division. Dr. Garrett is coauthor of Women Alone (1976) and Manny: A Criminal-Addict's Story (1977); he has contributed numerous articles to professional journals as well as to books on criminology, womens' studies, sociology from Whitman College and an M.A. and Ph.D. in sociology from Washington State University.

GLORIA LAUER GRACE is a Project Head Senior at System Development Corporation, Santa Monica, California. Prior to joining this corporation, she taught at the University of California (Berkeley), Grinnell College, Barnard College, and the Ohio State University. Dr. Grace is President-elect of the Human Factors Society, and she has published widely in the areas of psychology and organizational effectiveness. Her articles have appeared in the Journal of Applied Psychology, the Journal of Genetic Psychology, and the Human Factors

Journal. She is also the author of many technical reports. Dr. Grace holds a B.A. and an M.A. from the Ohio State University, and a Ph.D. from Columbia University, New York.

ROBERT HAYLES is an Assistant Program Director in the Psychological Sciences Division of the Office of Naval Research, Arlington, Virginia. Until 1976 he was a Research Scientist at the Battelle Human Affairs Research Center in Seattle, Washington. Dr. Hayles has published in the areas of minority student education and intergroup relations. His works have appeared in Measurement and Evaluation in Guidance and Overview of Intercultural Education, Training and Research. Dr. Hayles holds B.A. and M.A. degrees from the University of Kansas in Lawrence and a Ph.D. from the University of Colorado in Boulder.

DONALD A. LUND is Assistant Commissioner for Mental Health with the Department of Mental Hygiene of the State of New York. He previously served as Director of Program Evaluation of the department. Until 1974, he was Executive Director of the North Central Florida Community Mental Health Center in Gainesville, Florida, and a member of the faculty of the University of Florida. From 1971 to 1972 Dr. Lund served as an officer in the United States Army Military Police Corps. He has published articles on the management of civil disorder and techniques of program evaluation. He presently serves on the editorial board of Evaluation and Program Planning. Dr. Lund earned a B.A. from Middlebury College in Middlebury, Vermont, and an M.Ph. and Ph.D. from Yale University, New Haven, Connecticut.

WADE W. NOBLES is an experimental social psychologist and is currently the Research Scientist for Children and Youth Programs at Westside Community Mental Health Center, Inc., and the principal investigator for Black Family Research Projects. Dr. Nobles has studied and traveled in Africa; was awarded a Postdoctoral National Endowment to the Humanities Fellowship in Afro-American Studies. In addition to coediting the book, African Philosophy: Assumptions and Paradigms for Research on Black People, he has published articles in the Journal of Social Issues, the Journal of Social and Behavioral Sciences, the Black Scholar, and the edited textbook, Black Psychology. Dr. Nobles holds a B.A. from San Francisco State College, and an M.A. and Ph.D. from Stanford University, Palo Alto, California.

DENNIS K. ORTHNER is Assistant Professor of Family Studies at the University of North Carolina, Greensboro. He is also associated with the Family Research Center and is Director of the Single-Parent Research Project at the university. Dr. Orthner has been a member of the Executive Committee on the National Council on Family Relations and is author of numerous articles in family sociology. His contributions have appeared in The Journal of Marriage and the Family, The Family Coordinator, The Journal of Sex Research, and other publications. Dr. Orthner received his B.A., M.A. and Ph.D. degrees from Florida State University, Tallahassee, Florida.

BETTY PARKER earned her bachelor's degree in sociology at the University of Maryland, European Division. She has held teaching posts with city colleges of Chicago and is currently active in women's organizations in Fort Worth, Texas.

W. BARNETT PEARCE is Associate Professor of Communication Studies at the University of Massachusetts. Dr. Pearce has published widely in the area of interpersonal communication. His work has appeared in the journals Human Communication Research and the Journal of Communication; and in the books Explorations in Interpersonal Communication, New Models for Communication Research, Communicating Personally, and An Overview of Communication and Interpersonal Relations. Dr. Pearce holds a B.A. from Carson-Newman College, and M.A. and Ph.D. degrees from Ohio University.

JANICE G. RIENERTH is presently an Assistant Professor of Sociology at Appalachian State University, Boone, North Carolina. Dr. Rienerth received a B.S. in mathematics and a B.A. in sociology from Ohio University and an M.A. and Ph.D. in sociology from Southern Illinois University.

JOEL M. SAVELL, a research psychologist with the Army Research Institute for the Behavioral and Social Sciences, is currently serving as team leader for a group of social scientists conducting research on the role of women in the army. Before coming to ARI in 1971, he taught at Catholic University, where he served as codirector of the doctoral program in personality and social psychology. Dr. Savell's articles have appeared in a number of professional journals including Journal of Personality and Social Psychology, Sociometry, and Psychonomic Science. He holds an A.B. from Emory University, an A.M. from Ohio University, and a Ph.D. from Columbia University.

ALICE IVEY SNYDER is a contractor for the Office of Naval Research. She is currently investigating the effects of family separation and reunion upon navy wives. Dr. Snyder holds a B.A. and M.A. from the University of Hawaii.

MARY B. STEINER is a Congressional Staff Assistant in the District Office of California Congressman Robert K. Dornan. She previously served on the staff at System Development Corporation with major responsibility for field work in the navy wives' study. Ms. Steiner is the author of a number of technical reports. She holds a B.A. from the University of California at Los Angeles and has been active in the Human Factors Society at the local level.

ELLWYN R. STODDARD is Professor of Sociology and Anthropology at the University of Texas at El Paso. He has published several dozen professional books, chapters, articles, and major research reports. Dr. Stoddard is the organizer and President of the Association of Borderlands Scholars, a multi-disciplinary, learned society including members from more than 12 academic disciplines, three countries, and 20 states. He has presented more than 50 papers through national, international, and regional professional conferences. Military service includes World War II and Korea. He is a lifetime member of Delta Tau Kappa, an international social science honor society.

SUSAN S. STUMPF is a survey statistician at the Navy Personnel Research and Development Center, San Diego, California. She has conducted sociological research for the navy and army since 1966, covering a broad variety of topics of concern to military personnel and their families. She has also represented both the navy and the army in joint service research projects sponsored by the Office of the Secretary of Defense. Ms. Stumpf holds a B.A. in sociology from Tufts University, Medford, Massachusetts, and has done graduate work at American University in Washington, D.C. and San Diego State University.

JACQUELYN VAN METER is currently at the University of North Carolina and has been active in numerous organizations, focusing on women's issues in the military.

EDWIN W. VAN VRANKEN is a Social Work Officer in the Medical Service Corps of the United States Army Medical Department with the rank of Major. Currently Dr. Van Vranken is the U.S. Army Liaison Officer at the Center for Prisoner of War Studies, Naval Health Research Center, San Diego, California. His research efforts at the center have focused on the longitudinal studies of the health and adjustment of returned prisoners of war, their families, and the fami-

lies of servicemen missing in action. Dr. Van Vranken holds a
B.A. from San Jose State University, an M.S.W. from Florida State
University, and a D.S.W. from the University of Denver.

JAMES D. WATKINS is a Vice Admiral in the United States Navy
and is presently the Chief, Bureau of Naval Personnel, Washington,
D.C. He attended the University of California at Berkeley prior to
entering the U.S. Naval Academy, Annapolis, Maryland, where he
was graduated and commissioned ensign in 1949. In addition to the
Legion of Merit with two Gold Stars, the Bronze Star Medal with
Combat "V", the Navy Commendation Medal, Navy Unit Commenda-
tion with Bronze Star and the Meritorious Unit Commendation Ribbon,
Vice Admiral Watkins has earned and is authorized to wear the Navy
Expeditionary Medal, World War II Victory Medal, China Service
Medal, Navy Occupation Service Medal, National Defense Service
Medal with Bronze Star, Korean Service Medal, Vietnam Service
Medal with four Bronze Stars, United Nations Service Medal, and
the Vietnam Campaign Medal.

JOHN W. WILLIAMS, JR., is Professor and Head, Department
of Behavioral Sciences, at the United States Air Force Academy,
Colorado Springs, Colorado. Dr. Williams is an active-duty Air
Force Colonel and holds a Ph.D. in sociology. His publications
include articles on divorce in the military, liberal education at
service academies, and the military and society. His present research efforts center around alternative family styles in the military
environment.

JOHN C. WOELFEL is a research sociologist with the Army
Research Institute for the Behavioral and Social Sciences. He is
currently studying the performance and adjustment of women in the
United States Army. Dr. Woelfel's most recent publications have
appeared in Sex-Roles, Youth and Society, and Communication
Research. He holds a B.S. from Canisius College, an M.A. from
the University of Illinois, and a Ph.D. from the University of Michigan.

NANCY K. YORK is on active duty as a Captain in the United
States Marine Corps. Currently she serves as a Military Judge
Advocate at the United States Marine Corps Base, Camp Pendleton,
California. Captain York received her Doctorate of Jurisprudence
from the University of San Diego School of Law and has been an active
member of the State of California Bar Association since 1975.